Computer Graphics

Computer Graphics

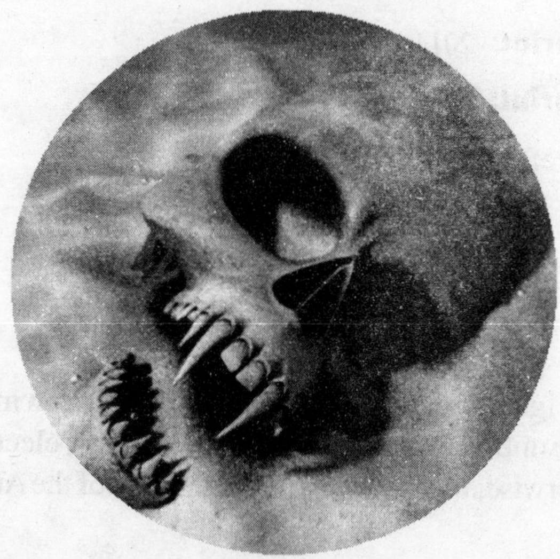

KULDEEP SINGH KOHAR

Assistant Secretariat

Department of Computer Engineering,
Directorate of Technical Education,
Chandigarh

AN ISO 9001:2008 CERTIFIED COMPANY

VAYU EDUCATION OF INDIA

2/25, Ansari Road, Darya Ganj, New Delhi-110 002

Computer Graphics

ISBN: 978-93-80712-74-1

First Edition: 2011

Reprint: 2014

Reprint: 2015

Price: ₹160.00

Printed & bound in India

Published by:

AN ISO 9001:2008 CERTIFIED COMPANY

VAYU EDUCATION OF INDIA

2/25, Ansari Road, Darya Ganj, New Delhi-110 002

Ph.: 91-11-47236600, 41564445

Fax: 91-11-41564440

E-mail: vei@veiindia.com

Web: www.veiindia.com

Preface

Today computers and computer-generated images touch many aspects of our daily life. Computer imagery is found on television, in newspapers, in weather reports, and during surgical procedures.

Computer graphics techniques provide the primary means by which we are able to view the results of wide ranging computational processes. Additionally, these techniques play a pivotal role in our interaction with the digital word.

This book is designed to be a course text for students studying computer graphics and related subjects at the introductory level within the context of an undergraduate or graduate degree programme. The content is presented in such a way as to ensure that it is accessible to the widest possible audience and wherever feasible a trans-disciplinary approach is adopted. Use of examples and graphical representation is the basic feature of the book.

Chapter wise composition of the book is as follows:

Chapter 1 introduces Computer Graphics. It also covers few application areas, type of images and few basic concepts in computer graphics.

Chapter 2 is about raster algorithms covering border-following algorithms, fill algorithms, discrete curves, the aliasing problem, halftoning, thresholding, and dithering, drawing algorithms etc.

Chapter 3 covers the concept of clipping. it includes line-clipping algorithms, polygon-clipping algorithms and text clipping.

Chapter 4 is about Transformations and the Graphics Pipeline. Chapter covers topics like vanishing points, view ports, Clip coordinate system, clipping, stereo views and parallel projections.

Chapter 5 talks about two-dimensional computer graphics. It covers graphical output devices, drawing straight lines, text in graphics, two-dimensional transformations, shading of polygons, clipping and windowing, interactive graphics

Chapter 6 covers 3d-transformations talking about points and lines and transformations in 3D.

Chapter 7 covers few basics of graphics programming in C language.

Contents

1

INTRODUCTION TO GRAPHIC SYSTEM

1.1 INTRODUCTION

Computer graphics are graphics created using computers and, more generally, the representation and manipulation of pictorial data by a computer.

The term computer graphics includes almost everything on computers that is not text or sound. Today nearly all computers use some graphics and users expect to control their computer through icons and pictures rather than just by typing [1]. The term Computer Graphics has several meanings:

- The representation and manipulation of pictorial data by a computer.
- The various technologies used to create and manipulate such pictorial data.
- The images so produced, * the sub-field of computer science which studies methods for digitally synthesizing and manipulating visual content.

Today, computers and computer-generated images touch many aspects of our daily life. Computer imagery is found on television, in newspapers, in weather reports, and during surgical procedures. A well-constructed graph can present complex statistics in a form that is easier to understand and interpret. Such graphs are used to illustrate papers, reports, thesis, and other presentation material. A range of tools and facilities are available to enable users to visualize their data, and computer graphics are used in many disciplines [2].

Computer Graphics systems could be *active* or *passive.* In both cases, the input to the system is the scene description and output is a static or animated scene to be displayed. In case of *active* systems, the user controls the display with the help of a GUI, using an input device. Computer Graphics is now-a-days, a significant component of almost all systems and applications of computers in every field of life.

Computer graphics techniques provide the primary means by which we are able to view the results of wide ranging computational processes. Additionally, these techniques play a pivotal role in our interaction with the digital word. As indicated in Figure 1.1, computer graphics underpins the modern human-computer interface. Here, we indicate a collection of hardware and software (which we loosely refer to as 'graphics elements') that provide a vital interface between underlying digital data and the human operator. These elements support the synthesis and depiction of pictorial imagery that is presented to the complex human visual system.

Although visual stimuli provide an extremely powerful means by which we visualise our surroundings (i.e. gain insight and understanding), other senses also play a crucial role.With this in mind, in Figure 1.1 we indicate that human visualisation processes may take input not only from the computer display but also from other interface mechanisms (such as the generation of sound and in the case of a growing number of applications). These sources of input to the human sensory systems are used to support the cognitive process of visualisation whereby we are able to form some type of mental image and thereby extract information, understand, and decide upon any appropriate responses that should be made.

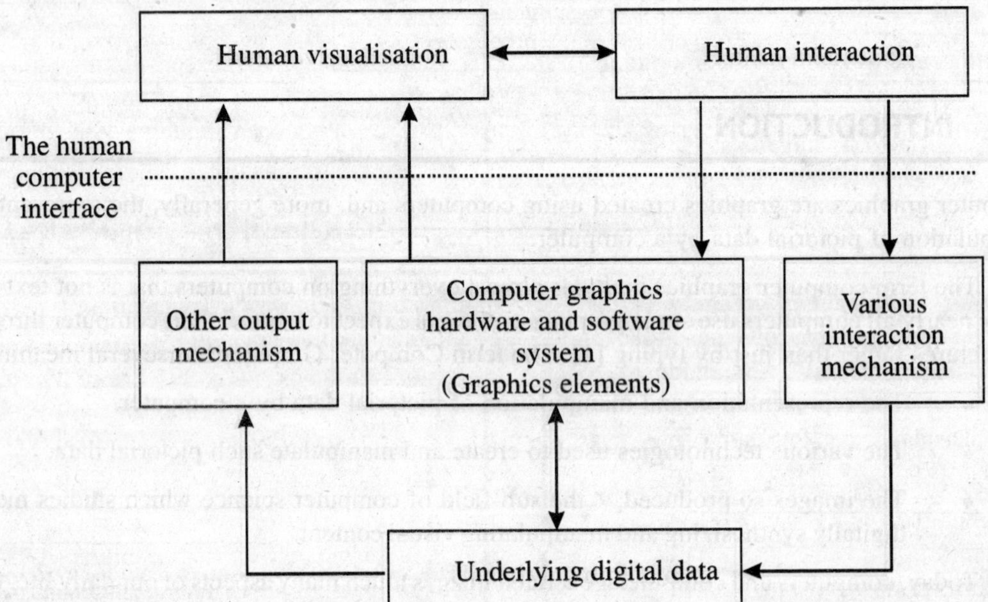

Figure 1.1 Aspects of the human-computer interface. Computer graphics techniques play a vital role in providing a window onto the digital world and in supporting interaction.

Real time interaction is critical to modern computing. For example, in the case of a video game, flight simulator or the like, we anticipate true real time performance and perceptible delays (latencies) that may occur as a result of the computational tasks that must be performed in order to execute an interactive operation, detract from the sense of immersion and are likely to negatively impact on the experience. Consequently, we cannot simply consider computer graphics software in isolation but must also bear in mind the architecture of the underlying hardware and interactions that occur between the graphics software and other elements within the system.

In other situations small delays that follow the initiation of an interactive operation and the system's response to it may be more readily tolerated. For example, when presented with some form of image (perhaps a graph indicating the change of one or more quantities with time), we may zoom on a feature of particular interest or manipulate image characteristics so as to facilitate the extraction of information. Here, slight pauses that can occur between the initiation of an operation and its completion may be deemed tolerable.

Computer graphics embraces all aspects of the synthesis, depiction and manipulation of pictorial representations by computational machines together with their presentation to the human visual system.

In Figure 1.2, we indicate some of the areas which (to a greater or lesser extent) influence the design and implementation of graphics systems and which must therefore be embraced by the computer graphics developer.

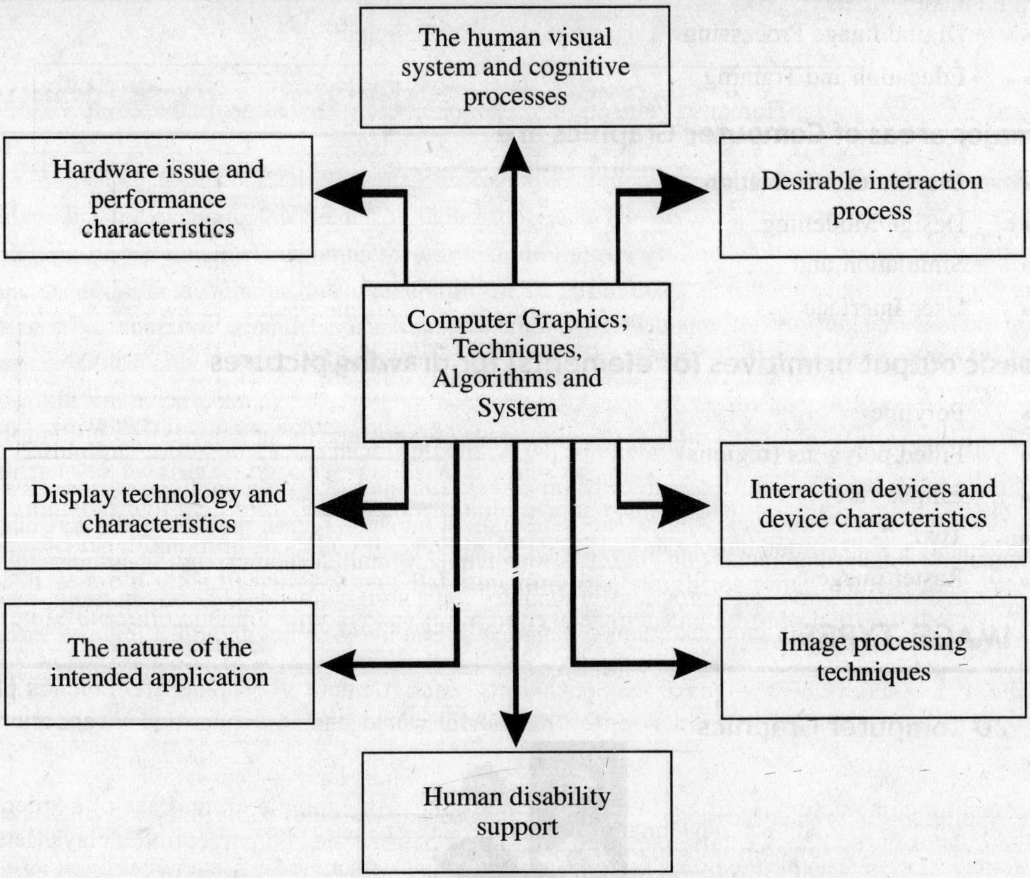

1.2 APPLICATIONS AREAS

- Plotting in business
- Plotting in science and technology

- GUI
- Scientific Visualization
- Office automation
- Desktop publishing
- Web/business/commercial publishing and advertisements
- CAD/CAM design (VLSI, Construction, Circuits
- Entertainment (movie, TV Advt., Games etc.)
- Virtual reality
- Process Monitoring
- Digital Image Processing
- Education and Training

Four major areas of Computer Graphics are

- Display of information,
- Design/Modelling,
- Simulation and
- User Interface.

Four basic output primitives (or elements) for drawing pictures

- Polyline
- Filled polygons (regions)
- Ellipse (arc)
- Text
- Raster image

1.3 IMAGE TYPES

1.3.1 2D Computer Graphics

Figure 1.3 Raster graphic sprites (left) and masks (right)

2D computer graphics are the computer-based generation of digital images—mostly from two-dimensional models, such as 2D geometric models, text, and digital images, and by techniques specific to them. The word may stand for the branch of computer science that comprises such techniques, or for the models themselves.

2D computer graphics are mainly used in applications that were originally developed upon traditional printing and drawing technologies, such as typography, cartography, technical drawing, advertising, etc.. In those applications, the two-dimensional image is not just a representation of a real-world object, but an independent artifact with added semantic value; two-dimensional models are therefore preferred, because they give more direct control of the image than 3D computer graphics, whose approach is more akin to photography than to typography.

1.3.2 Pixel art

Pixel art is a form of digital art, created through the use of raster graphics software, where images are edited on the pixel level. Graphics in most old (or relatively limited) computer and video games, graphing calculator games, and many mobile phone games are mostly pixel art.

1.3.3 Vector graphics

Figure 1.4 Example showing effect of vector graphics versus raster graphics.

Vector graphics formats are complementary to raster graphics, which is the representation of images as an array of pixels, as it is typically used for the representation of photographic images.[5] There are instances when working with vector tools and formats is best practice, and instances when working with raster tools and formats is best practice. There are times when both formats come together. An understanding of the advantages and limitations of each technology and the relationship between them is most likely to result in efficient and effective use of tools.

1.3.4 3D computer graphics

3D computer graphics in contrast to 2D computer graphics are graphics that use a three-dimensional representation of geometric data that is stored in the computer for the purposes of performing calculations and rendering 2D images. Such images may be for later display or for real-time viewing.

Despite these differences, 3D computer graphics rely on many of the same algorithms as 2D computer vector graphics in the wire frame model and 2D computer raster graphics in the final rendered display. In computer graphics software, the distinction between 2D and 3D is occasionally blurred; 2D applications may use 3D techniques to achieve effects such as lighting, and primarily 3D may use 2D rendering techniques.

3D computer graphics are often referred to as 3D models. Apart from the rendered graphic, the model is contained within the graphical data file. However, there are differences. A 3D model is the mathematical representation of any three-dimensional object (either inanimate or living). A model is not technically a graphic until it is visually displayed. Due to 3D printing, 3D models are not confined to virtual space. A model can be displayed visually as a two-dimensional image through a process called *3D rendering,* or used in non-graphical computer simulations and calculations.

1.3.5 Computer animation

Figure 1.5 An example of Computer animation produced using Motion capture

Computer animation is the art of creating moving images via the use of computers. It is a subfield of ***computer graphics*** and animation. Increasingly it is created by means of 3D computer graphics, though 2D computer graphics are still widely used for stylistic, low bandwidth, and faster real-time rendering needs. Sometimes the target of the animation is the computer itself, but sometimes the target is another medium, such as film. It is also referred to as CGI (Computer-generated imagery or computer-generated imaging), especially when used in films.

To create the illusion of movement, an image is displayed on the computer screen then quickly replaced by a new image that is similar to the previous image, but shifted slightly. This technique is identical to the illusion of movement in television and motion pictures.

1.4 CONCEPTS AND PRINCIPLES

1.4.1 Image

In common usage, an image or picture is an artifact, usually two-dimensional, that has a similar appearance to some subject—usually a physical object or a person. Images may be two-dimensional, such as a photograph, screen display, and as well as a three-dimensional, such as a statue. They may be *captured* by optical devices—such as cameras, mirrors, lenses, telescopes, microscopes, etc. and natural objects and phenomena, such as the human eye or water surfaces.

A digital image is a representation of a two-dimensional image using ones and zeros (binary). Depending on whether or not the image resolution is fixed, it may be of vector or raster type. Without qualifications, the term "digital image" usually refers to raster images.

1.4.2 Pixel

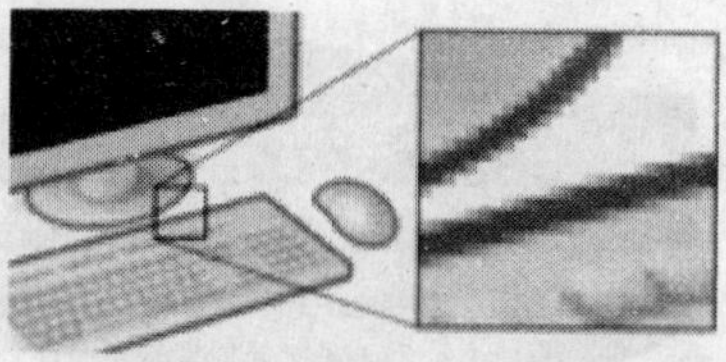

Figure 1.6 In the enlarged portion of the image individual pixels are rendered as squares and can be easily seen.

In digital imaging, a pixel is the smallest piece of information in an image [6]. Pixels are normally arranged in a regular 2-dimensional grid, and are often represented using dots or squares. Each pixel is a sample of an original image, where more samples typically provide a more accurate representation of the original. The intensity of each pixel is variable; in color systems, each pixel has typically three or four components such as red, green, and blue, or cyan, magenta, yellow, and black.

1.4.3 Graphics

Graphics are visual presentations on some surface, such as a wall, canvas, computer screen, paper, or stone to brand, inform, illustrate, or entertain. Examples are photographs, drawings, line art, graphs, diagrams, typography, numbers, symbols, geometric designs, maps, engineering drawings, or other images. Graphics often combine text, illustration, and color. Graphic design may consist of the deliberate selection, creation, or arrangement of typography alone, as in a brochure, flier, poster, web site, or book without any other element. Clarity or effective communication may be the objective, association with other cultural elements may be sought, or merely, the creation of a distinctive style.

1.4.4 Rendering

Rendering is the process of generating an image from a model, by means of computer programs. The model is a description of three dimensional objects in a strictly defined language or data structure. It would contain geometry, viewpoint, texture, lighting, and shading information. The image is a digital image or raster graphics image. The term may be by analogy with an "artist's rendering" of a scene. 'Rendering' is also used to describe the process of calculating effects in a video editing file to produce final video output.

3D projection

3D projection is a method of mapping three dimensional points to a two dimensional plane. As most current methods for displaying graphical data are based on planar two dimensional media, the use of this type of projection is widespread, especially in computer graphics, engineering and drafting.

Ray tracing

Ray tracing is a technique for generating an image by tracing the path of light through pixels in an image plane. The technique is capable of producing a very high degree of photorealism; usually higher than that of typical scanline rendering methods, but at a greater computational cost.

Shading

Figure 1.7 Example of shading

Shading refers to depicting depth in 3D models or illustrations by varying levels of darkness. It is a process used in drawing for depicting levels of darkness on paper by applying media more densely or with a darker shade for darker areas, and less densely or with a lighter shade for lighter areas. There are various techniques of shading including cross hatching where perpendicular lines of varying closeness are drawn in a grid pattern to shade an area. The closer the lines are together, the darker the area appears. Likewise, the farther apart the lines are, the lighter the area appears. The term has been recently generalized to mean that shaders are applied.

Texture mapping

Texture mapping is a method for adding detail, surface texture, or colour to a computer-generated graphic or 3D model. Its application to 3D graphics was pioneered by Dr Edwin Catmull in 1974. A texture map is applied (mapped) to the surface of a shape, or polygon. This process is akin to applying patterned paper to a plain white box. Multitexturing is the use of more than one texture at a time on a polygon[7].

1.4.5 Volume Rendering

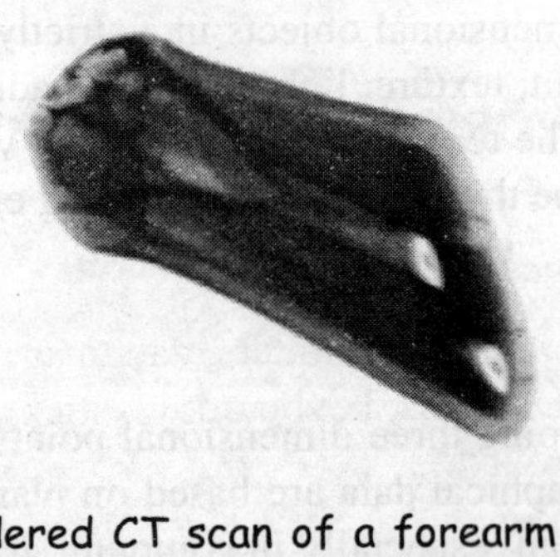

Figure 1.8 Volume rendered CT scan of a forearm with different colour schemes for muscle, fat, bone, and blood.

Volume rendering is a technique used to display a 2D projection of a 3D discretely sampled data set. A typical 3D data set is a group of 2D slice images acquired by a CT or MRI scanner.

Usually these are acquired in a regular pattern (e.g., one slice every millimeter) and usually have a regular number of image pixels in a regular pattern. This is an example of a regular volumetric grid, with each volume element, or voxel represented by a single value that is obtained by sampling the immediate area surrounding the voxel.

1.4.6 3D Modeling

3D modeling is the process of developing a mathematical, wireframe representation of any three-dimensional object via specialized software. The product is called a "3D model". It can be displayed as a two-dimensional image through a process called *3D rendering* or used in a computer simulation of physical phenomena. The model can also be physically created using 3D Printing devices. Models may be created automatically or manually. The manual modeling process of preparing geometric data for 3D computer graphics is similar to plastic arts such as sculpting.

1.5 COMPONENTS OF A GRAPHICS SYSTEM

Typical graphics system comprises of a host computer with support of fast processor, large memory, frame buffer and

- Display devices (color monitors),
- Input devices (mouse, keyboard, joystick, touch screen, trackball)
- Output devices (LCD panels, laser printers, Color printers. Plotters etc.)
- Interfacing devices such as, video I/O, TV interface etc.

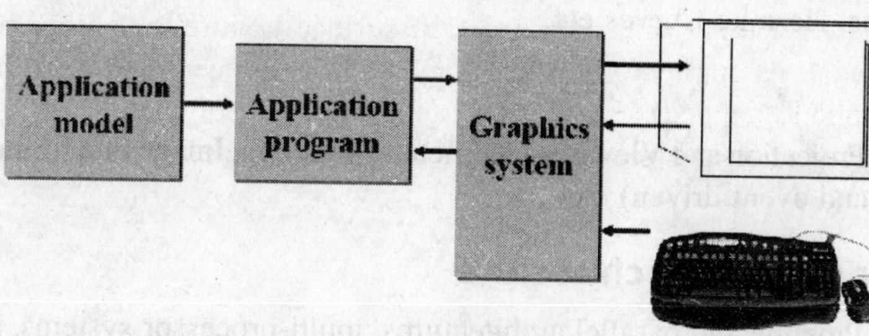

CONCEPTUAL FRAMEWORK FOR INTERACTIVE GRAPHICS

Examples of Computer Graphics Devices:

CRT, EGA/CGA/VGA/SVGA monitors, plotters, data matrix, laser printers, Films, flat panel devices, Video digitizers, scanners, LCD panels, keyboard, joystick, mouse, touch screen, track ball, etc.

IMPORTANT DEFINITIONS

Display Systems

Storage displays, Random scan, Raster refresh displays, CRT basics, video basics, Flat panel displays.

Transformations

Affine (2-D and 3-D): Rotation, Translation, Scale, Reflection and Shear.

Viewing: The Camera Transformations -perspective, orthographic, isometric and stereographic views, Quaternion.

Scan Conversion and Clipping

Drawing of Points, Lines, Markers, Curves, Circles, Ellipse, Polyline, Polygon. Area filling, fill-style, fill pattern, clipping algorithms, anti-aliasing etc.

Hidden Surface Removal

Back face culling, Painter's algorithm, scan-line algorithm, BSP-trees, Z-buffer/sorting, Ray tracing etc.

Shading & Illumination

Phong's shading model, texture mapping, bump mapping, Gouraud shading, Shadows and background, Color models etc.

Solid Modeling

Wire-frame, Octrees, Sweep, Boundary representations. Regularized Boolean set operations, Constructive Solid Geometry.

Curves and Surfaces

Bezier (Bernstein Polynomials) Curves, BSplines, Cubic-Splines, Quadratic surfaces, parametric and non-parametric forms, Hermite Curves etc.

Miscellaneous

Animation, Fractals, Projection and Viewing, Geometry, Modeling, Image File formats, Image Morphing, Interaction (sample and event-driven) etc.

Advanced Raster Graphics Architecture

Display Processors, Pipeline and parallel architectures, multi-processor systems, hybrid architectures.

REFERENCES

1. What is Computer Graphics? Cornell University Program of Computer Graphics. Last updated 04/15/98.
2. ISS (2002). "What are computer graphics?" Last updated: 22 Sep. 2008
3. Wayne Carlson, 2003. A Critical History of Computer Graphics and Animation. The Ohio State University
4. History of computer graphics 1960-69.
5. Ira Greenberg, 2007. *Processing: Creative Coding and Computational Art.* Apress. ISBN 159059617X.
6. http://books.google.com/books?id=WTl_7H5HUZAC&pg=PA115&dq=raster+vector+graphics+photographic&lr=&as_brr=0&ei=llOVR5LKCJL0iwGZ8-ywBw&sig=YEjfPOYSUDIf1CUbL5S5Jbzs7M8.

7. Rudolf F. Graf (1999). *Modern Dictionary of Electronics.* Oxford: Newnes. pp. 569. ISBN 0-7506-4331-5.

8. http://books.google.com/books?id=o2I1JWPpdusC&pg=PA569&dq=pixel+intitle:%22Modern+Dictionary+of+Electronics%22+inauthor:graf&lr=&as_brr=0&ei=5ygASM3qHoSgiwH45-GIDA&sig=7tg-LuGdu6Njypaawi2bbkeq8pw.

9. Blythe, David. *Advanced Graphics Programming Techniques Using OpenGL.* Siggraph 1999. (see: Multitexture)

10. *Computer Graphics:* Principles and practice; 2nd Edn. in C; J. Foley, A. Van Dam, Feiner and Hughes; Addison Wesley, 1997.

11. *11 Mathematical elements for Computer Graphics; 2nd Edn.;* D. F. Rogers and J. A. Adams; McGraw-Hill International. Edn., 1990.

12. *Computer Graphics - C version;* D. Hearn and M. P. Baker; Pearson Education, 2004.

13. *Computer Graphics using OpenGL;* 2nd Edn.; F. S. Hill Jr.; Pearson Education, 2003.

14. *Procedural Elements for Computer Graphics; 2nd Edn.,* D. F. Rogers, Tata McGraw-Hill, 2002.

FURTHER READING

- James D. Foley, Andries Van Dam, Steven K. Feiner and John F. Hughes (1995). *Computer Graphics: Principles and Practice.* Addison-Wesley
- Donald Hearn and M. Pauline Baker (1994). *Computer Graphics.* Prentice-Hall.
- Francis S. Hill (2001). *Computer Graphics.* Prentice Hall.
- John Lewell (1985). *Computer Graphics: A Survey of Current Techniques and Applications.* Van Nostrand Reinhold.
- Jeffrey J. McConnell (2006). *Computer Graphics: Theory Into Practice.* Jones & Bartlett Publishers.
- R. D. Parslow, R. W. Prowse, Richard Elliot Green (1969). *Computer Graphics: Techniques and Applications.*
- Peter Shirley and others. (2005). *Fundamentals of Computer Graphics.* A.K. Peters, Ltd.
- M. Slater, A. Steed, Y. Chrysantho (2002). *Computer Graphics and Virtual Environments: from Realism to Real-time.* Addison-Wesley

2 RASTER ALGORITHMS

2.1 INTRODUCTION

The only real implementation constraint that the hardware places on us is that all geometric objects eventually need to be represented by a collection of points in a two-dimensional grid (a raster). The subject matter of this chapter is to analyze the geometry of discrete sets and to describe some important algorithms that map continuous planar objects to discrete ones. Insofar as it is possible, one would like the discrete world to be a mirror image of the continuous one.

2.2 DISCRETE TOPOLOGY

This section defines the discrete analogs of a number of important continuous concepts. Probably the most basic of these is the idea of continuity itself, and central to that is the idea of a neighborhood of a point. Neighborhoods define the "topology" of a space. Now a raster can be modeled in an obvious way as a subset of $\mathbf{Z}^2$ and so this leads us to describe some possible definitions of a neighborhood of a point in $\mathbf{Z}^2$, or more generally in $\mathbf{Z}^n$. Although we are only interested in the case n = 2 in this chapter, there is nothing special about that case (except for the terminology), and it is useful to see what one can do in general.

Definition. In $\mathbf{Z}^2$, the *4-neighbors* of (i,j) are the four large grid points adjacent to (i,j) shown in Figure 2.1(a). The *8-neighbors* of (i,j) are the eight large grid points adjacent to (i,j) in Figure 2.1(b). More precisely, the 4-neighbors of (i,j) are the points (i,j + 1), (i - 1,j), (i,j - 1), and (i + 1,j). The 8-neighbors can be listed in a similar way. In order to generalize this definition to higher dimensions, think of the plane as tiled with 1 * 1 squares that are centered on the grid points of $\mathbf{Z}^2$ and whose sides are parallel to the coordinate axes (see Figure 2.1 again). Then, another way to define the neighbors of a point (i,j) is to say that the 4-neighbors are the centers of those squares in the tiling that share an edge with the square centered on (i,j) and the 8-neighbors are the centers of those squares in the tiling that share **either** an edge **or** a vertex with that square. Now think of $\mathbf{R}^n$ as tiled with n-dimensional unit cubes whose centers are the points of $\mathbf{Z}^n$ and whose faces are parallel to coordinate planes.

Definition. In $\mathbf{Z}^3$, the *6-neighbors* of (i,j,k) are the grid points whose cubes meet the cube centered at (i,j,k) in a face. The *18-neighbors* of (i,j,k) are the grid points whose cubes meet that cube in either a face **or** an edge. The *26-neighbors* of (i,j,k) are the grid points whose cubes meet that cube in either a face **or** an edge **or** a point.

Figure 2.2(a) shows the cubes of the 6-neighbors of the center point. Figure 2.2(b) shows those of the 18-neighbors and Figure 2.2(c), those of the 26-neighbors. More generally,

(a) (b)

Figure 2.1. The 4- and 8-neighbors of a point.

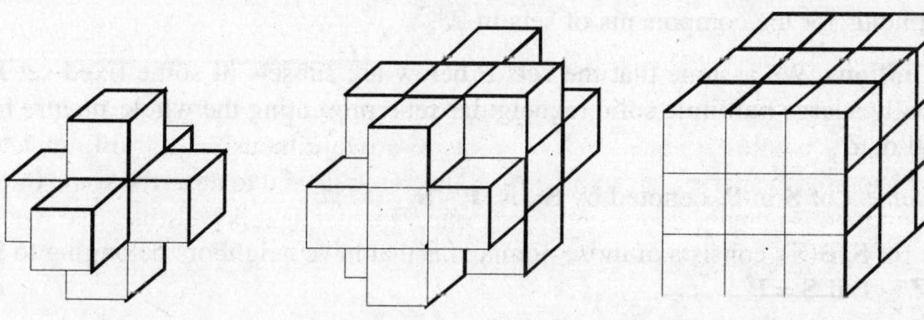

(a) (b) (c)

Figure 2.2. The 6-, 18-, and 26-neighbors of a point.

Definition. Let **p** å $\mathbf{Z}^n$ and let d be a fixed integer satisfying 0 <= d <= n - 1. Suppose that k is the number of points of $\mathbf{Z}^n$ that are the centers of cubes that meet the cube with center **p** in a face of dimension larger than or equal to d. Each of those points will be called a *k-neighbor* of **p** in $\mathbf{Z}^n$.

Note: The general definition for k-neighbor is not very satisfying because it is relatively complicated. It would have made more sense to call the point a "d-neighbor." Unfortunately, the terminology as stated is too well established for the two- and three dimensional case to be able to change it now.

Definition. Two points in $\mathbf{Z}^n$ are said to be *k-adjacent* if they are k-neighbors. k-adjacency is the key topological concept in the discrete world. All the terms defined below have an implicit "k-" prefix. However, to simplify the notation this prefix will be dropped. For example, we shall simply refer to "adjacent" points rather than "k-adjacent" points. It must be emphasized though that everything depends on the notion of adjacency that is chosen, that is, for example, whether the intended k is 4 or 8, in the case of $\mathbf{Z}^2$, or 6, 18, or 26, in the case of $\mathbf{Z}^3$. To make this dependency explicit, one only needs to restore the missing "k-" prefix. There is a nice alternate characterization of k-adjacency in two special cases that could have been used as the definition in those cases.

Definition. A (*discrete* or *digital*) *curve* from point **p** to point **q** in **Zn** is a sequence **rs**, 1 £ s £

k, of points such that $\mathbf{p} = \mathbf{r}_1$, $\mathbf{q} = \mathbf{r}_k$, and $\mathbf{r}_s$ is adjacent to $\mathbf{r}_{s+1}$, 1 <= s <= k - 1. Furthermore, with this notation, we define the *length* of the curve to be k - 1. For example, the points $\mathbf{p}_1$, $\mathbf{p}_2$, $\mathbf{p}_3$, and $\mathbf{p}_4$ in Figure 2.3 form a discrete curve of length 3 with respect to 8-adjacency but not with respect to 4-adjacency because $\mathbf{p}_1$ and $\mathbf{p}_2$ are not 4-adjacent.

Definition. A set **S** is *connected* if for any two points **p** and **q** in **S** there is a curve from **p** to **q** that lies entirely in **S**. A maximal connected subset of **S** is called a *component*.

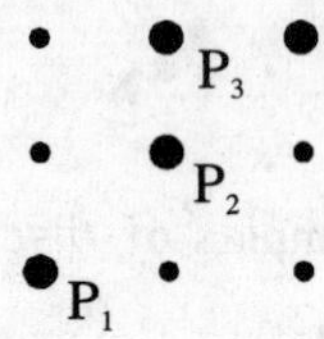

Figure 2.3. An 8-connected discrete curve.

Because of the difference between 4- and 8-connected, note the difference between a 4-component and an 8-component. It is easy to show that every 8-component is the union of 4-components. A similar comment holds for the components of sets in $\mathbf{Z}^3$.

Some Definitions. We assume that the sets **S** below are subsets of some fixed set **P** in $\mathbf{Z}^n$. In practice, **P** is usually a large but finite solid rectangular set representing the whole *picture* for a scene, but it could be all of $\mathbf{Z}^n$

The *complement* of **S** in **P**, denoted by $\mathbf{S}^c$, is, **P** - **S**.

The *border* of S, B(S), consists of those points of **S** that have neighbors belonging to $\mathbf{S}^c$ if $\mathbf{S} \neq \mathbf{P}$ or neighbors in $\mathbf{Z}^n$ - **P** if **S** = **P**.

The *background* of **S** is the union of those components of **Sc** that are either unbounded in $\mathbf{Z}^n$ or that contain a point of the border of the picture **P**.

The *holes* of **S** are all the components of $\mathbf{S}^c$ that are not contained in the background of **S**.

S is said to be *simply connected* if **S** is connected and has no holes.

The *interior* of S, iS, is the set S - B(S).

An *isolated point* of **S** is a point of **S** that has no neighbors in **S**.

If **S** is a finite set, then the *area* of **S** is the number of points in **S**.

Definition. There are several ways to define the *distance* d between two points (i,j) and (k,l) in $\mathbf{Z}^2$, or, more generally, between points **p** and **q** in $\mathbf{Z}^n$:

(a) *Euclidean distance*: $d = \sqrt{(i-k)^2 + (j-1)^2}$ or $d = |pq|$.

(b) *taxicab distance*: $d = |k-i| + |k-1|$ or $d = \sum_{i=1}^{n} |q_i - p_i|$

This distance function gets its name from the fact that a taxi driving from one location to another along orthogonal streets would drive that distance.

(c) *max distance*: $d = \max\left(|k-i|, |j-1|\right)$ or $d = \max_{1 \le i \le n}\left\{|q_i - p_i|\right\}$

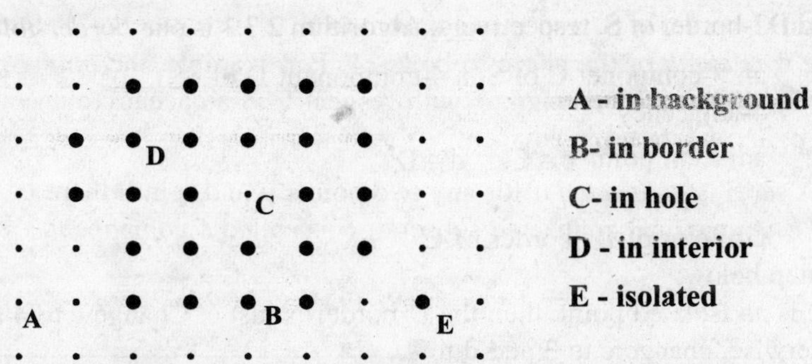

Figure 2.4. Examples of discrete concepts.

All three of these distance functions define a metric on $\mathbf{Z}^n$, called the *Euclidean*, *taxicab*, and *max metric*, respectively. (They actually also define a metric on $\mathbf{R}^n$.) For example, consider the points $\mathbf{p} = (2,1)$ and $\mathbf{q} = (5,3)$. Then the distances between these two points are:

Euclidean distance: $\sqrt{13}$

Taxicab distance: 5

Max distance: 3

The points that are a distance of 1 from a given point are its 4-neighbors when we use the taxicab distance and the 8-neighbors when we use the max distance. Finally, the rest of this chapter deals with two-dimensional sets and, unless stated otherwise, all our sets will be (discrete) subsets of some given picture **P** in $\mathbf{Z}^2$. We shall use the terminology above.

2.3 BORDER-FOLLOWING ALGORITHMS

Algorithms that can compute the borders of regions in a picture are important in a variety of places, in particular in animation. We describe one such algorithm here to give the reader a flavor of what they are like. Assume that each point of a picture has a value associated to it and that in our case this is either 0 or 1, with the region of interest in it being the points with value 1. We shall show pictures by showing the values at their points and, to simplify the discussion, we often identify the point with its value. ("Setting a point to 3" will mean setting its value to 3.)

Definition. If **C** is a component of **S**, **D** a component of **Sc**, then the ***D-border of C*** is the set of points of **C** that are adjacent to a point of **D**. For example, consider the connected set **S** of 1's below:

1 1 1 1
1 0 1 1 1
1 1 1 1

Let **D**1 and **D**2 be the components of **Sc** that contain the left and right "0," respectively. Then

1 1 1   **1 1 1 1**
1   1   and   **1   1**
1 1 1   **1 1 1 1**

are the **D**1-border and **D**2-border of **S**, respectively. Algorithm 2.3.1 is one *border-following* algorithm.

Input : an 8-componet C of S, a 4-component D of S^C
4-adjacency
adjacent point $c \in$ **C**, $d \in$ **D**

Output: all point of **D**- border of **C**

Follow the step below:

(1) If C is an isolated point, then the D-border is just c. Change c to 4 and stop. Otherwise, change c to 3 and d to 2.

(2) List the 8-neighbours of c in clockwise order starting with d and ending with first occurrence of 1, 3, or 4:
$e_1, e_2 \ldots . e_k$

(3) If c is 3, e_k is 4 and e_h is 2 for some h < k, then set c to 4, e_h to 0, and stop; otherwise, set c to 4 only if it was 1 and not 3), take e_k as the new c, take e_{k-1} as the new d, and go back to (2)

When the algorithm stops, the 4's will be the **D**-border of **C**.

Algorithm 2.3.1. A border-following algorithm.

2.3.1 Example

We show the various stages of Algorithm 2.3.1 for a set **S**. The values of points in the pictures below are shown in boldface and **S** starts off as the points marked with 1's. The current c and d are shown in parentheses to the left of the point to which they refer. The numbering of the 8-neighbors of c is shown in parentheses to the right of the point. We also show the value of k that we get in step (2) of the algorithm.

```
(d)0(1)  0(2)  0        2  (d)0(2)  0(2)       2   0       0        0          2      0       0
(c)1     1(3)  0   →    3  (c)1     0(3)  →    3   4(8)  (d)0(1)   0(2)   →   3    (c)4     0  →
  1        0   1        1    0      1(4)       1   0(7)  (c)1      0(3)       1(2) (d)0(1)  4
                                               0   0(6)   0(5)     0(4)        0      0       0

     k = 3                  k= 4                          k = 8                       k = 2

  0      2        0       0          0(2)     2(3)  0(4)0        0  0  0
0(6)   3(7)       4       0   →   (d)0(1)   (c)3   4(5)0   →    4  4  0
0(5)  (c)1    (d)0(1)     4          0        4      0  4        4  0  4
0(4)   0(3)     0(2)      0

              k = 7                          k =5 , h =3
```

Finally, the configuration

$$\begin{array}{ccccc} 1 & 1 & 1 & 1 & \\ 1 & 1 & 0 & 1 & \\ 1 & 1 & 1 & 0 & 1 \\ & & & 1 & \end{array}$$

shows that the choice of adjacency is important. The algorithm fails if **C** is a 4-component and must be changed. Algorithm 2.3.1 can be used to find **all** border points of a set **S**. It provides a way of marking its border points so that one can then fill the interior of **S** using a fill algorithm of the type discussed in the next section

2.4 FILL ALGORITHMS

Contour-filling algorithms are used in many places. For example, in pattern recognition problems integrals may have to be computed over areas; in photo typesetting, fonts are described by contours that are later filled; in animation, the cel painter who fills figures has the next most time-consuming job after the animator.

There are two broad classes of such algorithms – *polygon-based* (*edge-filling*) algorithms and *pixel-based* algorithms. The former can be used in the case where the regions to be filled are defined by polygons and we can use the equations for the edges. The latter are, in a sense, more general because they can be used both for polygonal regions and also arbitrary regions whose boundaries are defined on the pixel level. There is also a distinction as to how the algorithm decides whether a point is in the interior of a region. Some use a *parity check* that is based on the fact that lines intersect a closed curve an even number of times (if one counts intersections at certain special points such as at points of tangency correctly). This test is always used in case of polygon-based algorithms, but can also be used for pixel-based ones. Other algorithms, called *seed fill* algorithms, use connectivity methods. Here it is assumed that one is given a starting point or seed. Then one sees which pixels can be reached from this one without crossing the contour. The bounding curves can be quite general. This approach applies only to pixel-based algorithms. Also, one needs to know an interior point. This is okay in interactive situations (where one picks one using a mouse, for example), but if one wants to automate the process, note how border-following algorithms become relevant.

In this section we shall describe the pixel-based seed fill algorithms. Section 2.9.1 will look at polygon-based fill algorithms.

The Flood Fill Problem

Given distinct colors c and c', a set A of the same color c bounded by points whose colors are different from c and c', find an algorithm that changes all points of A and only those to the color c'. An algorithm that solves this problem is called a *flood fill* algorithm. There are a number of related fill problems and associated algorithms. For example, *boundary fill* algorithms assume that all points of the boundary have the same color, which is different from the color inside the region, where the *boundary* of a set S means here the set of points of Sc that are adjacent to S.

```
Procedure BFA (Integer x, y)
If Inside (x, y) then
        begin
                Set (x, y)
                BFA (x,y –1); BFA (x, y+1);
                BFA (x –1, y); BFA (x+1, y);
        end;
```

Algorithm 2.4.1. The basic fill algorithm.

In the algorithms of this section, the Boolean-valued function **Inside**(x,y) determines whether or not the pixel at (x,y) has the property one wants. The procedure **Set**(x,y) sets the value of the pixel at (x,y) to its desired value. For example, to get a flood fill algorithm let **Inside**(x,y) be true if the value of the pixel at (x,y) agrees with the value of the pixels in the region and let **Set**(x,y) set the pixel value to its new value (the same as **Draw**(x,y,c¢)). Using the functions **Inside** and **Set** will make our algorithms more general and applicable to a variety of fill algorithms. There is one constraint on the **Inside** function however: **Inside**(x,y) **must** return **false** after an operation **Set**(x,y).

Assume 4-adjacency is chosen and that our regions are 4-connected. The BFA procedure in Algorithm 2.4.1 shows that the basic idea behind a fill algorithm is very simple. Notice that 4-connected is important and that the algorithm will not work if the region is not 4-connected.

Although the BFA algorithm is simple, the recursion is expensive. One of the earliest nonrecursive algorithms is due to Smith. It is not very efficient because pixels are visited twice, but many of the better algorithms are based on it. It will be worthwhile to describe Smith's algorithm, Algorithm 2.4.2, first before we present theone due to [Fish90b]. In this algorithm and the next, the constants XMIN, XMAX, YMIN, and YMAX define the minimum and maximum values for the x- and ycoordinates of pixels in the viewport. The procedures **Push** and **Pop** push and pop a pair (x,y) onto and from a stack, respectively. The function **StackNotEmpty** tests whether this stack is empty or not. The procedures **Inside** and **Set** are as described above.

For example, suppose that in Figure 2.5 our starting point is (7,3). After the first **FillRight** command the two-pixel segment from (7,3) to (8,3) would have been filled. The **FillLeft** command would fill (6,3). The **ScanHi** command would place the pixel coordinates (6,4) and (8,4) on the stack in that order. The **ScanLo** command would add (6,2). The segments of the region that (6,4), (8,4), and (6,2) belong to are usually called "shadows." The point of the **ScanHi** and **ScanLo** procedures is to find these shadows that still need to be filled. We now return to the beginning of the main **while** loop, pop (6,2), and make that our new starting point. The next **FillRight** and **FillLeft** would fill the segment from (2,2) to (8,2). The **ScanHi** and **ScanLo** would

```
{Global variables}
integer x, y, lx, rx;
a stack of pixel coordinates (x, y)

procedure Fill (integer seedx, seedy)
begin
        x:=seedx; y := seedy;
        if not (Inside (x,y)) then Exit;
        Push (x, y);
```

```
        while StackNotEmpty () do
            begin
                PopXY ();
                if Inside (x, y) then
                    begin
                        FillRight (); FillLeft ();
                        ScanHi (); Scan ();
                    end
            end
        end;
procedure FillRight ()
begin
        integer tx;

        tx:=x
        {move rigth setting all pixel of sgement as we go}
        while Inside (tx,y) and (tx ≤ XMAX) do
            begin
                Set (tx,y); tx := tx+1;
            ends;
        rx := tx–1; {save index of rigth most pixel in segment}
end;
procedure FillLeft ()
begin
        integer tx;
        tx := x
        {Move left setting all pixels of segment as we go}
        while Inside (x,y) and (tx ≥ XMIN) do
            begin
                Set (tx,y); tx := tx –1;
            end;
        lx :=tx+1; {save index of left most pixel in segment}
end;
Procedure ScanHi ()
{Scan the pixels between lx and rx in the scan line above the current one.
 Stack the left most of these for any segment of our region that we find.
 We do not set any pixel in this pass.}
begin
        integer tx;
        if y + 1 > YMAX then Exit;
        tx := lx;
        while tx ≤ rx do
            begin
                {Scan past any pixel not in region}
                while not (Inside (tx, y+1)) and (tx ≤ rx) do tx := tx+1;
                if tx ≤ rx then
                    begin
```

```
                    Push (tx, y+1);
                    {We just saved first point of a sgement in region,
                     Now scan past the rest of the pixel in this sgement.}
                    while Inside (tx, y+1) and (tx ≤ rx) do tx := tx +1;
                end;
            end
end;
procedure ScanLo ()
{Scan the pixels between lx and rx in the scan line below the current one.
 Stack the left most of these for any segment of our region that we find.
 We do not set any pixel in this pass.}
begin
        integer tx;
        if y – 1 > YMIN then Exit;
        tx := lx;
        while tx ≤ rx do
            begin
                {Scan past any pixel not in region}
                while not (Inside (tx, y–1)) and (tx ≤ rx) do tx := tx+1;
                if tx ≤ rx then
                    begin
                        Push (tx, y–1);
                        {We just saved first point of a sgement in region,
                         Now scan past the rest of the pixel in this sgement.}
                        while Inside (tx, y–1) and (tx ≤ rx) do tx := tx +1;
                    end;
            end
end;
```

Algorithm 2.4.2. The Smith seed fill algorithm.

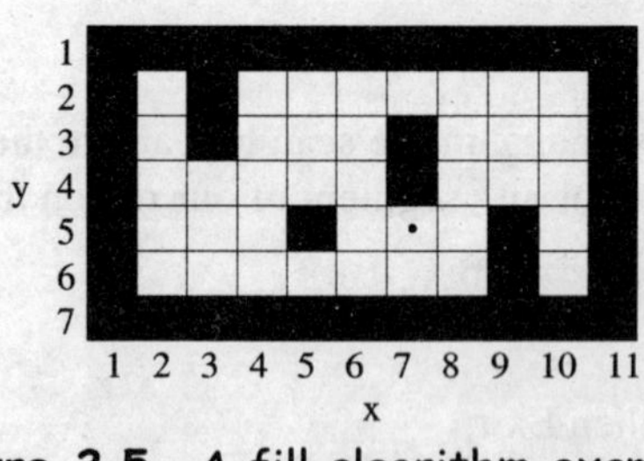

Figure 2.5. A fill algorithm example.

Figure 2.6. Pixel shadows.

put (2,3) and (6,3) on the stack. The loop would start over and pop (6,3). This time, since (6,3) has already been filled, we immediately jump back to the beginning and pop (2,3), and so on. The problem with Smith's basic algorithm is that we look at some pixels twice, as we saw in the case of (2,3) in the previous example. This happens because we automatically put coordinates from both the line above and the line below the current one on the stack. When we then, say, deal with the line above, the algorithm will have us look at the current line again because it will be the line below that one. For a fast algorithm we need to prevent this duplicate effort. Algorithm 2.4.3 from involves more bookkeeping because it differentiates between the three different types of possible shadows shown in Figure 2.6, but it will read each pixel only slightly more than once on the average and also has good worst-case behaviour. Fishkin points out that it is optimal if the region has no holes. An alternative improvement to Smith's seed fill algorithm is described by Heckbert.

Finally, another distinction that is made between flood fill algorithms is whether we are dealing with *hard* or *soft* area flooding. The algorithms we have described so far were hard area flooding, which basically assumed that the region to be filled was demarcated by a "solid" boundary, that is, a curve of pixels all of the same color. Such a boundary would be a jagged curve. To get a smoother looking boundary one typically would blur or "shade" it by assigning a gradation of colors in a neighbourhood of it. (The causes of the "jaggies" and solutions to the aliasing problem are discussed later in Section 2.6.) If boundaries are shaded, then we would like filling algorithms to maintain this shading. Soft area flooding refers to algorithms that do this and leave any "shading" intact. Smith's paper is a good reference for both hard and soft area flooding. The *tint fill* algorithm he describes in that paper is a soft area flooding algorithm. There are other types of pixel-based fill algorithms. Pavlidis describes a parity check type algorithm. Rogers describes various algorithms for filling regions bounded by polygons that he calls "edge fill" algorithms.

```
direction = (–1,+1)
stackRec = record          {a stackRec records the data for one shadow}
          integer myLx, myRx,    {endpoints of this shadow}
                  dadLx, dadRx,          {endpoints of my parent}
                  myY;                          {scan line of shadow}
          direction myDirection; {–1 means below parent, +1 means above}
end;

{Global variable}
Stack of stackRec shadowStack;

procedure Fill (integer seedx. seedy)
begin
          label       1,2
          integer     x, lx, rx, dadLx, dadRx, y;
          direction   dir;
          boolean     walin;
          Initialize shadowStack to empty;
          Find the span [lx, rx] containing the seed point;

          Push (lx, rx, lx, rx, seedy+1,1);
          Push (lx, rx, lx, rx, seedy–1,–1);

          while StackNotEmpty () do
```

```
1.          Pop ();
            if ( y<YMIN) or (y > YMAX) then Goto 1;
            x := lx+1;
            wasln := Inside (lx,y);
            if wasln then
               begin
                   Set (lx, y); lx := lx–1;
                   {If the left edge of the shadow touches a span, then move to its
                    left end setting pixels as we go}
                   while Inside (lx, y) and lx ≥ XMIn do
                       begin
                           Set (lx, y); lx := lx–1;
                       end
            end;
            {Start the main loop. Moving to the right starting from the current position
             x, if wasln is true, then we are inside a spam whose left edge is at lx.}
        while x ≤XMAX do
            if wasIn
               then
                   begin
                       if Inside (x, y)
                           then Set (x, y) {was inside and still inside}
                       else
                           begin
                               {was inside but not anymore, i.e., we
                               just passed the rigth edge of a span}
                               Stack (dadLx, dadRx, lx, xÝ, y, dir);
                               wasIn := false;
                           end
               end
            end
               begin
                       if x > rx then Goto 2;
                       if Inside (x,y) then
                           begin
                               {we weren't inside but are now i.e.
                                we just found the left edge of a new span}
                               Set (x, y);
                               wasIn :=true
                               lx := x;
                           end
                   x := x+1;
               end;
2.          If wasIn then
               {we just hit the edge of the viewport while in a span}
               Stack (dadLx, dadRx, lx, x–1, y, dir);
        end
```

```
end;

boolean function StackNotEmpty ()
{Return true if shadowStack is empty and false otherwise}

procedure Push (Integer myl, myr, dadl, dadr, y; direction  dir)
{Pushes record onto shadowStack}

procedure Pop ()
{Pops top of shadoStack into local variables lx, rx, dadLx, dadRx, y, dir}

procedure Stack (integer dadLx, dadRx, lx, rx, y; direction dir)
{Pushes an extra shadow onto shadowStack, given a newly discovered span
 and its parent. This is where the three types of shadows are differentiated}

begin
        Integer pushrx, pushlx;

        pushrx:= rx+1; pushlx := lx–1;
        Push (lx, rx, pushlx, pushrx, y+dir, dir);
        If rx > dadRx then Push (dadRx+1, rx, pushlx, pushrx, y–dir, dir);
        If lx < dadLx then Push (lx, dadLx–1, pushlx, pushrx, y–dir, dir);
end;
```

Algorithm 2.4.3. The Fishkin seed fill algorithm.

2.5 GENERATING DISCRETE CURVES

Now, we start a central topic of this chapter, namely, curves and the problem that one runs into when one tries to represent them with a discrete set of points. Clearly, we want any mapping of continuous structures into discrete ones to preserve the visual shape properties, such as smoothness and uniform thickness, as much as possible but this is not easy. We shall look at the problem of defining and generating discrete lines first and then conics.

Lines, or more accurately segments, are the most basic of computer graphics objects because most modeling systems use linear approximations to all objects so that displaying them reduces to drawing lots of lines. It is possible to actually give a formal definition of a discrete "straight" line. Not surprisingly, such definitions get complicated, but from a practical point of view we are not really interested in a definition. Rather, we are happy with an algorithm that generates a satisfactory set of points for a line. What is satisfactory? Well, that is not very precise, but some attributes that we want the generated discrete lines to have are:

(1) Visually, the line should appear as straight as possible.

(2) The line should start and end accurately, so that, for example, if several contiguous line segment are drawn, then there is no gap between them.

(3) Each line should appear to have an even visual thickness, that is, it should have as constant a density as possible, and this thickness should be independent of its length and slope.

(4) The conversion process must be fast.

In Sections 2.5.1–2.5.3 we look at line-drawing algorithms for the monochrome case, that is, where the raster is an array of 0's and 1's and the line consists of those pixels that are set to 1. Section 2.6 looks at some deeper problems that one encounters in the process of discretizing continuous objects and making them look smooth. Section 2.9.1 looks at a scan line algorithm for lists of lines and fill algorithm for polygons.

Conics are the next most common curve after the "straight" line. The circle is one obvious such curve, but the other conics are also encountered frequently. Their geo-metric properties and relatively low degree (when compared with the popular cubic splines) make them attractive for use in designing shapes such as fonts. Because of this, a great deal of effort has been spent on devising efficient algorithms for computing them. We shall look at a few of these in Sections 2.9.2 and 2.9.3.

Because one common theme of some of the algorithms that generate discrete curves is derived from the geometric approach to solving differential equations, we start with that subject.

2.5.1 Digital Differential Analyzers

Consider the basic first order differential equation of the form

$$\frac{dy}{dx} = f(x, y) = \frac{g(x, y)}{h(x, y)}$$

If y(x) is any solution, then f(x,y(x)) specifies the slope of the graph of y(x) at the point (x,y(x)). In other words, if one thinks of the function f as specifying a *vector field* over the entire plane (to (x,y) in the plane we associate the vector (1,f(x,y))), then solving equation (2.1) corresponds to finding a parameterized curve x -> (x,y(x)) whose tangent vectors agree with the vectors from this vector field. Mathematicians call such curves "integral curves." In general, given a vector field, a curve whose tangent vectors agree with the vectors of that vector field at every point on the curve is called an *integral curve* for that vector field. See Figure 2.7. The reason for this nomenclature is that solving for the curve basically involves an integration process.

This idea of vector fields and integral curves leads to the following approach to finding numerical solutions to differential equations called *Euler's method.* Suppose that we want the solution to pass through $\mathbf{p}_0 = (x_0,y_0)$. Since we know the tangent vector to the solution curve there and since the tangent line is a good approximation to the curve, moving a small distance along the tangent, say by å$(h(x_0,y_0),g(x_0,y_0))$, where e is a small positive constant, will put us at a point $\mathbf{p1} = (x_1,y_1)$, which hopefully is not too far away from an actual point on the curve. Next, starting at **p1** we repeat this process. In general, let

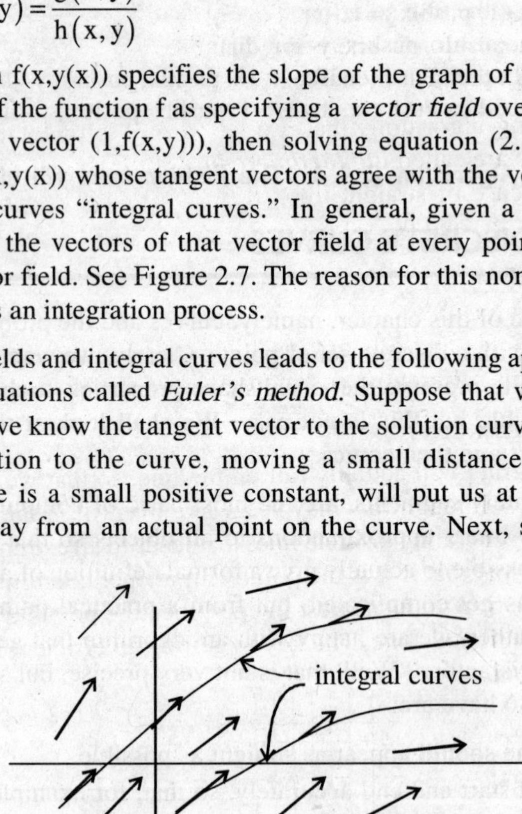

Figure 2.7. Integral curves of a vector field.

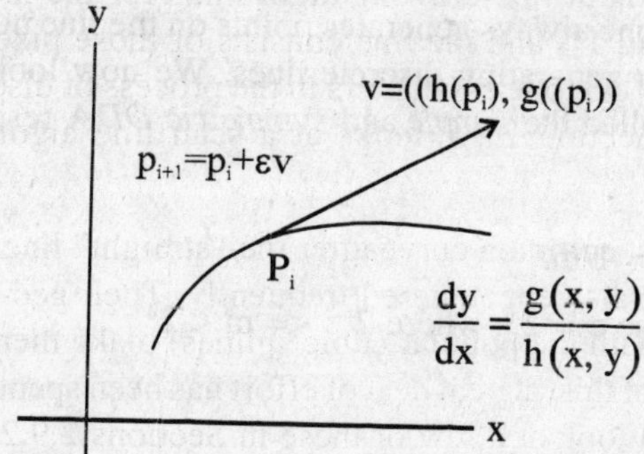

Figure 2.8. Generating an integral curve approximation.

$$p_{i+1} = p_i\varepsilon\left(h\left(x_i, y_i\right), g\left(x_i, y_i\right)\right)$$

See Figure 2.8. The sequence of points $\mathbf{p}_0$, $\mathbf{p}_1$, . . . , $\mathbf{p}_n$ obtained in this way becomes our approximation to the actual integral curve passing through $\mathbf{p}_0$. Unfortunately, as we move from point to point we start drifting away from the actual curve and so our approximation will, in general, get further and further away from the true solution. To make the method work we need to compensate for any possible error as we move along. There are some very good algorithms that solve differential equations with basically this approach by using some fancy error-correcting terms.

Discrete curve-drawing algorithms that are based on the qualitative solutions to differential equations as described above are called *digital differential analyzer* or *DDA* type algorithms. Let us see what we get in the special case of straight lines. The differential equation for the straight line that passes through the points (x_0,y_0) and (x_1,y_1) is

$$\frac{dy}{dx} = \frac{\Delta y}{\Delta x} = \frac{\varepsilon\Delta y}{\varepsilon\Delta x},$$

where "y = y_1 - y_0, "x = x_1 - x_0, and e is any positive real number. Specializing the approximation formula, equation (2.2), to this differential equation gives us a sequence of points $\mathbf{p}_i$ defined by

$$p_{i+1} = p_i + \left(\varepsilon\Delta x, \varepsilon\Delta y\right)$$

In fact, the points **pi** we generate will actually fall on the line, so that we do not have to worry about compensating for any errors. Although this may seem like overkill in the case of continuous lines, it does motivate an approach to generating discrete lines that leads to an extremely efficient such algorithm (the Bresenham algorithm). Note that if $\mathbf{q}_i$ is the point with integer coordinates that is gotten from $\mathbf{p}_i$ by rounding each real coordinate of $\mathbf{p}_i$ to its nearest integer, then the points $\mathbf{q}_i$ define a discrete curve that is an approximation to the continuous one. The key to getting an efficient line drawing algorithm is to be able to compute the $\mathbf{q}_i$ efficiently.

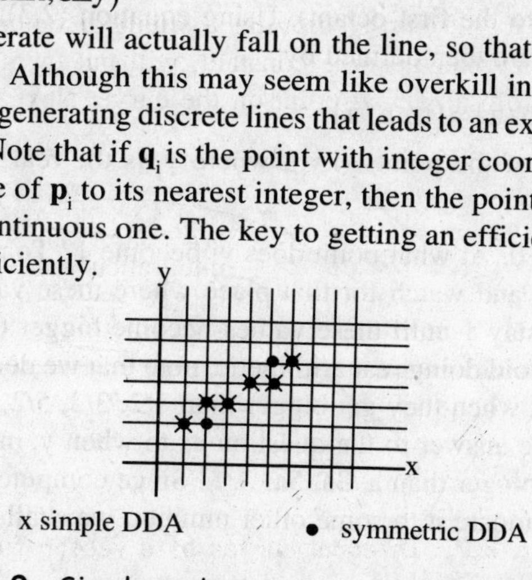

Figure 2.9. Simple and symmetric DDA generated lines.

In the continuous case one always generates points on the line no matter what e is chosen but the choice of e does matter when generating discrete lines. We now look at two possible choices for e. These give rise to what are called the *simple* and *symmetric DDA*, respectively.

Let m = max(|"x|,|"y|).

The simple DDA: Choose e = 1/m.

The symmetric DDA: Choose e = 2^{-n}, where 2^{n-1} <= m < 2^n.

2.5.1.1 Example

Suppose that we want to generate the discrete line from (1,2) to (6,5).

Solution. In this case (D_x,D_y) = (5,3). For the simple DDA we have

e=1 5,eDx=1,eDy = 3 5, and **pi**+1 =**pi**+(1,3 5).

In the case of the symmetric DDA, we have

e=1 8,e Δ x=5 8,e Δ y =3 8, and $\mathbf{p}_{i+1}$ =$\mathbf{p}_i$+(5 8,3 8).

The points that are generated are shown in Figure 2.9. The points of the simple DDA are shown as X's and those of the symmetric DDA are shown as solid circles.

2.5.2 The Bresenham Line-Drawing Algorithm

Although the DDA algorithms for drawing straight lines are simple, they involve **real** arithmetic. Some simple modifications result in an algorithm that does only **integer** arithmetic, and only additions at that.

Note that in the case of the simple DDA, either x or y will always be incremented by 1. For simplicity, assume that the start point of our line is the origin. If we also restrict ourselves to lines whose endpoint is in the first octant in the plane, then it will be the x that always increases by 1. Therefore, we only need to worry about computing the y coordinates efficiently.

Suppose therefore that we want to draw a line from (0,0) to (a,b), where a and b are integers and 0 £ b £ a (which puts (a,b) into the first octant). Using equation (2.3), the points **pi**, 0 < = i < = a, generated by the simple DDA are then defined by

$$p_i = p_{i-1} + (1, b/a) = (i, i\,b/a)$$

and the discrete line consists of the points (i,y_i), where y_i is the real number i(a/b) rounded to the nearest integer.

Now the y coordinates start at 0. At what point does yi become 1? To answer this question, we must compute b/a, 2b/a, 3b/a, . . . , and watch for that place where these values become bigger than 1/2. Furthermore, the y_i will then stay 1 until these values become bigger than 3/2, at which time y_i will become 2. Since we want to avoid doing real arithmetic, note that we do not really care what the actual values are but only care about when they get bigger than 1/2, 3/2, 5/2, ... This means that we can multiply through by 2a and the answer to the question as to when y_i increases by 1 is determined by when 2b, 4b, 6b, . . . become bigger than a, 3a, 5a, ... Since computers can compare a number to 0 in less time than it takes to compare it to some other number, we shall start off by subtracting a. Our first question now is

"When does 2b - a, 4b - a, 6b - a, . . . become bigger than 0?"

and only involves repeated integer additions of 2b to an initial sum d = 2b - a. After the sum d has become bigger than 0 and y has switched to 1, we need to check when the sum becomes bigger than 2a. By subtracting 2a, we again only need to keep checking for when the sum gets to be bigger than 0 by successive additions of 2b. In general, whenever y is incremented by 1, we subtract 2a from the current sum d. In that way we always need to check d simply against 0. For example, suppose we want to draw the line from (0,0) to (15,3). In this case, 2a = 30, 2b = 6, and the initial d is 6 - 15 = -9. The table below shows the points (x_i,y_i) that are drawn and the changes to the sum d as i ranges from 0 to 8:

i	0	1	2	3	4	5	6	7	8
d	−9	−3	−27	−21	−15	−9	−3	−27	
(x_i,y_i)	(0,0)	(1,0)	(2,0)	(3,1)	(4,1)	(5,1)	(6,1)	(7,1)	(8,2)

The code in Algorithm 2.5.2.1 implements the algorithm we have been describing. In our discussion above we have restricted ourselves to lines that start at the origin and end in the first octant. Starting at another point simply amounts to adding a constant offset to all the points. Lines that end in a different octant can be handled in a similar way to the first octant case – basically by interchanging the x and y. What this boils down to is that an algorithm which handles all lines is not much harder, involving only a case statement to separate between the case where the absolute value of the slope is either larger or less than or equal to 1.

We have just described the basis for the *Bresenham line-drawing algorithm.* It, or some variation of it, is the algorithm that is usually used for drawing straight lines. Bresenham showed that his algorithm generated the bestfit discrete approximation to a continuous line. The variation that is Algorithm 2.5.2.2

```
Code for drawing the discrete line from (0,0) to the point (a, b) in the first octant:
begin
        integer d, x, y;

        d := 2*b–a
        x := 0;
        y := 0;
        while true do
            begin
                Draw (x, y);
                if x= a then Exit;
                if d ≥ 0 then
                    begin
                        y := y +1;
                        d := d–2*a;
                    end
                x := x +1;
                d := d +2*b;
            end
end
```

Algorthm 2.5.2.1. Basic line-drawing algorithm.

comes from works for all lines. It generates the same points as the original Bresenham line-drawing algorithm but is slightly more efficient. To further improve the efficiency of DDA-based algorithms, there are n-step algorithms that compute several pixels of a line at a time. The first of these was based on the idea of double stepping. There are also algorithms that use a 3- or 4-step process. See [BoyB00] for an n-step algorithm that automatically uses the optimal n and claims to be at least twice as fast as earlier ones.

2.5.3 The Midpoint Line-Drawing Algorithm

Because drawing lines efficiently is so important to graphics, one is always on the lookout for better algorithms. Another well-known line-drawing algorithm is the so called *midpoint line-drawing algorithm*. It produces the same pixels as the Bresenham algorithm, but is better suited for generalizing to other implicitly defined curves such as conics and also to lines in three dimensions.

Assume that a **nonvertical** line **L** is defined by an equation of the form

$$f(x,y) = ax + by + c = 0,$$

```
procedure DrawLine (Integer x0, y0, x1, y1)
begin
        Integer dx, ax, sgnx, dy, ay, sgny, x, y, d;
        dx :=x1–x0; ax := abs (dx)*2; sgnx := Sign (dx);
        dy :=y1–y0; ay := abs (dy)*2; sgny := Sign (dy);
        x := x0; y := y0;
        if ax > ay
            then   {x increases faster than y}
              begin
                d := ay –ax/2;
                while true do
                  begin
                    Draw (x, y);
                    if x = x1 then Exit;
                    if d ≥ 0 then
                       begin
                            y : y+sgny; d:= d–ax;
                       end
                    x : x+sgnx; d := d+ay
                  end
                end
            else   {y increases faster than x}
                begin
                  d := ax –ay/2;
                  while true do
                    begin
                      Draw (x, y);
                      if y = y1 then Exit;
                      if d ≥ 0 then
```

```
                    begin
                        x : x + sgnx; d := d – ay;
                    end;
                y : y + sgny; d := d – ax;
            end
        end
end;
integer function Sign (real x)
if x < 0 then retrun (–1)
      else retrun (+1)
```

Algorithm 2.5.2.2. A Bresenham line-drawing algorithm.

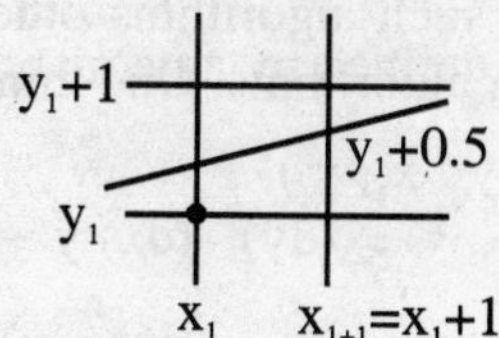

Figure 2.10. The midpoint line-drawing algorithm decision.

where -b e” a e” 0. This assumption implies that our line has slope between 0 and 1. Lines with other slopes are handled in a symmetric way like in Bresenham's algorithm. Vertical lines are a very special case that would be handled separately. Another important consequence of our assumptions is that f(x,y) will be positive for points (x,y) below the line and negative for points above the line. Also like in the Bresenham algorithm, the points **pi** = (xi,yi) that we will generate for the line will have the property that the x-coordinate will be incremented by 1 each time, xi+1 = xi + 1, so that we only have to determine the change in the y coordinate.

See Figure 2.10. The only possible value for yi+1 is yi or yi + 1. The decision will be based on the sign of If $d_i > 0$, then the line **L** crosses the line $x = x_i + 1$ above the point $(x_i + 1, y_i + 0.5)$ and we need to let y_i+1 be $y_i + 1$. If $d_i < 0$, then we should let y_i+1 be y_i. If $d_i = 0$, then either y value would be satisfactory. We shall choose yi in that case. Choosing our points p_i in this way is what constitutes the basic idea behind the midpoint line-drawing algorithm.

The only thing that is left is to describe some optimizations that can be made in the computations. First, the di can be computed efficiently in an incremental way. By definition, if $d_i <= 0$, then

$$d_{i+1} = f(x_i + 2, y_i + 0.5)$$

$$= a(x_i+2) + b(y_i+0.5)+c$$

$$= d_i + a$$

On the other hand, if $d_i > 0$, then

$$d_{i+1} = f(x_i + 2, y_i + 1.5)$$

$$= a(x_i+2) + b(y_i+1.5)+c$$

$$= d_i + a+b$$

This shows that the next value of the decision variable can be computed by simple additions to the previous value. If our line **L** starts at the point $\mathbf{p}_0 = (x_0,y_0)$, then

$$d_0 = f(x_0+1, y_0 +0.5) = f(x_0, y_0) +a+b/2$$

This gives us the starting value for the decision variable and all the rest are computed incrementally. We can avoid the fraction in the starting value and do all our computations using purely integer arithmetic by multiplying the equation for our line by 2, that is, let us use

$$F(x,y) = 2f(x, y) = 2(ax + by + c) = 0.$$

This has the effect of multiplying our starting value for the decision variable and its increments by 2. Since only the sign of the variable was important and not its value, we have lost nothing. Putting all this together leads to Algorithm 2.5.3.1. Finally, before leaving the subject of line-drawing algorithms, we should point out that there are other such algorithms other than the ones mentioned here. For example, there are run-based line drawing algorithms. One thing to keep in mind

```
procedure DrawLine (integer x0, y0, x1, y1)
{we have chosen the equation f(x, y) = (dy) –(dx) y +c=0 as tje equation for the line}
begin
        integer dx, dy, d, posInc, negInc, x, y;

        dx := x1 –x0;
        dy := y1 –y0;
        d := 2*dy – dx;    {Initial value of decision variable}
        posInc := 2*dy;
        negInc := 2*(dy–dx);
        x := x0; y :=y0;
        Draw (x, y)
        while x < x1 do
             begin
                 if (d≤0)
                     then d : d + posInc
                     else
                        begin
                            d : = d + negInc; y := y+1;
                        end
                 x := x+1;
                 Draw (x,y);
             end
end;
```

Algorithm 2.5.3.1. The midpoint-line drawing algorithm.

though is that the time spent in line drawing algorithms is often dominated by the operation of setting pixels in the frame buffer, so that software improvements alone may be less important.

2.6 THE ALIASING PROBLEM

No matter how good a line drawing algorithm is, it is impossible to avoid giving most discrete lines a staircase effect (the "jaggies"). They just will not look "straight." Increasing the resolution of the raster helps but does not resolve the problem entirely.

In order to draw the best looking straight lines one has to first understand the "real" underlying problem which is one of **sampling**.

The geometric curves and surfaces one is typically trying to display are continuous and consist of an infinite number of points. Since a computer can only show a finite (discrete) set of points, how one chooses this finite set that is to represent the object is clearly important. Consider the sinusoidal curve in Figure 2.11. If we sample such a sine wave badly, say at the points **A**, **B**, **C**, and **D**, then it will look like a straight line. If we had sampled at the points **A**, **E**, **F**, and **D**, then we would think that it has a different frequency.

The basic problem in sampling theory: How many samples does one have to take so that no information is lost?

This is a question that is studied in the field of signal processing. The theory of the *Fourier transform* plays a big role in the analysis.

Definition. A function whose Fourier transform vanishes outside a finite interval is called a *band-limited* function. One of the basic theorems in sampling theory is the following:

The Whittaker-Shannon Sampling Theorem. Let f(x) be a band-limited function and assume that its Fourier transform vanishes outside [-w,w]. Then f(x) can be reconstructed exactly from its samples provided that the sampling interval is no bigger than 1/(2w).

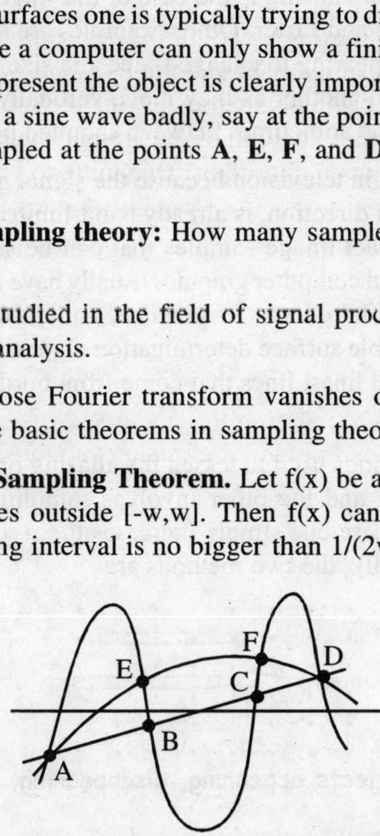

Figure 2.11. Aliasing caused by bad sampling.

If T is a sampling interval, then 1/T is called the *sampling frequency* and 1/(2T) is called the *Nyquist limit*. The Whittaker-Shannon Theorem says that if a function is sampled less often than its Nyquist limit, then a complete recovery is impossible. One says that the function is *undersampled* in that case. Undersampling leads to a phenomenon referred to as *aliasing*, where fake frequencies or patterns appear that were not in the original object. The two-dimensional situation is similar, but in practice one must sample a lot more because of limitations of available reconstruction algorithms.

Now in the discussion above, it was assumed that we were taking an infinite number of samples, something that we obviously cannot do in practice. What happens if we only take a finite number of samples? Mathematically, this corresponds to where we multiply the sampled result by a function that vanishes outside a finite interval. The main result is that it is in general **impossible** to faithfully reconstruct a function that has only been sampled over a finite range. To put it in another way, no function that is nonzero over only a finite interval can be band-limited and conversely, any band-limited function is nonzero over an unbounded set.

The practical consequences of the theory sketched above can be seen in lots of places. Aliasing is most apparent along edges, near small objects, along skinny highlights, and in textured regions. Ad hoc schemes for dealing with the problem may be disappointing because of the human visual system's extreme sensitivity to edge discontinuities (*vernier acuity*). Aliasing is also a problem in animation. The best-known example of temporal aliasing is the case of the wagon wheel appearing to reverse its direction of motion as it spins faster and faster. Other examples are small objects flashing off and on the screen, slightly larger objects appearing to change shape and size randomly, and simple horizontal lines jumping from one raster line to another as they move vertically. See Figure 2.12. This happens because objects fall sometimes on and sometimes between sampled points.

Jaggies do not seem to appear in television because the signal generated by a television camera, which is sampled only in the vertical direction, is already band-limited before sampling. A slightly out of focus television camera will extract image samples that can be successfully reconstructed on the home television set. People working in computer graphics usually have no control over the reconstruction process. This is part of the display hardware. In practice, antialiasing techniques are imbedded in algorithms (like line-drawing or visible surface determination algorithms). The approaches distinguish between the case of drawing isolated lines, lines that come from borders of polygons, and the interior of polygons.

There are essentially two methods used to lessen the aliasing problem. Intuitively speaking, one method treats pixels as having area and the other involves sampling at a higher rate. The obvious approach to the aliasing problem where one simply increases the resolution of the display device is a special case of the latter. athematically, the two methods are

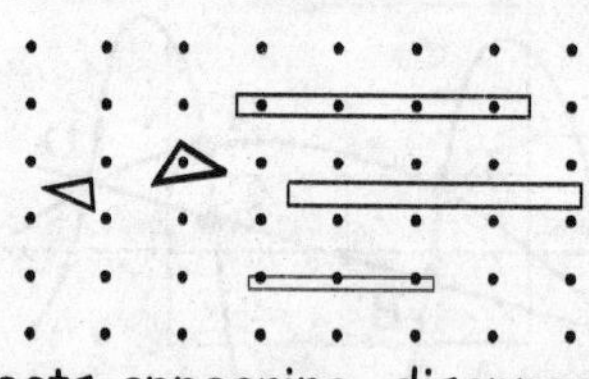

Figure 2.12. Objects appearing, disappearing, changing size.

(1) prefiltering, and

(2) supersampling or postfiltering

Prefiltering. This amounts to treating each sample point as representing a finite area rather than simply a dot. Because lines often fall between pixels, this would avoid concentrating everything at a pixel in a hit-or-miss fashion. Mathematically, the process corresponds to applying a convolutional filter before sampling. One must make sure that the highest frequency of a signal in a scene does not exceed one-half the sampling rate. Two widely used models for computing the area subtended by a pixel are

(1) One considers the image a square grid as in Figure 2.13 with the pixels in the centers of the squares.

(2) One computes the area using a weighting function similar to a Gaussian function. This in fact models the effect of the electron beam of a CRT and printing processes more closely. The pixels are larger and overlap. Details near the center now count more heavily than those near the edge.

Model (1) is easier than (2), but (2) produces better pictures. Internal details, such as highlights, are harder to handle.

In the case of boundaries of polygons we can use shading to suggest the position of the edges and can make the picture look as if it had higher resolution than it in fact has. Therefore, associate to each pixel an intensity proportional to the percentage of its area that is covered by the polygon. For example, if the intensity values ranged from 0 to 15, then we might assign pixel **A** in Figure 2.13 a value of 2 and pixel **B**, a value of 8. This approach could obviously substantially increase the amount of computation one has to do. However, by using an efficient approximation of the area that is needed, it turns out that all it takes is a slight modification to the Bresenham algorithm to get an efficient implementation of it, namely, the Pitteway-Watkinson algorithm. Another approach for drawing antialiased lines treats the lines as having a thickness. An algorithm of this type is the Gupta-Sproull algorithm. It also starts with the standard Bresenham algorithm and then adds some checks for nearby pixels above and below each pixel that would be drawn by that algorithm.

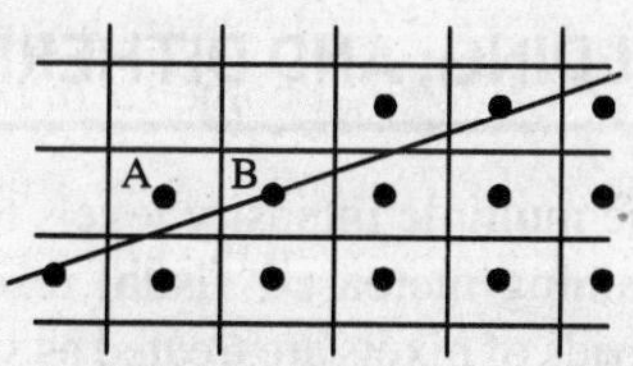

Figure 2.13. Pixel intensities based on percentage of *area covered.*

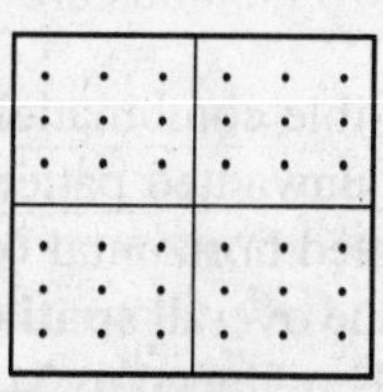

Figure 2.14. Supersampling with scaling factor 3.

More precisely, we sample at n uniformly situated points within the region associated to each pixel and then assign the average of these values to the pixel. One usually oversamples the same amount in each direction so that n = s2 for some *scaling factor* s.

For example, to create a 512 * 512 image we would sample at 1536 *1536 points if s is 3. The samples would be taken 1/3 of a pixel width apart. In Figure 2.14, each square corresponds to a pixel in the final image and the dots show the location of the nine samples per pixel.

Postfiltering. In supersampling the sample values for each pixel are **averaged**. This gives each sample the same weight. Postfiltering uses the same approach but allows each sample to have a different weight. Supersampling is therefore a special case of postfiltering. Different weighting or "window" functions can be used. For example, if we represent the weighting operation in matrix form with the ij'th entry being the weighting factor for the ij'th sample, then rather than using the supersampling matrix

$$(1/9)\begin{pmatrix}1 & 1 & 1\\ 1 & 1 & 1\\ 1 & 1 & 1\end{pmatrix}$$

We could use

$$(1/8)\begin{pmatrix}0 & 1 & 0\\ 1 & 4 & 1\\ 0 & 1 & 0\end{pmatrix} \text{ or } (1/16)\begin{pmatrix}1 & 2 & 1\\ 2 & 4 & 2\\ 1 & 2 & 1\end{pmatrix}$$

Mathematically, postfiltering corresponds to a convolution and filtering operation on the samples. The cost of generating an image with supersampling and postfiltering is proportional to the number of scan lines. The cost of calculations involving shading is proportional to the square of the number of scan lines. This means that the algorithm is particularly expensive for visible surface determination algorithms. In conclusion, antialiasing techniques add a large amount of computation time to any algorithm that uses them. To minimize this extra work, one tries to do it only for areas where problems occur and makes no special computations for the rest. Of course, this assumes that one knows all about the picture, say a jar defined via many polygons.

2.7 HALFTONING, THRESHOLDING, AND DITHERING

In contrast to antialiasing where we use multiple intensity levels to increase the resolution, *halftoning* (or *patterning*) is a technique for obtaining increased **visual** resolution with a minimum number of intensity levels. Basically, rectangular grids of pixels are treated as single pixels. This is how photographs are usually reproduced for magazines and books. For example, using a 2 * 2 grid we can get five different intensities.

See Figure 2.15(a). Not all of the possible combinations are used (basically symmetric patterns are to be avoided) in order not to introduce unwanted patterns into the picture. Using the patterns in Figure 2.15(b) could easily introduce unwanted horizontal or vertical lines in a picture. Normally 2 * 2 or 3 *3 grids are used. Halftoning reduces the overall **spatial** resolution of a system. For example, the resolution of a 1024 * 1024 monitor would be reduced to 512 * 512 with 2 * 2 grids. This means that such a technique is best applied when the resolution of the original scene is less than that of the output device.

Another technique called *thresholding* deals with the problem where we have a digital image with the same resolution as our monochrome display device but with more intensity levels. The simplest form of thresholding is to use a fixed threshold for each pixel. If the intensity exceeds that value, the pixel is drawn white, otherwise it is drawn black. Such a simple scheme can lose a lot of detail.

Finally, *dithering* is a technique applying to monochrome displays that is used with halftoning or thresholding methods to smooth edges of objects by introducing random noise into the picture. It increases the visual resolution without reducing the spatial resolution. One adds a random error to each pixel value before comparing to the threshold value (if any has been selected). Good error patterns have to be chosen carefully. *Ordered dithering* is where a square **dither matrix** is added to the picture. Alternatively, rather than adding noise using the same threshold for each pixel one can vary the threshold. With this approach, an optimum 2 * 2 matrix has been shown to be

$$\begin{pmatrix} 0 & 2 \\ 3 & 1 \end{pmatrix}$$

The entries of the matrix are used as the threshold for the corresponding pixel. There are recursive formulas for higher dimensional dither matrices.

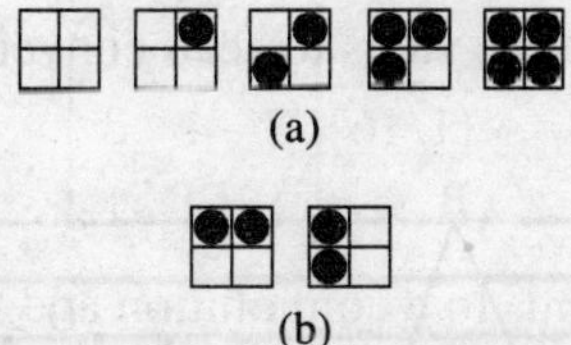

Figure 2.15. Halftone patterns.

2.8 CHOOSING THE COORDINATES OF A PIXEL

Before going on to discuss another scan conversion algorithm we pause to take up a subject that probably did not occur to the reader as being an issue. However, since pixels should be treated as having area, if we consider our image as corresponding to a grid as we have, where should the pixels be placed? Should they be at the intersection of the grid lines or in the center of the grid squares? Equivalently, when we consider scan lines, do their y-coordinates fall on integers or half-integers? Whatever choice one makes, it **does** matter. The real issue here is how one maps reals to integers. Should one round or truncate?

Rounding corresponds to placing pixels at the integers because the whole interval [n - 0.5,n + 0.5) will map to n. Truncating corresponds to placing the pixels at half-integers because the whole interval [n,n + 1) will map to n. To use an example, if one rounds, then the interval [-.5,2.5) maps to {0,1,2}, whereas if one truncates, then [0,3) maps to {0,1,2}. The second approach is a cleaner choice because there are no .5's to worry about. By truncating one simplifies some mathematics. We shall therefore use the following correspondence if we need to map back and forth between the continuous and discrete world:

real c $\rightarrow$ integer n = Floor (c)

integer n $\rightarrow$ real (n + 0.5)

(Mathematically it is the Floor function that returns an integer whereas the Trunc function returns a real.) In two dimensions this means that when we have a pixel with coordinates (x,y), its center will be at continuous coordinates (x + 0.5,y + 0.5). Note that this was the choice we made when discussing antialiasing. Now we know why. In the future, whenever we scan a **continuous** object the scan lines will fall on half-integers.

2.9 MORE DRAWING ALGORITHMS

2.9.1 Scan Converting Polygons

The Bresenham line-drawing algorithm discussed in Section 2.5.2 dealt with scan converting a **single** segment. There may be several segments we want to scan convert such as the boundary of a polygon. In that case one can use the **coherence** inherent in that problem and use an algorithm that is more efficient that simply scan converting each bounding edge separately. Consider the edges in Figure 2.16. As we move down from the top of the picture one scan line at a time we do not need to compute the intersections of the edges with the scan line each time. These can be computed incrementally. Since not every edge will intersect current scan line, by using an *active edge list* (AEL), we do not have to look at every edge each time. Here are the steps to scan convert these edges efficiently:

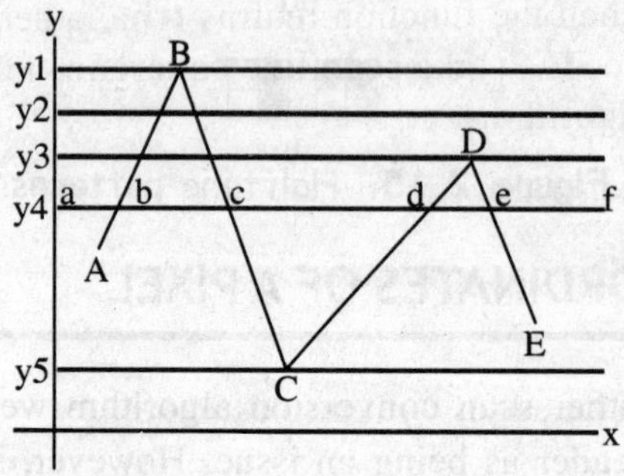

Figure 2.16. Scan converting a polygon.

Step 1. Associate a "bucket" to each scan line and initialize it to empty.

Step 2. Find the largest y value for each edge and put the edge into the corresponding scan line's bucket.

Step 3. For each edge **e** maintain the following information:

x – initially the x-coordinate of the highest point of the edge **e** (in general the x-coordinate xe of the intersection of **e** with the current scan line)

dx – change in x from line to line (the reciprocal of the slope of the line)

dy – initially the number of scan lines crossed by **e**

Step 4. Initialize the active edge list to empty. Set y to the height of the top scan line.

Step 5. Add any edges in the bucket for y to the active edge list.

Step 6. For each edge in the active edge list draw (x,y), change the x to x + dx, and decrement dy. If dy becomes 0, then remove that edge from the list.

Step 7. Decrement y. If y is 0, then quit; otherwise, go back to Step 5.

In Figure 2.16, when we reach scan line y1, the edges **AB** and **BC** will be added to the active edge list. At scan line y2 nothing special happens. When we get to scan line y3, the edges **CD** and **DE** will be added to the list. Finally, at scan line y5 there are only the two edges **BC** and **CD** on the list and they will now be removed. To avoid having fixed bucket sizes and limiting the amount of data for each scan line, one stores pointers only and stores all information sequentially in an array. Alternatively, one can use a **linked** list to be able to add and delete easily.

A problem related to scan converting lists of edges which is of more practical importance is scan converting **solid** polygons. This leads to polygon based fill algorithms. The pixel-based analog was already discussed earlier in Section 2.4. Assume that XMIN, XMAX, YMIN, and YMAX are the minimum and maximum values for the x- and y-coordinates of pixels. The basic idea here is the following:

```
for i: =YMIN to YMAX do
for j: =XMIN to XMAX do
if Inside (polygon,j,i) then Draw (j,i);
```

The Boolean-valued function "Inside" counts the intersections of the line from (j,i) to (– • ,i) with the polygon. If this number is odd, then the function returns **true**, other-wise it returns **false**. Of course, this algorithm is too slow. One needs to take **scan line coherence** into account. This leads us to what are called *ordered edge list* fill algorithms.

They have the following general form:

```
for each scan line do
begin
Find all intersections of edges with the scan line;
Sort the intersections by increasing x;
Fill alternate segments;
end;
```

For example, consider the scan line y4 in Figure 2.16. Notice how filling the alternate segments [b,c] and [d,e] does in fact fill what we want. That this works is justified by a parity type argument. An active edge list again helps. Algorithm 2.9.1.1 shows a more detailed version.

```
linerec = record
        real x, dx;
        integer dy;
end

linerecs = linerec list;

begin
        linerecs array [0..] edges;    {edges of the polygons}
        linerecs ael;                  {the active edge list}
        integer y;

        Scan the polygon and set up the edges table;
        ael :=nil;

        for y := YMIN to YMAX do
                begin
                        Add all edges in edges [y] to ael;
                        if ael ≠ nil then
                                begin
                                        Sort ael by increasing x;
```

```
                    Fill pixels along y by scanning ael and filling alternate x segments;
                    Delete from ael edges for which dy = 0;
                    Update each x in ael by dx;
                end
            end
end;
```

Algorithm 2.9.1.1. An ordered edge list fill algorithm.

The following points need to be made about Algorithm 2.9.1.1:

(1) The polygon is assumed to lie entirely in window.

(2) Horizontal edges need not be considered because they get filled automatically.

(3) There is a problem with parity at vertices unless one takes precautions.

To understand the parity problem at vertices consider Figure 2.16 again. At vertices, their x values would be listed twice in the active edge list. In the case of a local maximum like vertex **B** = (x_B,y_B), the algorithm would fill the segments $[XMIN,x_B]$, $[x_B,x_B]$, and $[x_B,XMAX]$ on the scan line $y = y_B$ to the background color, the color of the polygon, and the background color, respectively. This is as we would want it. On the other hand, when the algorithm gets to vertex **A** = (x_A,y_A), assuming that there was another edge below this vertex, it would fill $[XMIN,x_A]$ to the background color, $[x_A,x_{BA}]$ to the color of the polygon, and $[x_{BA}, x_{BC}]$ to the background color, etc. This is **not** correct. Furthermore, we cannot simply skip duplicate x-coordinates as we scan the active edge list. If we did, then vertices like **A** would be handled correctly, but the algorithm would now fail at local maxima and minima like **B**. The way that this parity problem is usually resolved is to shorten one of the (two) edges that meet in a vertex that is **not** at a local extremum. For example, change the lower vertex (x,y) of the upper edge to (x,y + 1) (leaving the upper vertex of the lower edge in tact). **No** shortening takes place at vertices that are local extrema. With this change to the edges, Algorithm 2.9.1.1 will now work correctly, but we need a test for when vertices are local extrema.

Here is one:

if adjacent edges have the same sign for their slope

then the common vertex is not a local extremum

else test the opposite endpoints for whether or not they lie on the same side of the scan line as the vertex: if they do, then the vertex is a local extremum, otherwise, not

To see that a further test is required in the **else** case, consider Figure 2.17 and the two pairs of segments ([(-1,-1),(0,0)],[(0,0),(1,-1)]) and ([(-1,-1),(0,0)],[(0,0),(-1,1)]). In both pairs, the segments have opposite slopes, but (0,0) is a local extremum for the first pair but not for the second. One can tell the two apart however because the endpoints (-1,-1) and (-1,1) for the first pair lie on opposite sides of the scan line for (0,0), whereas the endpoints (-1,-1) and (1,-1) both lie on the same side of the scan line.

Finally, note that the ordered edge list fill algorithm "works" for polygons with self-intersections and/or holes. See Figure 2.18. One needs to understand what "works"

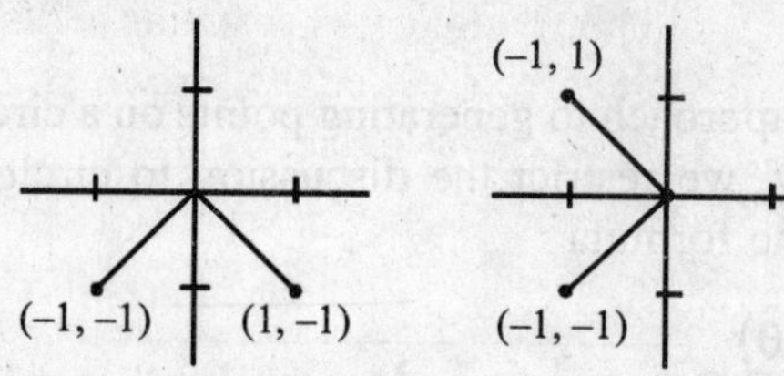

Figure 2.17. Testing for local extrema.

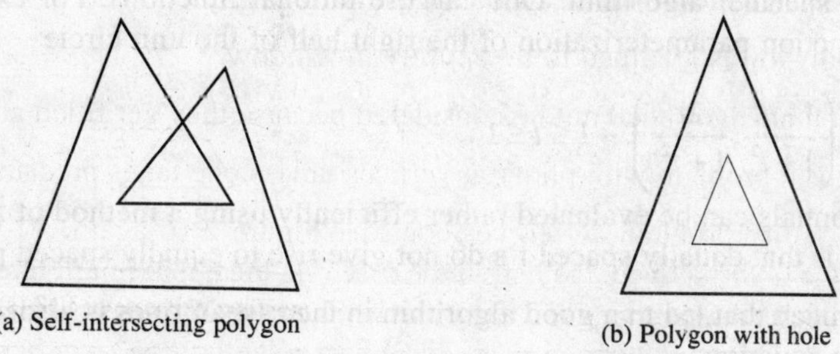

Figure 2.18. Various types of polygon.

means though. For example, the inside of the inner loop of Figure 2.18(a) will be drawn in the background color. We can deal with multiple polygons here if we have an associated priority number with each, where having a higher priority means being in front of or not obscuring. In the algorithm above, as we go along we must now keep track of the polygon to which the "current" segment "belongs." One way to do this is to maintain the following additional data:

(1) Covers – a Boolean array so that covers[i] is **true** for the ith polygon if it covers the current segment.

(2) Numcover – the number of polygons covering the current segment.

(3) VisiblePoly – a pointer to the foremost polygon, if any.

As we move from segment to segment in a scan line, numcover is incremented or decremented appropriately. The array covers is initialized to **false** and every time that

one runs into an edge of the ith polygon, covers[i] is negated. The pointer visiblePoly tells us the color of the current segment.

In conclusion, here are some points to consider when deciding on a fill algorithm. The main advantages of ordered edge list algorithms are that pixels are visited only once and they are well suited for shading algorithms since both ends of a span are computed before the span is drawn so that one can interpolate intensities. The main disadvantage is the large amount of processing required maintaining and sorting various lists. The main advantage to seed fill algorithms is that they can fill arbitrary planar contours, not just those bounded by polygonal curves. The main disadvantages are that some pixels are visited many times and one requires an initial interior point. The latter is not a problem in interactive situations but would be in a fully automated one. One would then have to invoke another algorithm to find such a point. Basically, fill time tends to be dominated by the time required to set pixels making the ordered edge list algorithms the most attractive overall.

2.9.2 Drawing Circles

Probably the most straightforward approach to generating points on a circle is to use a polar coordinate parameterization. If, for simplicity, we restrict the discussion to circles of radius *r* centered at the origin, then this map is given by the formula

$$\theta \to (r\cos\theta, r\sin\theta)$$

The only problem with this is that the sine and cosine functions are relatively complicated to evaluate. We want a speedier algorithm. One can use rational functions. For example, there is the following rational function parameterization of the right half of the unit circle

$$t \to \left(\frac{1-t^2}{1+t^2}, \frac{2t}{1+t^2}\right), -1 \le t \le 1$$

These rational polynomials can be evaluated rather efficiently using a method of forward differences, but the problem now is that equally spaced t's do not give rise to equally spaced points on the circle.

The DDA approach that led to a good algorithm in the case of lines is also applicable to circles. By differentiating the equation

$$x^2 + y^2 = r^2$$

for a circle of radius r about the origin implicitly with respect to x, one sees that

$$\frac{dy}{dx} = -\frac{x}{y}$$

is the differential equation for that circle. This means that a circle-generating DDA can be written in the form

$$x_{n+1} = y_n + \varepsilon y_n$$

$$y_{n+1} = y_n - \varepsilon x_n$$

A natural choice for e is 2^{-n}, where $2^{n-1} <= r < 2^n$. Unfortunately, if one were to plot the points that are generated by these equations, one would find that they spiral outward. From a mathematical standpoint one should not have been surprised because the determinant of the matrix

$$\begin{pmatrix} 1 & -\varepsilon \\ \varepsilon & 1 \end{pmatrix}$$

for this linear transformation is 1 +å². An ad hoc way to correct this determinant problem is to make a slight change and note that the matrix

$$\begin{pmatrix} 1 & -\varepsilon \\ \varepsilon & 1-\varepsilon^2 \end{pmatrix}$$

has determinant equal to 1. The points that are generated by the corresponding transformation produce a much better result. The equations for this transformation are

$$x_{n+1} = x_n + \varepsilon y_n$$

$$y_{n+1} = (1-\varepsilon^2) y_n - \varepsilon x_n$$

which reduces to

$$x_{n+1} = x_n + \varepsilon y_n$$
$$y_{n+1} = y_n - \varepsilon x_{n+1}$$

Notice how the equation for the (n + 1)st value for y now also involves the (n + 1)st value of x. The coordinates of the new point have to be computed sequentially, first the x value, then the y value. Before we could compute them in parallel. Furthermore, what we have here is a simple example of an error-correcting term. All good methods for numerical solutions to differential equations have this, something that was alluded to in Section 2.5.1.

Returning to our problem of generating points on a circle, our new system of equations produces points that no longer spiral out. However, having determinant equal to 1 is only a necessary requirement for a transformation to preserve distance. It is not a sufficient one. In fact, the points generated by our new transformation form a slight ellipse. To get a better circle-generating algorithm we start over from scratch with a new approach. Assume that the radius r is an integer and define the "error" function E by

$$E=r^2-x^2-y^2.$$

This function measures how close the point (x,y) is to lying on the circle of radius r. As we generate points on the circle we obviously want to minimize this error. Let us restrict ourselves to the octant of the circle in the first quadrant, which starts at (0,r) and ends at (r/÷2,r/÷2). Note that in this octant as we move from one point to the next the x-coordinate will always increase by 1 and the y-coordinate will either stay the same or decrease by 1. Any other choice would not minimize E. The two cases are illustrated in Figure 2.19. We shall call the two possible moves an **R-move** or a **D-move**, respectively.

As we move from point to point, we choose that new point which minimizes E. However, we can save computation time by computing the new E incrementally. To see this, suppose that we are at (x,y). Then the current E, Ecur, is given by

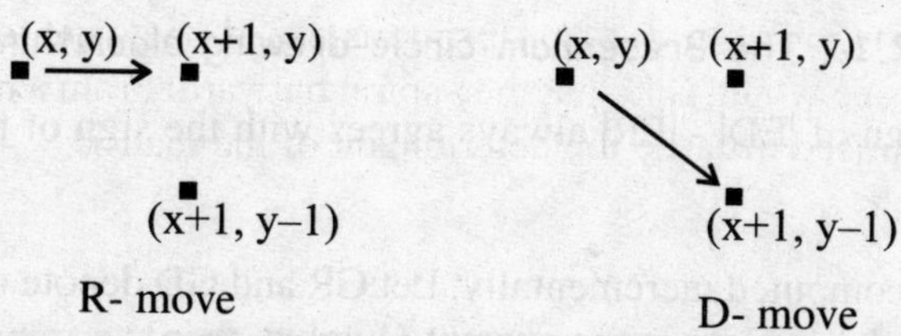

Figure 2.19. Moves in circle-generating algorithm.

$$E_{cur} = r^2 - x^2 - y^2$$

After an R-move the new E, call it E_R, is

$$E_R = r^2 - (x+1)^2 - y^2$$
$$= E_{cur} - (2x+1)$$

After a D-move the new E, call it E_D, is

$$E_D = r^2 - (x+1)^2 - (y-1)^2$$
$$= E_{cur} - (2x+1) + (2y-1)$$

One algorithm for drawing a circle is to choose that move which makes our new error, either E_R or E_D, have the opposite sign of our current one. The idea is that if we find ourselves outside the circle we should move as quickly as possible back into the circle and vice versa. This leads to Algorithm 2.9.2.1, the Bresenham circle-drawing algorithm.

The only problem with Algorithm 2.9.2.1 is that we were using a heuristic that does not always minimize the real error E. To get a better algorithm, we have to make that our goal. Choosing the move that minimizes the error can be done by testing the sign of |ED| - |ER|. To gain efficiency we want to avoid having to compute absolute values of numbers. Consider the possible outcomes shown in following table:

E_D	E_R	$\|E_D\| - \|E_R\|$
+	+	$E_D - E_R = 2y-1$, always positive
+	–	$E_D - E_R$
–	+	this case never happens
–	–	$-E_D + E_R = -(2y-1)$, always negative

```
x:=0; y : = r; E:=0;
while x ≤ y do
    begin
        If E < 0 then
            begin
                E:= E + y + y –1;
                y := y –1;
            end;
        E :=E –x –x –1;
        x := x +1
        Draw (x, y);
    end;
```

Algorithm 2.9.2.1. The Bresenham circle-drawing algorithm (one octant).

This table shows that the sign of |ED| - |ER| always agrees with the sign of the auxiliary Variable

$$G=E_D+E_R$$

Furthermore, G can also be computed incrementally. Let GR and GD denote the values of G after an R-move or D-move, respectively. If Gcur is the current G value, then

$$G_R=G_{cur} - 4x - 6$$

And

$$G_D=G_{cur} - 4x+ 4y - 10$$

It is easy to derive formulas (2.4) and (2.5). We prove formula (2.4) for GR in case we move right. Recall that

$$E_R=E_{cur} - (2x+1),$$

$$E_D=E_{cur} - (2x+1)+(2y-1), \text{ and}$$

$$G_{cur} = E_D + E_R = 2E_{cur} - (4x+2)+(2y-1)$$

On an R-move,

$$\begin{aligned}
E_{new} &= E_{cur} - (2x+1), \\
\text{new } E_R &= E_{new} - [2(x+1)+1], \\
\text{new } E_D &= E_{new} - [2(x+1)+1]+(2y-1), \text{ and} \\
G_R &= \text{new}E_D - \text{new}E_R \\
&= 2E_{new} - (4x+2) - 2 + (2y-1) = 2E_{cur} - 2(2x+1) - (4x+2) - 2 + (2y-1) \\
&= G_{cur} - 4x - 6
\end{aligned}$$

The other cases are proved in a similar fashion.

Finally, going one step further, the increments to G_R and G_D themselves can be computed incrementally, producing an improved Algorithm 2.9.2.2. It can be shown that the algorithm produces a best-fit curve for the circle when either the radius r or its square is an integer, but that may not be the case if one tries the same approach when r2 is not an integer.

2.9.3 Drawing Ellipses and Other Conics

The equation for the standard ellipse centered at the origin is

$$\frac{x^2}{a^2}+\frac{y^2}{b^2}=1$$

```
x := 0;
y :=r;
g:= 2*r;
dgr := –6; dgd := 4*r –10;
while  x ≤ y do
     begin
          if g < 0
             then                    [go diagonal]
               begin
                  g :=g + dgd;
                  dgd := dgd–8; (–4(x+1)+4(y–1)–10=4x–4y–10–8)
                  y := y –1;
               end;
             else
               begin
                  g :=g + dgr;
                  dgd := dgd–4; (y stays the same, x increases by 1)
               end;
             dgr:=dgr –4; (x always get incremented: –4(x+1)–6=–4x–6–4)
             x : = x+1;
             Draw (x, y);
     end;
```

Algorithm 2.9.2.2. An improved Bresenham circle-drawing algorithm (one octant).

and we can generate points on it using the standard parameterization

$$\theta \rightarrow (a\cos\theta, b\sin\theta)$$

Differentiating equation (2.6) implicitly gives the differential equation

$$\frac{dy}{dx} = -\frac{xb^2}{ya^2}$$

This leads to a DDA approach similar to the case of a circle. Because ellipses are an important class of curves, many algorithms exist to draw them. The Bresenham approach to drawing a circle can be extended to ellipses, but that algorithm will no longer guarantee a minimum linear error between the ellipse and the chosen pixels. Alternatively, a version of the midpoint algorithm described in Section 2.5.3 produces an efficient and more accurate algorithm . Special algorithms for generating parabolas and hyperbolas are also known. We shall not describe any here but instead jump directly to the case of a general conic. Every conic can be defined implicitly by an equation of the form

$$ax^2 + bxy + cy^2 + dx + ey + f = 0$$

Given a starting pixel **on** the conic, one can determine which adjacent pixel to pick next similar to what we did in the case of circles by looking at an error function. Each possible move will have an error associated to it and we simply choose the move with the least error. It is easy to show that the error functions have the same form as the equation of the conic and that they can be computed incrementally.

EXERCISES

Section 2.2

2.2.1 Find the various integers k so that there are k-neighbors in **Z**4.

2.2.2 Prove that every 8-component of a subset of **Z**2 is the union of 4-components.

Section 2.5.1

2.5.1.1 Determine the points generated by the simple and symmetric DDA for the line segment from (2,6) to (-1,1). Make a table and also plot these points (both the real **and** integer ones).

2.9.2.1 Give an example showing that the first Bresenham circle-drawing algorithm (Algorithm 2.9.2.1) is **not** optimal but that the improved Bresenham algorithm (Algorithm 2.9.2.2) gives the correct results in this case.

PROGRAMMING PROJECTS

For some of the projects below you will first have to have a program, like GM, which lets a user define boundaries for arbitrary regions by dragging the cursor across the screen (either with a mouse or by using the arrow keys on the keyboard). Alternatively, deal only with polygonal regions that the user specifies by picking its vertices.

Section 2.4

2.4.1 Fill the region with a user selected color using the Fishkin algorithm.

Section 2.9.1

2.9.1.1 Implement the algorithm for scan converting polygons described in this section. More generally, implement this algorithm for multiple polygons that admit a back-to-front ordering.

Section 2.10

2.10.1 Implement a program showing a bouncing ball using the color lookup table technique as indicated in Figure 2.24.

2.10.2 A billiard ball game

The object of this project is to simulate the motion of a billiard ball and a cue stick. See Figure 2.26. Specifically, you should

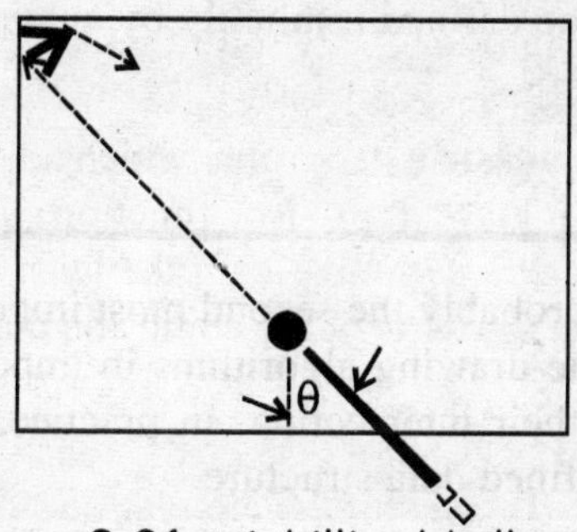

Figure 2.26. A billiard ball game.

(1) display a rectangular "table" with a single solid colored ball at some initial position
(2) show a cue stick (represented as a long, thin rectangular object) hitting the ball at various angles specified by the user
(3) show the movement of the ball after it is hit as it bounces from wall to wall
(4) have the balls slow down and finally come to a halt to make things look somewhat Realistic

Experiment with different animation techniques on your own, such as double buffering. Hand in the one that you think gives the best results. *Be sure to explain* why it was chosen over other approaches. Optionally, have one or more other balls on the table and

(5) if a moving ball hits another one, then it should come to a stop and the other one should move in the appropriate direction with the first one's velocity (if a ball hits k > 1 balls with velocity v, then they should start with velocity v/k)

Your program should have suitable menus and output explanations as to what is happening.

3 CLIPPING

3.1 INTRODUCTION

Planar clipping algorithms rank as probably the second most important type of algorithm in computer graphics, following right behind line-drawing algorithms in importance. Mathematically, to *clip* one set against another means to find their intersection. In practice, one usually wants also to get this intersection in terms of some predefined data structure.

This chapter discusses some of the well-known clipping algorithms along with some newer and more efficient ones. The algorithms fall into two types: the *line clipping* algorithms, which clip single line segments against rectangular or convex regions, and *polygon-clipping* algorithms, which clip whole polygons against other polygons. The following terminology is used:

Definition. The polygon being clipped is called the *subject* polygon and the polygon that one is clipping against is called the *clip* polygon. The choice of algorithms to discuss was motivated by the following considerations:

(1) It is currently one of the best algorithms of its type.

(2) It is not the best algorithm but still used a lot.

(3) The algorithm was interesting for historical reasons and easy to describe.

(4) It involved the use of some interesting techniques, even though it itself is no longer a recommended method.

Below we list the algorithms described in this chapter and categorize them by considerations (1)–(4) above. We also state any assumption regarding their clip polygon and make some comments about them. Some of the algorithms will be discussed in great detail. Others are only described very briefly, especially if they fall under heading (3) or (4) above.

Line-clipping algorithms

	Category	Clip Polygon	Comments
Cohen-Sutherland	(2)	Rectangular	The class line-clipping alogirthm, Still popular it is so easy to implement
Cyrys-Beck	(4)	Convex	Faster than Cohen-Sutherland
Liang-Barsky	(2)	Rectangular	Still Popular. Easy to implement
Nicholl-Lee-Nicholl	(1)	Rectangular	Purely two dimensional

Polygon-clipping algorithms

	Category	Clip Polygon	Comments
Sutherland-hodgman	(3)	Convex	
Weiler	(3), (4)	Arbitrary	
Liang-Barsky	(4)	Rectangular	
Maillot	(1)	Rectangular	
Vatti	(1)	Arbitrary	Fast, versatile, and can generate a trapezoidal decomposition of the intersection.
Greiner-Hormann	(1)	Arbitrary	As general as Vatti. Simpler and potential faster, but no trapezoidal decomposition

Line-clipping algorithms fall into two types: those that use encoding of the endpoints of the segment (Cohen-Sutherland) and those that use a parameterization of the line determined by the segment (Cyrus-Beck, Liang-Barsky, and Nicholl-Lee-Nicholl). In Section 4.6 we discuss a hybrid of the two approaches that works well for the clipping needed in the graphics pipeline.

Frequently, one needs to clip more than one edge at a time, as is the case when one wants to clip one polygon against another. One could try to reduce this problem to a sequence of line-clipping problems, but that is not necessarily the most efficient way to do it, because, at the very least, there would be additional bookkeeping involved. The clipped figure may involve introducing some vertices that were not present in the original polygon. In Figure 3.1 we see that the corners **A** and **B**

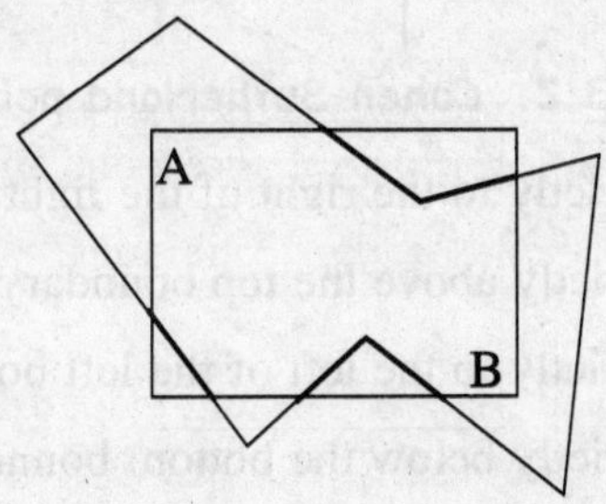

Figure 3.1. Turning points in polygon clipping.

of the window need to be added. These corners are called *turning points.* The term was introduced in [LiaB83] and refers to the point at the intersection of two clipping region edges that has to be added to preserve the connectivity of the original polygon. This is the reason that polygon clipping is treated separately from line clipping.

Polygon-clipping algorithms fall into roughly two categories: *turning-point-based algorithms* like the Liang-Barsky and Maillot algorithms, which rely on quickly being able to find turning points explicitly, and the rest. Turning-point-type algorithms scan the segments of the subject polygon and basically clip each against the **whole** window. The rest tend to find turning points implicitly, in the sense that one does not look for them directly but that they are generated "automatically" as the algorithm proceeds. The Sutherland-Hodgman algorithm treats the clip polygon as the intersection of halfplanes and clips the **whole** subject polygon against each of these halfplanes one at a time. The Weiler, Vatti, and Greiner-Hormann algorithms find the turning points from the clip polygon in the process of tracing out the bounding curves of the components of the polygon intersection, although they trace the boundaries in different ways.

3.2 LINE-CLIPPING ALGORITHMS

3.2.1 Cohen-Sutherland Line Clipping

This section describes an algorithm that solves the following planar clipping problem:

Given a segment [**P1**, **P2**], clip it against a rectangular window and return the clipped segment [**Q1**, **Q2**] (which may be empty if the original segment lies entirely outside the window). The Cohen-Sutherland line-clipping algorithm is probably the most popular of

such algorithms because of its simplicity. It starts out by encoding the nine regions into which the boundary lines of the window divide the whole plane with a 4-bit binary code. See Figure 3.2. If **P** is an arbitrary point, then let c(**P**) = $x_3x_2x_1x_0$, where x_i is either 0 or 1, define this encoding. The bits x_i have the following meaning:

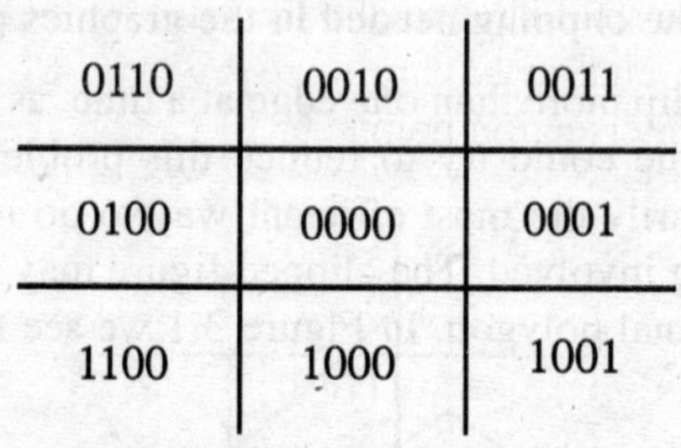

Figure 3.2. Cohen-Sutherland point codes.

x_0 = 1 if and only if **P** lies strictly to the right of the right boundary line.

x_1 = 1 if and only if **P** lies strictly above the top boundary line.

x_2 = 1 if and only if **P** lies strictly to the left of the left boundary line.

x_3 = 1 if and only if **P** lies strictly below the bottom boundary line.

The algorithm now has three steps:

Step 1. Encode $\mathbf{P}_1$ and $\mathbf{P}_2$. Let c_1 = c($\mathbf{P}_1$) and c_2 = c($\mathbf{P}_2$).

Step 2. Check if the segment can be trivially rejected, that is, using the bitwise logical **or** and **and** operators, test whether

(a) c_1 or $c_2 = 0$, or

(b) c_1 and $c_2 \neq 0$

In case (a), the segment is entirely contained in the window since both endpoints are and the window is convex. Return $\mathbf{Q}_1 = \mathbf{P}_1$ and $\mathbf{Q}_2 = \mathbf{P}_2$. In case (b), the segment is entirely outside the window. This follows because the endpoints will then lie in the half plane determined by a boundary line that is on the other side from the window and half planes are also convex. Return the empty segment.

Step 3. If the segment cannot be trivially rejected, then we must subdivide the segment. We clip it against an appropriate boundary line and then start over with Step 1 using the new segment. Do the following to accomplish this:

(a) First find the endpoint **P** that will determine the line to clip against. If c1 = 0000, then **P1** does not have to be clipped and we let **P** be $\mathbf{P}_2$ and **Q** be $\mathbf{P}_1$. If c1 '''0000, then let **P** be $\mathbf{P}_1$ and **Q** be $\mathbf{P}_2$.

(b) The line to clip against is determined by the left-most nonzero bit in c(**P**). For the example in Figure 3.3, $\mathbf{P} = \mathbf{P}_1$, $\mathbf{Q} = \mathbf{P}_2$, and the line to clip against is the left boundary line of the window. Let **A** be the intersection of the segment [**P**,**Q**] with this line.

(c) Repeat Steps 1–3 for the segment [**A**,**Q**].

The algorithm will eventually exit in Step 2. With respect to the efficiency of the Cohen-Sutherland algorithm, note that the encoding is easy since it simply involves comparing a number to some constant (the boundary lines of the window are assumed to be horizontal and vertical). Step 3 is where the real work might have to be done. We shall have to clip four times in the worst case. One such worst case is shown in Figure 3.3 where we end up having to clip successively against each one of the window boundary lines generating the intersection points **A**, **B**, **C**, and **D**.

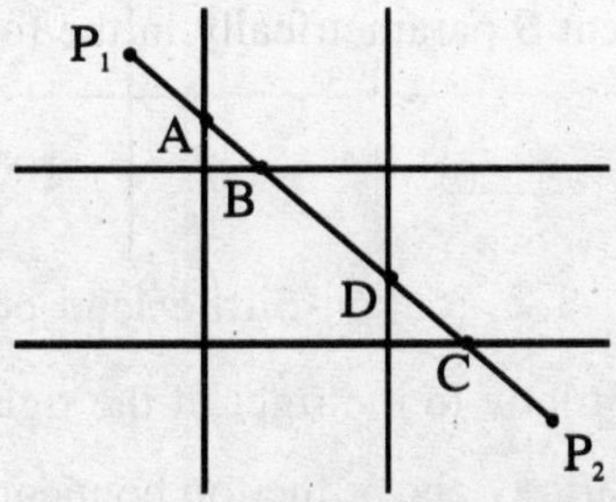

Figure 3.3. Cohen-Sutherland line-clipping example.

Algorithm 3.2.1.1 is an implementation of the just-described algorithm. To be more efficient, all function calls should be replaced by inline code. Finally, note that the encoding found in the Cohen-Sutherland line-clipping algorithm is driven by determining whether a point belongs to a halfplane. One can easily generalize this to the case where one is clipping a segment against an arbitrary convex set **X**. Assume that **X** is the intersection of halfplanes $\mathbf{H}_1, \mathbf{H}_2, \ldots, \mathbf{H}_k$.

The encoding of a point **P** is now a k-bit number c(**P**) = $X_K X_{K-1} \ldots X_1$, where X_i is 1 if **P** lies in $\mathbf{H}_i$ and 0 otherwise.

Using this encoding one can define a clipping algorithm that consists of essentially the same steps as those in the Cohen-Sutherland algorithm. One can also extend this idea to higher dimensions and use it to clip segments against cubes.

3.2.2 Cyrus-Beck Line Clipping

The Cyrus-Beck line-clipping algorithm clips a segment **S** against an arbitrary convex polygon **X**. Let **S** = $[\mathbf{P}_1,\mathbf{P}_2]$ and **X** = $\mathbf{Q}_1\mathbf{Q}_2 \ldots \mathbf{Q}_k$. Since **X** is convex, it is the intersection of halfplanes determined by its edges. More precisely, for each segment $[\mathbf{Q}_i,\mathbf{Q}_{i+1}]$, i = 1,2, . . . ,k, ($\mathbf{Q}_{k+1}$ denotes the point $\mathbf{Q}_1$) we can choose a normal vector $\mathbf{N}_i$, so that **X** can be expressed in the form

$$X = \bigcap_{i-1}^{k} H_i$$

where $\mathbf{H}_i$ is the halfplane

$$H_i = \{Q \mid N_i \bullet (Q - Q_i) \geq 0\}$$

With this choice, the normals will point "into" the polygon. It follows that

$$S \cap X = \bigcap_{i-1}^{k} (S \cap H_i)$$

In other words, we can clip the segment **S** against **X** by successively clipping it against the halfplanes $\mathbf{H}_i$. This is the first basic idea behind the Cyrus-Beck clipping algorithm. The second, is to represent the line **L** determined by the segment **S** parametrically in the form $\mathbf{P}_1 + t\mathbf{P}_1\mathbf{P}_2$ and to do the clipping with respect to the parameter *t*.

```
(Constants )
RIGHTBDRY     =1;
TOPBDRY       =2;
LEFTBDRY      =4;
BOTTOMBDRY =8;

Boolean function CS_Clip (ref real x0, y0, x1, y1; real xmin, yamin, xmax, ymax)
{This function clips the segment from (x0, y0) to (x1, y1) against the window
[xmin, xmax]X[ymin, ymax]. It returns false if the segments is entirely outside the
window
and true otherwise. In the latter case the variable z0, y0, z1, and y1 will also have been
modified to specify the final clipped segment.}
begin
        byet c0, c1, c;
        real x, y;
```

```
{First emcpde the points}
c0 := RegionCode (x0, y0);
c1 := RegionCode (x1, y1);

{Next the main loop}
while (c0 or c1) "' 0 do
    if (c0 and c1) "' 0
        then returns (false);
        else
            begin
                {Choose the first point not in the window}
                c := c0;
                if c = 0 then c := c1
                {Now clip against line corresponding to first nonzero bit}
                if (LEFTBDRY and c) "' 0
                    then
                        begin        {Clip against left bdry}
                            x:= xmin;
                            y := y0 + (y1 – y0)*(xmin – x0)/(x1-x0);
                        end
                    else If (RIGHTBDRY and c) "' 0
                        then
                            begin   {Clip against left bdry}
                                x := xmax;
                                y := y0 + (y1 – y0)*(xmax – x0)/(x1-x0);
                            end
                        else If (BOTTOMBDRY and c) "' 0
                            then
                                begin        {Clip against bottom bdry}
                                    x:= x0+(x1–x0)*(ymin– y0)/(y1– y0);
                                    y := ymin;
                                end
                        else If (TROPBDRY and c) "' 0
                            then
                                begin    [ Clip against top bdry]
                                    x:=x0+(x1– x0)*(ymax–y0)/(y1 – y0);
                                    y := ymax;
                                end;

        [ Next update the clipped endpoint and its code ]
        If c = 0
            then
                begin
                    x0 := x: y0 := y;
                    c0 := RegionCode (x0,y0);
```

```
                        end
                    else
                        begin
                            x1 := x; y1 := y;
                            c1 := Regioncode (x1,y1);
                        end
                end; [ While ]
        return ( true ) ;
end

bytes function RegionCode (real x,y);
{Return the 4-bit code for the point (x,y)}
begin
        byte c;

        c :=0;
        If x < xmin
                then c := c +LEFTBDRY
                else if x > xmax
                    then c := c +RIGHTBDRY;
        if y < ymin
                then c := c + BOTTOMBDRY
                else if y > ymax
                    then c := c +TROPBDRY;
        return (c);
end;            [ RegionCode ]
```

Algorithm 3.2.1.1. The Cohen-Sutherland line-clipping algorithm.

Let **Li** be the line determined by the segment $[\mathbf{Q}_i,\mathbf{Q}_{i+1}]$. Define intervals $\mathbf{I}_i = [a_i,b_i]$ as follows:

Case 1: L is parallel to $\mathbf{L}_i$.

(a) If **L** lies entirely in $\mathbf{H}_i$, then let $\mathbf{I}_i$ = (-", +").

(b) If **L** lies entirely outside of $\mathbf{H}_i$, then let $\mathbf{I}_i$ = f.

Case 2: L is not parallel to **Li**.

In this case **L** will intersect **Li** in some point $\mathbf{P} = \mathbf{P}_1 + t_i\mathbf{P}_1\mathbf{P}_2$. We distinguish between the case where the line **L** "enters" the halfplane $\mathbf{H}_i$ and where the line "exits" $\mathbf{H}_i$.

(a) (Line enters) If $\mathbf{P}_1\mathbf{P}_2 \bullet \mathbf{N}_i$ e ≥ 0, then let $\mathbf{I}_i = [t_i, +\infty)$.

(b) (Line exits) If $\mathbf{P}_1\mathbf{P}_2 \bullet \mathbf{N}_i < 0$, then let $\mathbf{Ii} = (-\infty, t_i]$.

See Figure 3.4, where a segment **S** = [**P**1,**P**2] is being clipped against a triangle $\mathbf{Q}_1\mathbf{Q}_2\mathbf{Q}_3$.

Note that finding the intersection point **P** in Case 2 is easy. All we have to do is solve the equation

$$N_i \bullet (P_1 + tP_1P_2 - Q_i) = 0$$

for t.

Now let $\mathbf{I}_0 = [a_0,b_0] = [0,1]$. The interval $\mathbf{I}_0$ is the set of parameters of points which lie is **S**. It is easy to see that the interval

$$I = \bigcap_{j-0}^{k} I_i$$

$$= \begin{bmatrix} \max a_j, & \min b_i \\ 0 \, \mathrm{si} \, sk & 0 sisk \end{bmatrix}$$

$$= [a, b]$$

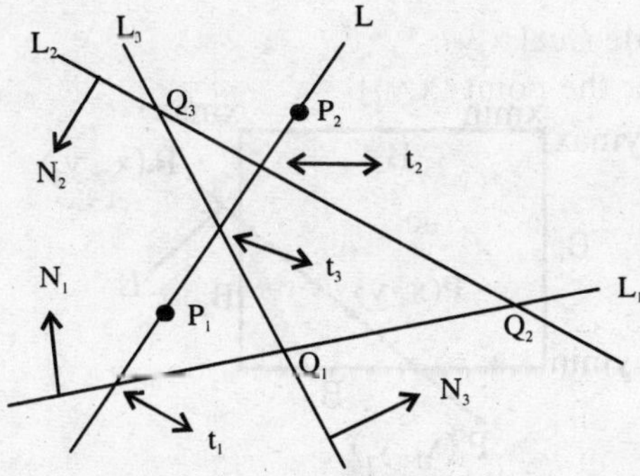

Figure 3.4. Cyrus-Beck line clipping.

is the set of parameters for the points in **S** ∩ **X**. In other words, if **I** is not empty, then

$$S \cap X = [P_1 + aP_1P_2, \; P_1 + bP_1P_2]$$

We shall explain this process with the example in Figure 3.4. In this example,

$$I = [0, 1] \cap [t_1, +\infty) \cap [t_3, +\infty) = [t_3, t_2],$$

which clearly gives the right answer.

3.2.3 Liang-Barsky Line Clipping

The Liang-Barsky line–clipping algorithm optimizes the Cyrus–Beck lineclipping algorithm in the case where we are clipping against a rectangle. It starts by treating a segment as a parameterized set. Let $\mathbf{P}_1 = (x_1, y_1)$ and $\mathbf{P}_2 = (x_2, y_2)$. A typical point $\mathbf{P} = (x, y)$ on the oriented line **L** determined by $\mathbf{P}_1$ and $\mathbf{P}_2$ then has the form $\mathbf{P}_1 + t\mathbf{P}_1\mathbf{P}_2$. If we let $\Delta_x = x_2 - x_1$ and $\Delta_y = y_2 - y_1$, then

$$x = x_1 + \Delta xt$$

$$y = y_1 + \Delta yt$$

If the window **W** we are clipping against is the rectangle $[x_{min}, x_{max}] * [y_{min}, y_{max}]$, then **P** belongs to **W** if and only if

$$x\min \le x_1 + \Delta xt \le x\max$$

$$y\min \le y_1 + \Delta yt \le y\max$$

That is

$$-\Delta xt \le x_1 - x\min$$

$$\Delta xt \le x_1 \max - x_1$$

$$-\Delta yt \le y_1 - \min$$

$$\Delta yt \le y\max - y_1$$

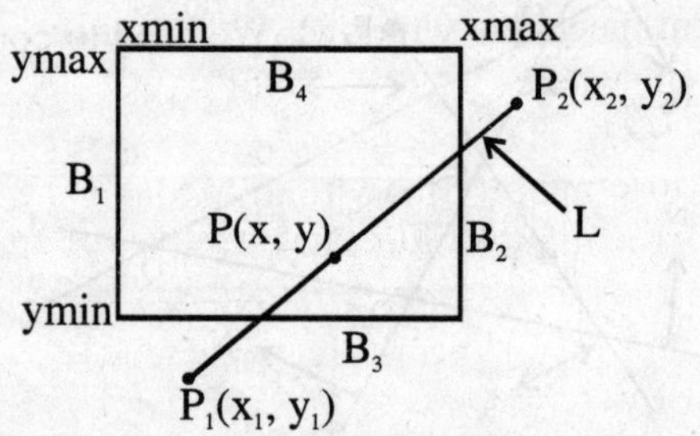

Figure 3.5. Liang-Barsky line clipping

To simplify the notation, we introduce variables ck and qk and rewrite these equations As

$$c_1 t \le q_1$$

$$c_2 t \le q_2$$

$$c_3 t \le q_3$$

$$c_4 t \le q_4$$

Set $t_k = q_k/c_k$ whenever ck $\neq 0$. Let $\mathbf{B}_1$, $\mathbf{B}_2$, $\mathbf{B}_3$, and $\mathbf{B}_4$ denote the left, right, bottom, and top boundary lines of the window, respectively. With this notation we can make the following observations:

(1) If $c_k > 0$, then **L** goes from the "inside" to the "outside" of the boundary line $\mathbf{B}_k$ as t increases and we shall call t_k an *exit* value.

(2) If $c_k < 0$, then **L** goes from the "outside" to the "inside" of the boundary line $\mathbf{B}_k$ as t increases and we shall call tk an *entry* value.

(3) If $c_k = 0$, the **L** is parallel to $\mathbf{B}_k$, which is outside the window if $q_k < 0$.

The clipping algorithm now proceeds by analyzing the three quantities q_k, c_k, and t_k. Algorithm 3.2.3.1 is a high-level version of the Liang-Barsky algorithm. Algorithm 3.2.3.2 gives the code for the actual Liang-Barsky algorithm.

3.2.3.1 Example

Consider the segment $[P_1,P_2]$ in Figure 3.6. We see that c_1, $c_4 < 0$ and c_2, $c_3 > 0$. In other words, t_1 and t_4 are entry values and t_2 and t_3 are exit values. The picture bears this out. One can also easily see that $t_1 < 0 < t_2 < t_4 < 1 < t_3$. Therefore, there is an entry value (t_4) that is larger than an exit value (t_2). Using the algorithm we conclude that the segment lies entirely outside the window, which is correct.

Reject the segment as soon as
an entry value is larger than 1 or
an exit value is less than 0 or
an entry value is larger than an exit value

Otherwise, the segment meets the window. We need to compute in intersection only if t0 > 0 and t1 <1, where

$$t0 = \max(0, \max[\text{ entry value } t_k]), \text{ and}$$
$$t1 = \min(1, \min[\text{ exit values } t_k]).$$

(The case where t0 = 0 or t1 = 1 means that we should use the endpoint, that is, no clipping is necessary,)

Algorithm 3.2.3.1. High-level Liang-Barsky line-clipping algorithm.

```
Boolean function LB_Clip (ref real x0, y0, x1, y1; real xmin ymin xmax, ymax)
{This clips the segment from (x0, y0) to x1, y1) against the window [xmin, xmax] X
[ymin, ymax]. It returns false if the segment is entirely outside the window and true
otherwise. In the later case the variables x0, y0, x1, and y1 will also have been modified
to specify the final clipped segment.}
begin
    real    t0, t1, dx, dy;
    boolean more;

    t0 :=0, t1 :=1, dx :=x1-x0;

    Findt (-dx, x0 - xmin,t0t1,more);                    [left bdry ]
    if more then
        begin
            Find (dx,xmax - x0,t0,t1,more);              {right bdry}
            if more then
                begin
                    dy :=y1 - y0;
                    Findt (-dy,y0-ymin,t0,t1,more); {bottombdry}
                    if more then
                        begin
                            Findt (dy, ymax - y0,t0,t1,more);     {top bdry}
```

```
                        if more then
                            begin           {clip the line}
                                if t1 < 1 then
                                    begin       {calculate exit point}
                                        x1 := x0 +t1*dx;
                                        y1 := y0 + t1*dy;
                                    end;
                                if t0 > 0 then
                                    begin           {calculate    entry
point}
                                        x0 := x0 + t0*dx;
                                        y0 := y0 + t0*dy;
                                    end
                            end
                    end
                end
            end
        return (more)
end
procedure Findt (real denom, num; ref real t0, t1; ref between more)
begin
        real r:

        more := true
        if denom < 0
            then
                begin       {line from outside to inside}
                    r := num/denom;
                    if r > t1
                        then more := false
                        else if r > t0 then t0 := r;
                end
            else if denom > 0
                then        {line from inside to outside }
                    begin
                        r := num/denom;
                        If r < t0
                            then more := false
                            else if r < t1 then t1 := r,
                    end
                else if num < 0             {line parallel to boundary}
                    then more := false
end;    [ Findt }
```

Algorithm 3.2.3.2. The Liang-Barsky line-clipping algorithm.

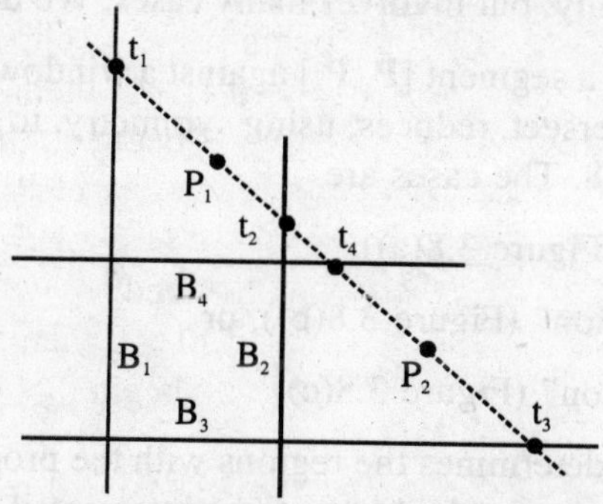

Figure 3.6. Liang-Barsky line-clipping example.

3.2.3.2 Example.

Consider the segment $[\mathbf{P}_1, \mathbf{P}_2]$ in Figure 3.7. In this example, $c_1, c_3 < 0$ and $c_2, c_4 > 0$, so that t_1 and t_3 are entry values and t_2 and t_4 are exit values. Furthermore, $t1 < 0 < t_3 < 1 < t_2 < t_4$. This time we cannot reject the segment and must compute $t_0 = \max(0, c_1, c_3) = c_3$ and $t_1 = \min(1, c_2, c_4) = 1$. The algorithm tells us that we must clip the segment at the $\mathbf{P}_1$ end to get **Q** but do not need to clip at the $\mathbf{P}_2$ end. Again this is clearly what had to be done.

In conclusion, the advantage of the Liang-Barsky algorithm over the Cohen-Sutherland algorithm is that it involves less arithmetic and is therefore faster. It needs only two subtractions to get q_k and c_k and then one division.

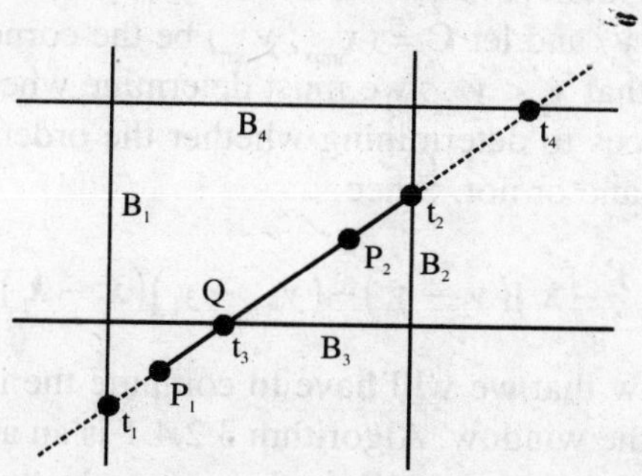

Figure 3.7. Liang-Barsky line-clipping example

3.2.4 Nicholl-Lee-Nicholl Line Clipping

One of the problems common to both the Cohen-Sutherland and the Liang-Barsky algorithm is that more intersections are computed than necessary. For example, consider Figure 3.6 again where we are clipping line segment $[\mathbf{P}_1, \mathbf{P}_2]$ against the window.

The Cohen-Sutherland algorithm will compute the intersection of the segment with the top boundary at t_4 even though the segment is later rejected. The Liang-Barsky algorithm will actually compute **all** the parameter values corresponding to the intersection of the line with the window. Avoiding many of these wasted computations is what the Nicholl-Lee-Nicholl line-clipping algorithm is all about. These authors also make a detailed analysis of the deficiencies of the Cohen-Sutherland and Liang-Barsky algorithms. Their final algorithm is much faster than either of these. It is not really much more complicated conceptually, but involves many cases. We describe one basic case below.

Assume that we want to clip a segment [$\mathbf{P}_1$,$\mathbf{P}_2$] against a window. The determination of the exact edges, if any, that one needs to intersect, reduces, using symmetry, to an analysis of the three possible positions of $\mathbf{P}_1$ shown in Figure 3.8. The cases are

(1) $\mathbf{P}_1$ is in the window (Figure 3.8(a)),

(2) $\mathbf{P}_1$ is in a "corner region" (Figure 3.8(b)), or

(3) $\mathbf{P}_1$ is in an "edge region" (Figure 3.8(c)).

For each of these cases one determines the regions with the property that no matter where in the region the second point $\mathbf{P}_2$ is, the segment will have to be intersected with the **same** boundaries of the window. These regions are also indicated in Figure 3.8. As one can see, these regions are determined by drawing the rays from $\mathbf{P}_1$ through the four corners of the window. The following abbreviations were used:

T – ray intersects top boundary	LT – ray intersects left and top boundary
L – ray intersects left boundary	LR – ray intersects left and right boundary
B – ray intersects bottom boundary	LB – ray intersects left and bottom boundary
R – ray intersects right boundary	TR – ray intersects top and right boundary
	TB – ray intersects top and bottom boundary

For example, suppose that the segment [$\mathbf{P}_1$,$\mathbf{P}_2$] is as shown in Figure 3.8(c). Here are the computations one has to perform. Let $\mathbf{Pi} = (x_i, y_i)$ and let $\mathbf{C} = (x_{max}, y_{min})$ be the corner of the window also indicated in Figure 3.8(c). After checking that $y_2 < y_{min}$, we must determine whether the vector $\mathbf{P}_1\mathbf{P}_2$ is above or below the vector $\mathbf{P}_1\mathbf{C}$. This reduces to determining whether the ordered basis ($\mathbf{P}_1\mathbf{C}$,$\mathbf{P}_1\mathbf{P}_2$) determines the standard orientation of the plane or not. Since

$$\det\begin{pmatrix}\mathbf{P}_1\mathbf{C}\\ \mathbf{P}_1\mathbf{P}_2\end{pmatrix} = (x_{max} - x_1)(y_2 - y_1) - (y_{min} - y_1)(x_2 - x_1) < 0,$$

$\mathbf{P}_1\mathbf{P}_2$ is below $\mathbf{P}_1\mathbf{C}$. We now know that we will have to compute the intersection of [$\mathbf{P}_1$,$\mathbf{P}_2$] with both the left and bottom boundary of the window. Algorithm 3.2.4.1 is an abstract program for the Nicholl-Lee-Nicholl algorithm in the edge region case ($\mathbf{P}_1$ in the region shown in Figure 3.8(c)). We assume a window $[x_{min}, x_{max}] * [y_{min}, y_{max}]$.

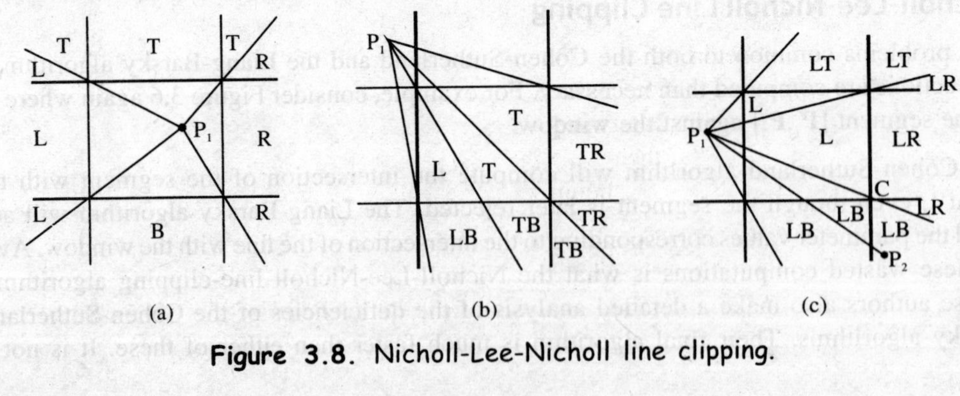

Figure 3.8. Nicholl-Lee-Nicholl line clipping.

```
procedure LeftEdgeRegionCase (ref real x1, y1, x2, y2; ref Boolean visible)
    begin
        real dx, dy;

        if x2 < xmin
            then visible := false
            else if y2 < ymin
                then LeftBottom (xmin, ymin, xmax, ymax, x1, y1, x2, y2, visible)
                else if y2 > ymax
                    then
                        begin       {Use symmetry to reduce to LeftBottom case}
                            y1 := y1;  y2 := y2;    [ reflect about x-axis ]
                            LeftBottom(xmin,–ymax,xmax,–ymin,x1,y1,x2,y2, visible);
                            y1 := y1;  y2 := -y2;  [ reflect back ]
                        end
                    else
                        begin
                            dx := x2 – x1;  dy := y2 – y1;
                            if x2 > xmax then
                                begin
                                    y2:= y1+dy*(xmax– x1)/dx; x2 := xmax;
                                end
                            y1:= y1+dy*(xmin– x1)/dx;   x1 := xmin;
                            visible := true;
                        end
end;
```

```
procedure LeftBottom {real xmin, ymin, xmax, ymax;
                      ref real x1, y1, x2, y2; ref Boolean visible}
begin
    real dx, dy, a, b, c;
    dx := x2 – x1;              dy := y2 – y1;
    a := (xmin – x1)*dy;        b := (ymin – y1)*dx;
    if b > a
        then visible := false {(x2,y2) is abelow ray from (x1,y1) to bottom left corner]
        else
            begin
                visible := true;
                if x2 < xmax
                    then
                        begin x2 := x1 - b/dy:   y2 := ymin;        end
                    else
                        begin
                            c := (xmax – x1)*dy;
                            if b> c
```

```
                    then {(x2,y2) is between rays from (x1,y1) to
                         bottom left and right corner}
                    begin x2 := x1 + b/dy:   y2 := ymin;      end
               else
                    begin y2 := y1 + c/dx;   x2 := xmax;      end
          end;
     end
  y1 := y1 + a/dx;  x1 := xmin;
end;
```

Algorithm 3.2.4.1. The edge region case of the Nicholl-Lee-Nicholl line-clipping algorithm.

To deal with symmetry only rotations through 90, 180, and 270 degrees about the origin and reflections about the lines x = -y and the x-axis are needed. These operations are extremely simple and involve only negation and assignment. This finishes our survey of line-clipping algorithms. Next, we turn our attention to polygon-clipping algorithms.

3.3 POLYGON-CLIPPING ALGORITHMS

3.3.1 Sutherland-Hodgman Polygon Clipping

One of the earliest polygon-clipping algorithms is the Sutherland-Hodgman algorithm. It is based on clipping the **entire** subject polygon against an edge of the window (more precisely, the halfplane determined by that edge which contains the clip polygon), then clipping the new polygon against the next edge of the window, and so on, until the polygon has been clipped against all of the four edges. An important aspect of their algorithm is that one can avoid generating a lot of intermediate data. Representing a polygon as a sequence of vertices $\mathbf{P}_1, \mathbf{P}_2, \ldots, \mathbf{P}_n$, suppose that we want to clip against a single edge **e**. The algorithm considers the input vertices $\mathbf{P}_i$ one at a time and generates a new sequence $\mathbf{Q}_1, \mathbf{Q}_2, \ldots, \mathbf{Q}_m$. Each $\mathbf{P}_i$ generates 0, 1, or 2 of the $\mathbf{Q}_j$, depending on the position of the input vertices with respect to **e**. If we consider each input vertex **P**, except the first, to be the terminal vertex of an edge, namely the edge defined by **P** and the immediately preceding input vertex, call it **S**, then the **Q**'s generated by **P** depend on the relationship between the edge [**S**,**P**] and the line **L** determined by **e**. There are four possible cases. See Figure 3.9. The window side of the line is marked as "inside." The circled vertices are those that are output. Figure 3.10 shows an example of how the clipping works. Clipping the polygon with vertices labeled $\mathbf{P}_i$ against edge $\mathbf{e}_1$ produces the polygon with vertices $\mathbf{Q}_i$. Clipping the new polygon against edge $\mathbf{e}_2$ produces the polygon with vertices $\mathbf{R}_i$.

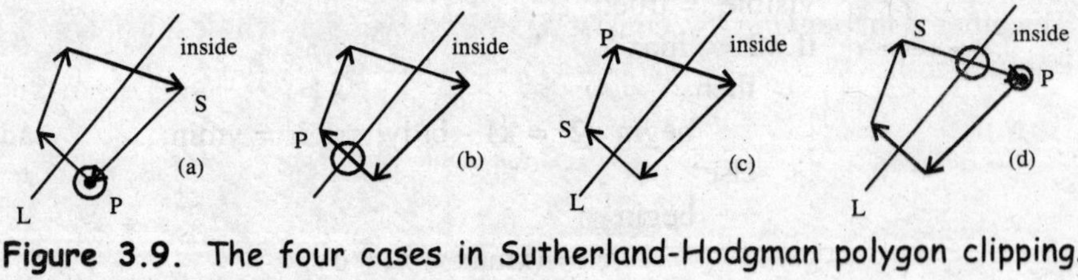

Figure 3.9. The four cases in Sutherland-Hodgman polygon clipping.

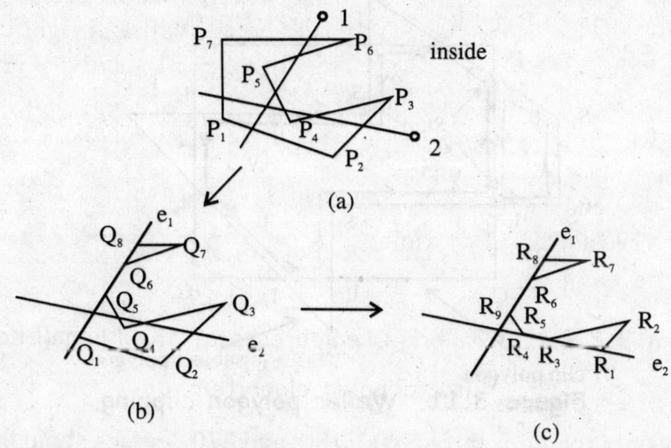

Figure 3.10. *A Sutherland-Hodgman polygon-clipping example.*

Note that we may end up with some bogus edges. For example, the edge $\mathbf{R_5R_6}$ in Figure 3.10 is not a part of the mathematical intersection of the subject polygon with the clip polygon. Eliminating such edges from the final result would be a nontrivial effort, but normally they do not cause any problems. We run into this bogus edge problem with other clipping algorithms also.

3.3.2 Weiler Polygon Clipping

Another early polygon clipping algorithm was developed in the context of the visible surface determination algorithm in [WeiA77]. Weiler and Atherton needed a new algorithm because the Sutherland-Hodgman algorithm would have created too many auxiliary polygons. An improved version of the algorithm can be found in [Weil80]. Here is a very brief description of the algorithm:

The boundaries of polygons are assumed to be oriented so that the inside of the polygon is always to the right as one traverses the boundary. Note that intersections of the subject and clip polygon, if any, occur in pairs: one where the subject *enters* the inside of the clip polygon and one where it *leaves*.

Step 1: Compare the borders of the two polygons for intersections. Insert vertices into the polygons at the intersections.

Step 2: Process the nonintersecting polygon borders, separating those contours that are outside the clip polygon and those that are inside.

Step 3: Separate the intersection vertices found on all subject polygons into two lists. One is the *entering list,* consisting of those vertices where the polygon edge enters the clip polygon. The other is the *leaving list,* consisting of those vertices where the polygon edge leaves the clip polygon.

Step 4: Now clip.

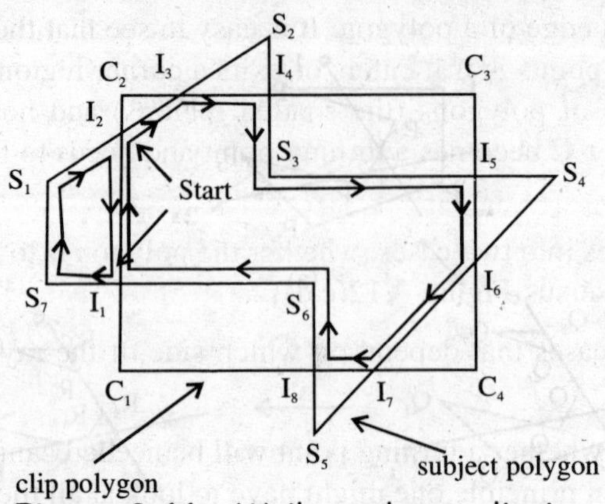

Figure 3.11. Weiler polygon clipping.

(a) Remove an intersection vertex from the entering list. If there is none, then we are done.

(b) Follow the subject polygon vertices to the next intersection.

(c) Jump to the clip polygon vertex list.

(d) Follow the clip polygon vertices to the next intersection.

(e) Jump back to the subject polygon vertex list.

(f) Repeat (b)–(e) until we are back to the starting point.

This process creates the polygons inside the clip polygon. To get those that are outside, one repeats the same steps, except that one starts with a vertex from the leaving list and the clip polygon vertex list is followed in the **reverse** direction. Finally, all holes are attached to their associated exterior contours.

3.3.2.1 Example

Consider the polygons in Figure 3.11. The subject polygon vertices are labeled **Si**, those of the clip polygon are labeled $\mathbf{C}_i$, and the intersections are labeled $\mathbf{I}_i$. The entering list consists of $\mathbf{I}_2$, $\mathbf{I}_4$, $\mathbf{I}_6$, and $\mathbf{I}_8$. The leaving list consists of $\mathbf{I}_1$, $\mathbf{I}_3$, $\mathbf{I}_5$, and $\mathbf{I}_7$. Starting Step 4(a) with the vertex $\mathbf{I}_2$ will generate the inside contour Starting Step 4(a) with vertices $\mathbf{I}_1$, $\mathbf{I}_3$, $\mathbf{I}_5$, and $\mathbf{I}_7$ will generate the outside contours

3.3.3 Liang-Barsky Polygon Clipping

This section gives a brief outline of the Liang-Barsky polygon-clipping algorithm. The algorithm is claimed to be twice as fast as the Sutherland-Hodgman clipping algorithm. This algorithm and the next one, the Maillot algorithm, base their success on their ability to detect turning points efficiently. Before we get to the algorithm, some comments on turning points are in order.

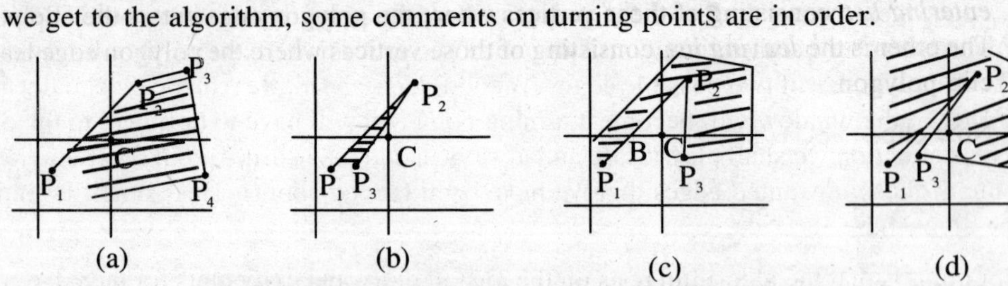

Figure 3.12. Different types of turning *points.*

Assume that $[\mathbf{P}_1,\mathbf{P}_2]$ is an edge of a polygon. It is easy to see that the only time that this edge is relevant to the issue of turning points is if it enters or exits a corner region associated to the window. Figure 3.12 shows some cases of polygons (the shaded regions) and how the exiting edge $[\mathbf{P}_1,\mathbf{P}_2]$ affects whether or not the corner **C** becomes a turning point and needs to be added to the output. One sees the following:

(1) The analysis divides into two cases: whether the polygon is to the right or left of the edge. (Figure 3.12(a,b) versus Figure 3.12(c,d))

(2) There are two subcases that depend on which side of the ray from $\mathbf{P}_2$ to **C** the segment $[\mathbf{P}_2,\mathbf{P}_3]$ is located.

(3) The decision as to whether a turning point will be needed cannot be made on the basis of only a few edges. In principle one might have to look at all the edges of the polygon first.

It is observation (3) that complicates life for polygon-clipping algorithms that process edges sequentially in one pass. One could simplify life and generate a turning point **whenever** we run into an edge that enters, lies in, or exits a corner region. The problem with this approach is that one will generate bogus edges for our clipped polygon. The polygon in Figure 3.12(c) would generate the "dangling" edge **[B,C]**. Bogus edges were already encountered in Sutherland-Hodgman clipping (but for different reasons). These edges might not cause any problems, as in the case where one is simply filling two-dimensional regions. On the other hand, one would like to minimize the number of such edges, but avoiding them entirely would be very complicated with some algorithms like the Liang-Barsky and Maillot algorithm. With this introduction, let us describe the Liang-Barsky algorithm. We shall be brief because it does not contain much in the way of new insights given the fact that

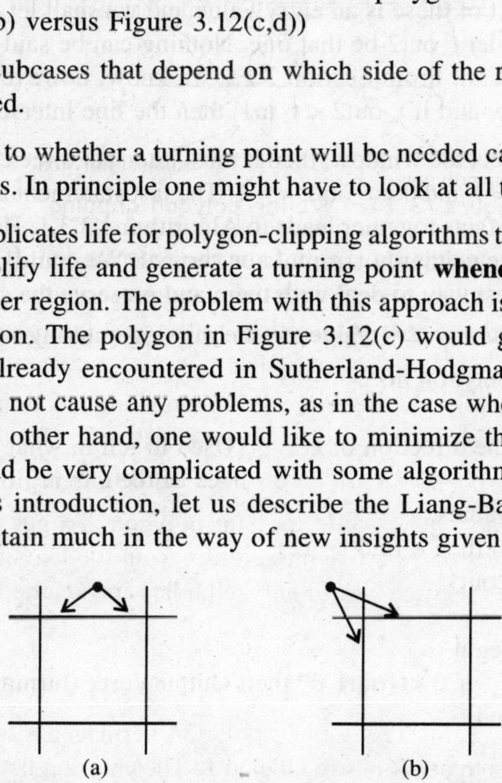

Figure 3.13. Testing for turning points.

it is built on the approach they use in their line-clipping algorithm. Furthermore, another algorithm, the Maillot algorithm, is better. Our discussion here will follow who have modified the algorithm so that it is easier to follow although it has the potential disadvantage of creating more bogus edges.

Consider Figure 3.13. We extend the edges of our rectangular window to divide the plane into nine regions. If we are at a point of the polygon that lies in one of the four outside regions that meet the window in an edge, then the next edge of the polygon can only meet the window in that edge. See Figure 3.13(a). On the other hand, if the point is in one of the four corner regions, then the next edge could meet the window in one of two possible edges. Without look-ahead, we really cannot tell whether the adjacent corner of the window will become a turning point and will have to be added to the output polygon. In such a situation we shall play it safe and always include the corner point (even though this may create some of these unwanted edges that we have been talking about). This is the first point to make about the algorithm.

The other point is that the algorithm rests on the idea of entry and exit points for the edges of the polygon that correspond to the entry and exit values used in the lineclipping algorithm described in

Section 3.2.3. By analyzing these points one can tell if an edge intersects the window or if it gives rise to a turning point. As we work our way through the edges of the polygon, assume that the current edge $\mathbf{e} = [\mathbf{p}_i, \mathbf{p}_{i+1}]$ is neither vertical nor horizontal. Then **e** will intersect all the boundary lines of our window. If we parameterize the line containing **e** in the form $\mathbf{p}_i + t\mathbf{p}_i\mathbf{p}_{i+1}$, then the four intersection points correspond to four parameter values and can again be classified as two entry and two exit points. We shall denote these associated parameter values by t_in1, t_in2, t_out1, and t_out2, respectively. It is easy to see that the smallest of these is an entry value and we shall let t_in1 be that one. The largest is an exit value and we shall let t_out2 be that one. Nothing can be said about the relative size of the remaining two values in general. From Section 3.2.3 we know, however, that if t_in2 < t_out1, then the line intersects the window and if t_out2 < t_in1, then the line intersects a corner region.

If a line does not intersect the window, then it must intersect three corner regions. The conditions for that are that 0 < t_out1 < = 1 and 0 < t_out2 < = 1. The last statement also holds if the line intersects the window. Putting all these facts together leads to Algorithm 3.3.3.1. However, we were assuming in the discussion that edges were neither horizontal nor vertical. We could deal with such lines by means of special cases, but the easiest way to deal with them and preserve the structure of Algorithm 3.3.3.1 is to use a trick and assign dummy $\pm\infty$ values to the missing entering and leaving parameters.

```
for each edge e of polygon do
        begin
        Determine the direction of e;      {Used to tell in what order of bounding
                                            lines of the clip region will be hit}
        Find exit t values;
        if t_out2 > 0 then e find t_in2;
        if t_in2 > t_out1
              then
                 begin
                    if 0 <t_out1 d" then OutputVertx (turning vertex);
                 end
              else
                 begin
                    if (0 < t_out1) and t _in2 d" 1) then
                       begin
                          if 0 d" t_in2
                                then OutputVertex (appropriate side intersection)
                                else OutputVertex (starting g vertex );
                          if t_out1 d" 1
                                then OutputVertex (appropriate side intersection)
                                else OutputVertex (ending vertex);
                       end
                 end;
              if 0 < t_out2 d" 1 then OutputVertex (appropriate corner);
        end;
```

Algorithm 3.3.3.1. Overview of a Liang-Barsky polygon-clipping algorithm.

3.3.4 Maillot Polygon Clipping

The Maillot clipping algorithm ([Mail92]) clips arbitrary polygons against a rectangular window. It uses the well-known Cohen-Sutherland clipping algorithm for segments as its basis and then finds the correct turning points for the clipped polygon by maintaining an additional bit of information. As indicated earlier, it is speedy determination of turning points that is crucial for polygon clipping, and this algorithm does it very efficiently. We shall use the same notation that was used in Section 3.2.1.

We also assume that the **same** encoding of points is used. This is very important; otherwise, the tables Tcc and Cra below **must** be changed. Let **P** be a polygon defined by the sequence of vertices $\mathbf{p}_0$, $\mathbf{p}_1$, . . . , $\mathbf{p}_n$, $\mathbf{p}_{n+1}$ = $\mathbf{p}_0$. Algorithm 3.3.4.1 gives a top-level description of the Maillot algorithm. In addition to the Cohen-Sutherland trivial rejection cases, Maillot's algorithm subjects all vertices of the polygon to one extra test, which he calls the "basic turning point test." This test checks for the case where the current point lies in one of the four

```
p := p_o; c_p := c(p);
for I := 1 to n + 1 do
    begin
        q := p; c_q := c(q);
        {Clip the segment [p,q] as in Cohen-Southerland algorithm}
        DoCSClip ();

        if segment [p,q] is outside clipping region then TestForComplexCase;

        DoBasicTurningPointTest ();

        p := q;    c_p := c_q
    end
```

Algorithm 3.3.4.1. *Overview of Maillot polygon-clipping algorithm.*

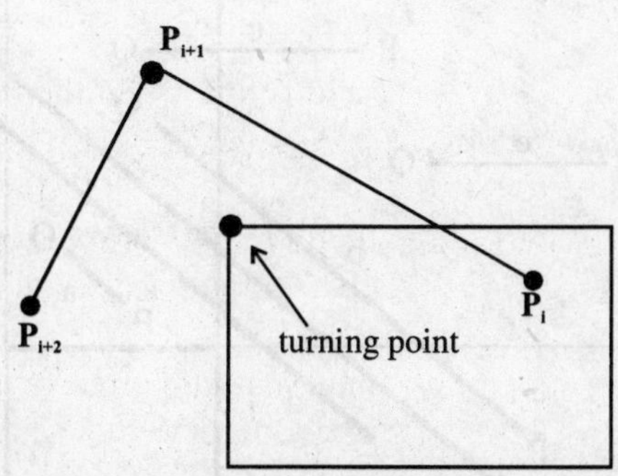

Figure 3.14. *A turning point case.*

corners outside the window. One probably needs to add a turning point to the clipped polygon in this case. See Figure 3.14. We said "probably" because if the current point is considered in isolation (without looking at its predecessors), then to always automatically add the point may cause us to add the same corner several times in a row.

See points $\mathbf{p}_i$, $\mathbf{p}_{i+1}$, and $\mathbf{p}_{i+2}$ in Figure 3.14. In the implementation of Maillot's algorithm, we do not try to eliminate such redundancies. If this is not desired, then extra code will have to be added to avoid it. If all of a polygon's edges meet the window, then the basic turning point test is all that is needed to clip it correctly. For polygons that have edges entirely **outside** the clipping region, one needs to do more. Figure 3.15 shows all (up to symmetry) generic cases that need to be handled in this more complex situation. The following terminology is useful for the case of edges outside the clipping region.

Notation. A point that lies in a region with code 0001, 0010, 0100, or 1000 will be called a 1-*bit point.* A point that lies in a region with code 0011, 0110, 1100, or 1001 will be called a 2-*bit point.* A segment is called an *x-y segment* if its start point is an x-bit point and its endpoint is a y-bit point. Knowing the type of segment that one has is important for the algorithm. This is why an extra bit is used in the encoding of points. It is stuck at the left end of the original Cohen-Sutherland code. Below is an overview of the actions that are taken in the Test For Complex Case procedure. Refer to Figure 3.15.

The 1–1 Segment Cases (Segments **a** and **b**). Either the two points have the same code (segment **a**) and no turning point needs to be generated or they have different codes (segment **b**). In the latter case there is one turning point that can be handled by the basic turning point test. The code for the corner for this turning point is computed from the **or** of the two codes and a lookup table (the Tcc table in the code).

The 2–1 and 1–2 Segment Cases (Segments **c** and **d**). In this case one point of the segment has a 1-bit code and the other, a 2-bit code.

(a) The endpoint is the point with the 1-bit code (segment **c**): If both codes **and** to a nonzero value (segment **[P,R]** in Figure 3.16(a)), there is no turning point. If both codes **and** to

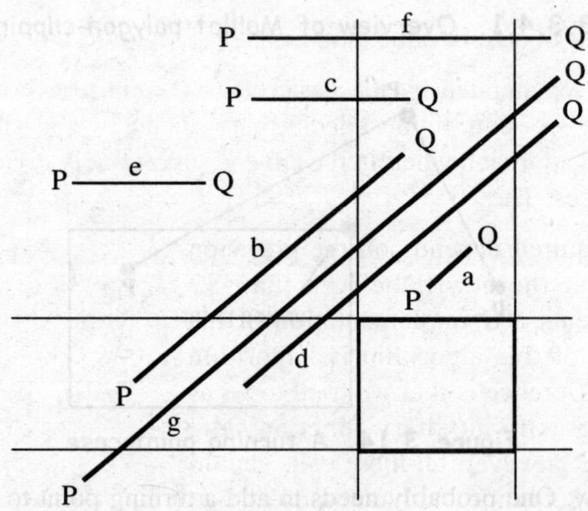

Figure 3.15. Turning point cases in Maillot Algorithm

zero, then we need to generate a turning point that depends on the two codes. A lookup table (Tcc in the code) is used for this.

(b) The endpoint has the 2-bit code (segment **d**): The case where the **and** of both codes is nonzero is handled by the basic turning point test (segment [**R**,**Q**] in Figure 3.16(b). If both codes **and** to zero, we need two turning points. The first one depends on the two codes and is determined by again using a lookup table (Tcc in the code). The other is generated by the basic turning point test (segment [**P**,**Q**] in Figure 3.16(b)).

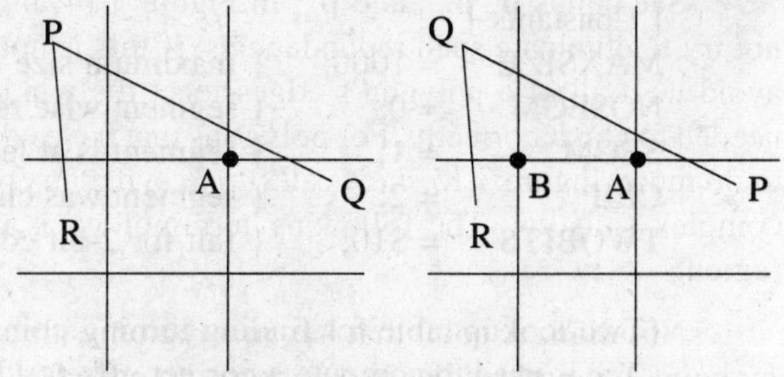

Figure 3.16. Turning point tests.

As an example of how the Tcc table is generated, consider the segment [**P**,**Q**] in Figure 3.16(b). In the figure there are two turning points **A** and **B**. The basic turning point test applied to **Q** will generate **B**. Let us see how **A** is generated. How can one compute the code, namely 3, for this turning point? Maillot defines the sixteen element Tcc table in such a way that the following formula works:

newCode = code(**Q**)+ Tcc[code(**P**)]

For the 1–1, 2–1, and 1–2 segment cases only four entries of Tcc are used in conjunction with this formula. Four other entries are set to 1 and used in the 2–2 segment case discussed below when it runs into a 1–1 segment. The remaining eight of the entries in Tcc are set to 0.

The 2–2 Segment Case (Segments **e, f** and **g**). There are three subcases.

(a) Both points have the same code (segment **e**): No turning point is needed here.

(b) Both codes **and** to a nonzero value (segment **f**): Apply the basic turning point test to the end point.

(c) Both codes **and** to a zero value (segment **g**): There will be two turning points.

One of them is easily generated by the basic turning point test. For the other one we have a situation as shown in Figure 3.17 and we must decide between the two possible choices **A** or **B**. Maillot uses a midpoint subdivision approach wherein the edge is successively divided into two until it can be handled by the previous cases. The

number of subdivisions required depends on the precision used. For 32-bit integers, there will be less than 32 subdivisions. Maillot presents a C implementation of his algorithm in. Our version of this algorithm is Algorithm 3.3.4.2 below. The main difference is that we tried to be as clear as possible by using extra auxiliary functions and procedures. To be efficient, however, all these calls should be eliminated and the code put inline. As mentioned earlier, Maillot's algorithm uses the Cohen-Sutherland clipping algorithm. One can use the implementation in Section 3.2.1 for this except that the extended encoding function (Extended Cs Code) shown in Algorithm 3.3.4.3 should be

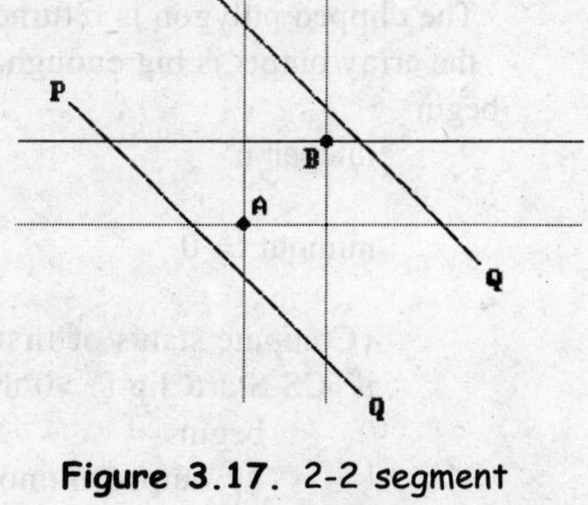

Figure 3.17. 2-2 segment

```
[ Constants ]
MAXSIZE     = 1000;    { maximum size of pnt2d array }
NOSEGM      = 0;       { segment wise reject }
SEGM        = 1;       { segment is at least partial visible}
CLIP        = 2;       { segment was clipped }
TWOBITS     = $10;     { falt for 2-bit code }

{Two lookup table for finding turning point
  Tcc is used to compute a correct offset,
  Cra gives an index into the clipRegion array for turning point coordinates}
Integer array [0..15] Tcc = (0, -3, -6, 1, 3, 0, 1,0,6,1,0,0,1,0,0,0,);
Integer array [0..15] Cra = (-1, -1, -1, 3, -1, -1, 2, -1, -1, 1, -1, -1, 0, -1, -1, -1);

pnt2d = record
        real x, y;
end

pnt2ds = pnt2d array [0..MAXSIZE];

{Global variables}
{The clipping region [ xmin,xmax]X[ymin,ymax] bounds listed in order;
(xmin,ymin),(xmax,ymin),(xmin,ymax),(xmax,ymax)}
array [0..3] of pnt2d clipRegion;

pnt2d   startPt;{ start point of segment }
Integer startC;     { code for start point }
Integer startC0;    { saves startC for next call to CS_EndClip }
Pnt2d   endPt;      { endpoint of segment }
Integer endC;       {code for endpoint }
Integer aC;         { used by procedure TwoBitEndPoint }

procedure M_Clip (refer pnt2ds inpts; integer numin);
                    ref pnt2ds outpts; ref integer numout"
{inpts[0..numin-1] defines the input polygon with input[ numin – 1 ] = inpts [0]
  The clipped polygon is returned in outputs[0.numout – 1 ]. It is assumed that
  the array outpts is big enough. }
begin
        integer i;

        numout := 0

        {Compute status of first point.  If it is visible, it is stored in outpts array.}
        if  CS-StartClip () >0 then
                begin
                    outpts[ numout ] := startPt;
```

```
            Inc ( numout);
            end

      { Now the rest of the points}
      for i := 1 to numin-1, do
            begin
               cflag := CS_EndClip (i);

               startC0 := endC; [ endC may get changed ]
               if SegMetWindow (cflag)
                  then
                     begin
                        if Clipped (cflag) then
                           begin
                              outpts [numout] := startPt;
                              Inc (numout);
                           end;
                        outpts [numout] := endpt;
                        Inc (numout);
                  end
               else if TwoBitCase (endC)
                  then TwoBitEndPoint ()
                  else OneBitEndPoint ();

               {The basic turning point test ]
               if TwoBitcase (endC) then
                  begin
                     outpts [numout] := clipRegion[Cra[C and not (TWOBITS)]];
                     Inc (numout);
                  end;

               startPt; := inpts[i];
            end;

      { Now close the output }
      If numout > 0 then
            begin
               outpts [numout] := outpts [0];
               Inc (numout);
            end
end; {M_Clip }

boolean function SegMetWindow (Integer cflag)
return (cflag and SEGM "' 0 );
```

```
boolean function Clipped (integer cflag)
{ Actually, this function should return true only if the first point is clipped;
 Otherwise we generate redundant points.}
return (cflag and CLIP) "' 0);

boolean function TwoBitCase (integer cflag)
return ((cflag and TWOBITS) "' 0);

procedure TwiBitEndPoint ()
{The line has been rejected and we have a 2-bit endpoint. ]
if (startC and endC and (TWOBITS – 1)) = 0 then
        begin
                {The points have no region bits in common. We need to generate
                an extra turning point – which one is specified by Cra table.}
                if TwoBitCase (startC)
                    then BothAreTwoBits ()          {defines aC for this case}
                    else aC := endC + Tcc [startC]; [ 1-bit start point. 2-bit endpoint ]

                outpts [numout] := clipRegion[Cra{aC and not (TWOBITS)]];
                Inc (numout);
        end; [ TwoBitEndPoint ]

procedure BothAreTwoBits ()
{Determines what aC should be by doing midpoint subdivision.}
begin
        boolean notdone;
        pnt2d Pt1, Pt2, aPt;

        notdone := true;
        Pt1 := startPt
        Pt2 := endPt
        while notdone do
                begin
                    aPt.x := (Pt1.x + Pt2.x)/2.0;
                    aPt.y := (Pt1.y + Pt2.y)/2.0;
                    aC := ExtenbdedCsCode (aPt);
                    If TwoBitCase (aC)
                        then
                            begin
                                if aC = endC
                                    then Pt2 := aPt
                                    else
                                        begin
                                            If aC = startC
                                                then Pt1 := aPt
```

```
                                        else notdone := false
                                   end
                          end
                      else
                          begin
                              if (aC and end C) ‘“ 0
                                   then aC := endC + Tcc [startC and not (TWOBITS)]
                                   else aC := startC + Tcc [endC and not (TWOBITS)];
                              notdone := false;
                          end
                 end
end; {Both AreTwoBits}

procedure OneBitEndPoint ()
{The line has been rejected and we have a 1-bit endpoint.}
If TwoBitCase (startC)
       then
             begin
                 if (startC and endC) = 0 then
                      endC := startC + Tcc[endC];
             end
       else
             begin
                 endC := endC or startC;
                 if Tcc[endC] =1 then endC:= endC or TWOBITS;
             end; [ OneBitEndPoint ]
```

Algorithm 3.3.4.2. The Maillot polygon-clipping algorithm.

```
Integer function ExtendedCsCode (pnt2d p)
{The Maillot extension of the Cohen-Sutherland encoding of points}
begin
         if p.x < clipRegion [0].x then
                 begin
                     if p.y > clipRegion[3].y then return (6 or TWOBITS);
                     if p.y < clipRegion[0].y then return (12 or TWOBITS);
                     return (4);
                 end;
         if p.x > clipRegioni[3].x then
                 begin
                     if p.y > clipRegion[3].y then return (3 or TWOBITS);
                     if p.y < clipRegion[0].y then return (9 or TWOBITS);
                     return (1);
                 end;
         if p.y > clipRegion[3].y then return (2);
```

```
        if p.y < clipRegion[0].y then return (8);
        return (0);
    end;
```

Algorithm 3.3.4.3. An extended clipping code function.

used. This function adds the extra bit (TWOBITS), which we talked about. Within the Cohen-Sutherland clipping the extra bit should be ignored. Two functions in the Maillot algorithm, Algorithm 3.3.4.2, make use of Cohen-Sutherland clipping:

CS_StartClip: This function defines global variables

startPt – the first point of the input polygon

startC – the extended Cohen-Sutherland code for startPt

and returns values SEGM or NOSEGM, where

SEGM means that the point is inside the clipping region

NOSEGM means that the point is outside the clipping region

CS_EndClip (**integer** i): This function uses the global variables startC0 and startPt, clips the segment [startPt,ith point of polygon], and defines the global variables

startC, endC – the extended Cohen-Sutherland code for the start and endpoint, respectively

startPt, endPt – these are the original endpoints if there was no clipping or are the clipped points otherwise

The function returns values SEGM, SEGM **or** CLIP, or NOSEGM, where

SEGM means that the segment is inside the clipping region

CLIP means that the segment is only partly inside the clipping region

NOSEGM means that the segment is outside the clipping region

In conclusion, Maillot claims the following for his algorithm and implementation:

(1) It is up to eight times faster than the Sutherland-Hodgman algorithm and up to three times faster than the Liang-Barsky algorithm.

(2) It can be implemented using only integer arithmetic.

(3) It would be easy to modify so as to reduce the number of degenerate edges.

With regard to point (3), recall again that the Sutherland-Hodgman and Liang-Barsky algorithms also produce degenerate edges sometimes. The Weiler and Vatti algorithm are best in this respect.

3.3.5 Vatti Polygon Clipping

Quite a few polygon-clipping algorithms have been published. We have discussed several. The Liang-Barsky and Maillot algorithms are better than the Sutherland-Hodgman algorithm, but these algorithms only clip polygons against simple rectangles.

This is adequate for many situations in graphics. On the other hand, the Sutherland-Hodgman and Cyrus-Beck algorithms are more general and allow clipping against any convex polygon. The restriction to convex polygons is caused by the fact that the algorithm clips against a sequence of halfplanes and therefore only applies to sets that are the intersection of halfplanes, in other words, convex (linear) polygons. There are situations however where the convexity requirement is too restrictive. The Weiler algorithm is more general yet and works for non-convex polygons. The final two algorithms we look at, the Vatti and Greiner-Hormann algorithms, are also extremely general. Furthermore, they are the most efficient of these general algorithms. The polygons are not constrained in any way now. They can be concave or convex. They can have self-intersections. In fact, one can easily deal with lists of polygons. We begin with Vatti's algorithm. Call an edge of a polygon a *left* or *right edge* if the **interior** of the polygon is to the right or left, respectively. Horizontal edges are considered to be both left and right edges. A key fact that is used by the Vatti algorithm is that polygons can be represented via a set of *left* and *right bounds*, which are connected lists of left and right edges, respectively, that come in pairs. Each of these bounds starts at a local minimum of the polygon and ends at a local $\mathbf{p}_0, \mathbf{p}_1, \ldots, \mathbf{p}_8$ shown in Figure 3.18(a). The two left bounds have vertices $\mathbf{p}_0, \mathbf{p}_8, \mathbf{p}_7, \mathbf{p}_6$ and $\mathbf{p}_4, \mathbf{p}_3, \mathbf{p}_2$, respectively. The two right bounds have vertices $\mathbf{p}_0, \mathbf{p}_1, \mathbf{p}_2$ and $\mathbf{p}_4, \mathbf{p}_5, \mathbf{p}_6$.

Note. In this section the y-axis will be pointing up (rather than down as usual for a viewport).

Here is an overview of the Vatti algorithm. The first step of the algorithm is to determine the left and right bounds of the clip and subject polygons and to store this information in a *local minima list* (LML). This list consists of a list of matching pairs

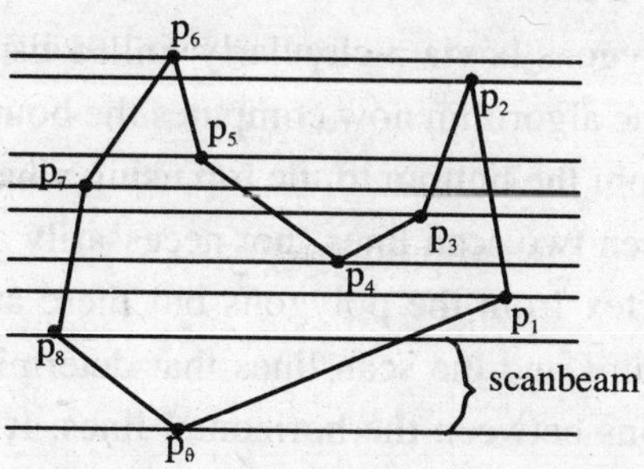

(a)

LML = ((B_1, B_2), (B_3, B_4))

where the bounds B_i are define by

$B_1 = (p_0p_8,\ p_8p_7,\ p_7p_6)$

$B_2 = (p_0p_1,\ p_1p_2)$,

$B_3 = (p_4p_5,\ p_5p_6)$, and

$B_4 = (p_4p_3,\ p_3p_2)$

(b)

Figure 3.18. Polygon bounds

of left-right bounds and is sorted in ascending order by the y-coordinate of the corresponding local minimum. It does not matter if initial horizontal edges are put into a left or right bound. Figure 3.18(b) shows the LML for the polygon in Figure 3.18(a). The algorithm for constructing the LML is a relatively straightforward programming exercise and will not be described here. It can be done with a single pass of the clip and subject polygons.

The bounds on the LML were specified to have the property that their edges are either **all** left edges or **all** right edges. However, it is convenient to have a more general notion of a left or right bound. Therefore, from now on, a *left* or *right bound* will denote any connected sequence of edges only whose **first** edge is required to be a left or right edge, respectively. We still assume that a bound starts at a local minimum and ends at a local maximum. For example, we shall allow the polygon in

Figure 3.18(a) to be described by one left bound with vertices **p0**, **p8**, **p7**, **p6**, **p5**, **p4**, **p3**, **p2** and one right bound with vertices **p0**, **p1**, **p2**. The clipped or *output* polygons we are after will be built in stages from sequences of "partial" polygons, each of which is a "V-shaped" list of vertices with the vertices on the left side coming from a left bound and those on the right side coming from a right bound with the two bounds having one vertex in common, namely, the one at the bottom of the "V", which is at a local minimum. Let us use the notation $P[\mathbf{p}_0\mathbf{p}_1 \ldots \mathbf{p}_n]$ to denote the partial polygon with vertices $\mathbf{p}_0$, $\mathbf{p}_1,\ldots,\mathbf{p}_n$, where $\mathbf{p}_0$ is the first point and $\mathbf{p}_n$ the last. The points $\mathbf{p}_0$ and $\mathbf{p}_n$ are the top of the partial left and right bound, respectively. Some vertex **pm** will be the vertex at a local minimum that connects the two bounds but, since it will not be used for anything, there is no need to indicate this index m in the notation. For example, one way to represent the polygon in Figure 3.18(a) would be as $P[\mathbf{p}_6, \mathbf{p}_7, \mathbf{p}_8, \mathbf{p}_0, \mathbf{p}_1, \mathbf{p}_2, \mathbf{p}_3, \mathbf{p}_4, \mathbf{p}_5, \mathbf{p}_6]$ (with m being 3 in this case).

Notice how the edges in the left and right bounds are **not** always to the right or left of the interior of the polygon here. In the case of a "completed" polygon, $\mathbf{p}_0$ and $\mathbf{p}_n$ will be the same vertex at a local maximum, but at all the other intermediate stages in the construction of a polygon the vertices $\mathbf{p}_0$ and $\mathbf{p}_n$ may **not** be equal. However, $\mathbf{p}_0$ and $\mathbf{p}_n$ will always correspond to top vertices of the current left and right partial bounds, respectively. For example, $P[\mathbf{p}_7\mathbf{p}_8\mathbf{p}_0\mathbf{p}_1]$ (with m equal to 2) is a legitimate expression describing partial left and right bounds for the polygon in Figure 3.18(a).

A good way to implement these partial polygons is via a circularly linked list, or cycle, and a pointer that points to the last element of the list. The algorithm now computes the bounds of the output polygons from the LML by scanning the world from the bottom to the top using what are called *scan beams*. A scan beam is a horizontal section between two scan lines (not necessarily adjacent), so that each of these scan lines contains at least one vertex from the polygons but there are **no** vertices in between them. Figure 3.18(a) shows the scan beams and the scan lines that determine them for that particular polygon. The scan beams are the regions between the horizontal lines. It should be noted here that the scan lines that determine the scan beams are not computed all at once but incrementally in a bottom up fashion. The information about the scan beams is kept in a *scan beam list* (SBL), which is an ordered list ordered by the y-coordinates of all the scan lines that define the scan beams. This list of increasing values will be thought of as a stack. As we scan the world, we also maintain an *active edge list* (AEL), which is an ordered list consisting of all the edges intersected by the current scan beam.

When we begin processing a scan beam, the first thing we do is to check the LML to see if any of its bound pairs start at the bottom of the scan beam. These bounds correspond to local minima and may start a new output polygon or break one into two depending on whether the local minimum starts with a left-right or right-left edge pair. After any new edges from the LML are added to the AEL, we need to check for intersections of edges within a scan beam. These intersections affect the output polygons and are dealt with separately first. Finally, we process the edges on the AEL. Algorithm 3.3.5.1 summarizes this overview of the Vatti algorithm. To understand the algorithm a little better we look at some more of its details. The interested reader can find a much more thorough discussion with abstract programs and explicit data structures in the document VattiClip on the accompanying CD. The UpdateLMLandSBL procedure in Algorithm 3.3.5.1 finds the bounds of a polygon, adds them to LML, and also updates SBL. Finding a bound involves finding the edges that make them up and initializing their data structure that maintains the information that we need as we go along. For example, we keep track of the x-coordinate of their intersection with the bottom of the current scan beam. We call this the *x-value* of the edge. The edges of the AEL are ordered by these values with ties being broken using their slope. We also record the *kind* of an edge which refers to whether it belongs to the clip or subject polygon. Two edges are called *like* edges if they are of the same kind and *unlike* edges otherwise. The partial polygons that are built and that, in the end, may become the polygons that make up the clipped polygon are called the *adjacent polygons* of their edges. Because horizontal edges complicate matters, in order to make dealing with horizontal edges easier, one assumes that the matching left and right bound pairs in the LML list are "normalized". A *normalized* left and right bound pair satisfies the following properties:

(1) All consecutive horizontal edges are combined into one so that bounds do not have two horizontal edges in a row.

(2) No left bound has a bottom horizontal edge (any such edges are shifted to the right bound).

(3) No right bound has a top horizontal edge (any such edges are shifted to the left bound).

```
{Global varibales}
real list          SBL;  {an ordered list of distinct reals thought of as a stack}
bound pair list LML;  {a list of pairs of matching polygon bounds}
edge list          AEL;  {a list of nonhorizontal edges ordered by x intercept
                           with the current scan line}
polygon list    PL;    {the finished output polygons are stored here as algorithm
                           progresses}

polygon list function Vatti_Clip (polygon subjectP; polygon clipP)
{The polygon subjectP is clipped against the polygon clipP,
 The list of polygons which are the intersection of subjctP and clipP is returned to the
  calling procedure.}
begin
        real yb, yt;

        Initialize LML, SBL to empty

        (Define LML and the initial SBL)
        UpdateLMLandSBL (subjectP, subject); {subject and clip specify a subject}
        UpdateLMLandSBL (clipP, clip); {or clip polygon, respectively}

        Initialize PL, AEl to empty;
```

```
        yb := PopSBL ();        {bottom of currentscan beam}
        repeat
                AddNewBoundPairs (yb);
                yt= PopSBL ();
                ProcessIntersections (yb, yt);
                ProcessEdgesInAEL (yb, yt);
                yn := yt;
        until Empty (SBL);

        return (PL);
end;
```

Algorithm 3.3.5.1. The Vatti polygon-clipping algorithm.

We introduce some more terminology. Some edges and vertices that one encounters or creates for the output polygons will belong to the bounds of the clipped polygon, others will not. Let us call a vertex or an edge a *contributing* or *non-contributing vertex* or *edge* depending on whether or not it belongs to the output polygons. With regard to vertices, if a vertex is not a local minimum or maximum, then it will be called a *left* or *right intermediate* vertex depending on whether it belongs to a left or right bound, respectively. Because the overall algorithm proceeds by taking the appropriate action based on the vertices that are encountered, we shall see that it therefore basically reduces to a careful analysis of the following three cases:

(1) The vertex is a local minimum.

(2) The vertex is a left or right intermediate vertex.

(3) The vertex is a local maximum.

Local minima are encountered when elements on the LML become active. Intermediate vertices and local maxima are encountered when scanning the AEL. Intersections of edges also give rise to these three cases.

Returning to Algorithm 3.3.5.1, the first thing that happens in the main loop is to check for new bound pairs that start at the bottom of the current scan beams. If any such pairs exist, then we have a case of two bounds starting at a vertex **p** that is a local minimum. We add their first nonhorizontal edges to the AEL and the top y-values of these to the SBL. The edges are flagged as being a **left** or **right** edge. We determine if the edges are **contributing** by a parity test and flag them accordingly. An edge of the subject polygon is contributing if there are an odd number of edges from the clip polygon to its left in the AEL. Similarly, an edge of the clip polygon is contributing if there are an odd number of edges from the subject polygon to its left in the AEL. If the vertex is contributing, then we create a new partial polygon P[**p**] and associate this polygon to both edges. Note that to determine whether or not an edge is contributing or noncontributing we actually have to look at the geometry only for the first nonhorizontal edge of each bound. The bound's other edges will be of the same type as that one.

The central task of the main loop in the Vatti algorithm is to process the edges on the AEL. If edges intersect, we shall have to do some preprocessing (procedure ProcessIntersections), but right now let us skip that and describe the actual processing, namely, procedure ProcessEdgesInAEL. Because horizontal edges cause substantial complications, we separate the discussion into two cases. We shall discuss the case where there are no horizontal edges first.

If an edge does not end at the top of the current scan beam, then we simply update its x-value to the x-coordinate of the intersection of the edge with the scan line at the top of the scan beam. If an edge **does** end at the top of the scan beam, then the action we take is determined by the type of the top end vertex **p**. The vertex can either be an intermediate vertex or a local maximum.

If the vertex **p** is a left or right intermediate vertex, then the vertex is added at the beginning or end of the vertex list of its adjacent polygon, depending on whether it is a left or right edge, respectively. The edge is replaced on the AEL by its successor edge which inherits the adjacent polygon and left/right flag of the old edge. If the vertex **p** is a local maximum of the original clip or subject polygons, then a pair of edges from two bounds meet in the point **p**. If **p** is a contributing vertex, then the two edges may belong either to the same or different (partial) polygons. If they have the same adjacent polygons, then this polygon will now be closed once the point **p** is added. If they belong to different polygons, say **P** and **Q**, respectively, then we need to merge these polygons. Let **e**1 and **e**2 be the top edges for **P** and **f**1 and **f**2, the top edges for **Q**, so that **e**1 and **f**1 meet in **p** with **f**1 the successor to **e**1 in the AEL. See Figure 3.19.

Figures 3.19(a) and (c) show specific examples and (b) and (d) generic cases. If **e**1 is a left edge of **P** (Figures 3.19(a) and (b)), then we append the vertices of **Q** to the beginning

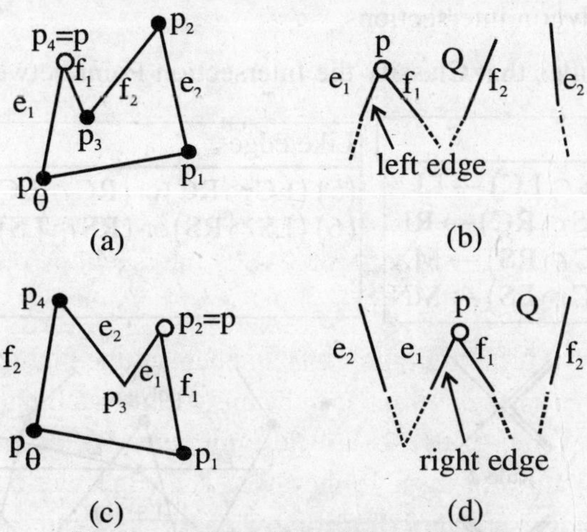

Figure 3.19. Merging polygons.

of the vertex list of **P**. If **e**1 is a right edge of **P** (Figures 3.19(c) and (d)), then we append the vertices of **P** to the end of the vertex list of **Q**. Note that each of the polygons has two top contributing edges. In either case, after combining the vertices of **P** and **Q**, the two edges $\mathbf{e}_1$ and $\mathbf{f}_1$ become noncontributing. If $\mathbf{e}_1$ was a left edge, then $\mathbf{f}_2$ will be contributing to **P** and the adjacent polygon of $\mathbf{f}_2$ will become **P**. If $\mathbf{e}_1$ was a right edge, then $\mathbf{e}_2$ will be contributing to **Q**. Therefore, the adjacent polygon of $\mathbf{e}_2$ will become **Q**.

When we find a local maximum we know two top edges right away, but if these have different adjacent polygons, then we need to find the other two top edges for these polygons. There are two ways to handle this. One could maintain pointers in the polygons to their current top edges, or one could do a search of the AEL. The first method gives us our edges without a search, but one will have to maintain the pointers as we move from one edge to the next. Which method is better depends on the number of edges versus the number of local maxima. Since there probably are relatively few local maxima, the second method is the recommended one.

Finally, we look at how one deals with intersections of edges within a scan beam. The way that these intersections are handled depends on whether we have like or unlike edges. Like intersections need only be considered if both edges are contributing and in that case the intersection point should be treated as both a left and right intermediate vertex. (Note that in the case of like intersections, if one edge is contributing, then the other one will be also.) Unlike intersections must always be handled. How their intersection point is handled depends on their type, side, and relative position in the AEL.

It is possible to give some precise rules on how to classify intersection points. The **classification rules** are shown in Table 3.3.5.1 in an encoded form. Edges have been specified using the following two-letter code: The first letter indicates whether the edge is a left (L) or right (R) edge, and the second letter specifies whether it belongs to the subject (S) or clip (C) polygon. The resulting vertex type is also specified by a two-letter code: local minimum (MN), local maximum (MX), left intermediate (LI), and right intermediate (RI). Edge codes are listed in the order in which their edges appear in the AEL. For example, Rule 1 translates into the following: The intersection of a left clip edge and a left subject edge, or the intersection of a left subject edge and a left clip edge, produces a left intermediate vertex. Rules 1–4 are shown graphically in Figure 3.20(a). Figure 3.20(b) shows an example of how the rules apply to some real polygon intersections.

Table 3.3.5.1 Rules that Classify the Intersection Point between Edges

Unlike edges
(1) $(LC \cap LS)$ or $(LS \cap LC) \rightarrow LI$
(2) $(RC \cap RS)$ or $(RS \cap RC) \rightarrow RI$
(3) $(LS \cap RC)$ or $(LC \cap RS) \rightarrow MX$
(4) $(RS \cap LC)$ or $(RC \cap LS) \rightarrow MN$

Like edges
(5) $(LC \cap RC)$ or $(RC \cap LC) \rightarrow LI$ and RI
(6) $(LS \cap RS)$ or $(RS \cap LS) \rightarrow LI$ and RI

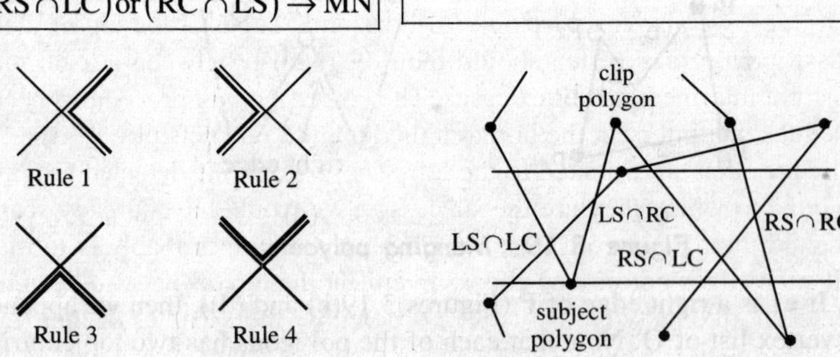

Figure 3.20. Intersection rules.

As one moves from scan beam to scan beam, one updates the x-values of all the edges (unless they end at the top of the scan beam). Although the AEL is sorted as one enters a new scan beam, if any intersections are found in a scan beam, the AEL will no longer be sorted after the x-values are updated. The list must therefore be resorted, but this can be done in the process of dealing with the intersections. Vatti used a temporary *sorted edge list* (SEL) and an *intersection list* (IL) to identify and store all the intersections in the current scan beam. The SEL is ordered by the x-coordinate of the intersection of the edge with the **top** of the scan beam similarly to the way that the AEL is ordered by the intersection values with the bottom of the scan beams. The IL is a list of nodes specifying the two intersecting edges and also the intersection itself. It is sorted in an increasing order by the y-coordinate of the intersection. The SEL is initialized to empty. One then makes a pass over the AEL comparing the top x-value of the current edge with the top x-values of the edges in the SEL starting at the **right** of the SEL. There will be an intersection each time the AEL edge has a smaller top x-value than the SEL edge. Note that the number of intersections that are found is the same as the number of edge exchanges in the AEL it takes to bring the edge into its correct place at the **top** of the scan beam. Intersection points of edges are basically treated as vertices. Such "vertices" will be classified in a similar way as the regular vertices. If we get a local maximum, then there are two cases. If two unlike edges intersect, then a contributing edge becomes a noncontributing edge and vice versa. This is implemented by simply swapping the output polygon pointers. If two like edges intersect, then a left edge becomes a right edge and a right edge becomes a left edge. One needs to swap the intersecting edges in the AEL to maintain the x-sort.

This finishes our discussion of the Vatti algorithm in the case where there are no horizontal edges. Now we address the more complicated general case that allows horizontal edges to exist. (However, we never allow edges to overlap, that is, where they share a common segment.) The only changes we have to make are in procedure ProcessEdgesInAEL. On an abstract level, it is easy to see how horizontal edges should be handled. The classification of vertices described above should proceed as if such edges were absent (had been shrunk to a point). Furthermore, if horizontal edges do not intersect any other edge, then for all practical purposes they could be ignored. The problems arise when intersections exist.

Imagine that the polygons were rotated slightly so that there were no horizontal edges. The edges that used to be horizontal would now be handled without any problem. This suggests how they should be treated when they are horizontal. One should handle horizontal edges the same way that intersections are handled. Note that horizontal edge intersections occur only at the bottom or top of a scan beam. Horizontal edges at local minima should be handled in the AddNewBoundPairs procedure. The others are handled as special cases in that part of the algorithm that tests whether or not an edge ends in the current scan beam. If it does, we also need to look for horizontal edges at the top of the current scan beam and the type classification of a vertex should then distinguish between a local maximum, left intermediate vertex, or right intermediate vertex cases. The corresponding procedures need to continue scanning the AEL for edges that intersect the horizontal edge until one gets past it. One final problem occurs with horizontal edges that are oriented to the left. These would be detected too late, that is, by the time one finds the edge to which they are the successor, we would have already scanned past the AEL edges that intersected them. To avoid this, the simplest solution probably is to make an initial scan of the AEL for all such edges before one checks events at the top of the scan beam and put them into a special left-oriented horizontal edge list (LHL) ordered by the x-values of their left endpoints. Then as one scans the AEL one needs to constantly check the top x-value of an edge for whether it lies inside one of these horizontal edges.

This completes our description of the basic Vatti algorithm. The algorithm can be optimized in the common case of rectangular clip bounds. Another optimization is possible if the clip polygon is fixed (rectangular or not) by computing its bounds only once and initializing the LML to these bounds at the beginning of a call to the clip algorithm.

An attractive feature of Vatti's algorithm is that it can easily be modified to generate trapezoids. This is particularly convenient for scan line–oriented rendering algorithms.

Each local minimum starts a trapezoid or breaks an existing one into two depending on whether the local minimum starts with a left-right (contributing case) or right-left (noncontributing case) edge pair. At a contributing local minimum we create a trapezoid. Trapezoids are output at local maxima and left or right intermediate vertices. A noncontributing local minimum should output the trapezoid it is about to split and update the trapezoid pointers of the relevant edges to the two new trapezoids. Vatti compared the performance of the trapezoid version of his algorithm to the Sutherland-Hodgman algorithm and found it to be roughly twice as fast for clipping (the more edges, the more the improvement) and substantially faster if one does both clipping **and** filling. Because Section 14.4 will describe a special case of the trapezoid form of the Vatti algorithm for use with trimmed surfaces, we postpone any further details on how to deal with trapezoids to there.

Finally, we can also use the Vatti algorithm for other operations than just intersection. All we have to do is replace the classification rules. For example, if we want to output the union of two polygons, use the rules

(1) $(LC \cup LS)\text{or}(LS \cup LC) \to LI$

(2) $(RC \cup RS)\text{or}(RS \cup RC) \to RI$

(3) $(LS \cup RC)\text{or}(LC \cup RS) \to MN$

(4) $(RS \cup LC)\text{or}(RC \cup LS) \to MX$

Local minima of the subject polygon that lie outside the clip polygon and local minima of the clip polygon that lie outside the subject polygon should be treated as contributing local minima. For the difference of two polygons (subject polygon minus clip polygon) use the rules

(1) $(RC - LS)\text{or}(LS - LC) \to LI$

(2) $(RS - LC)\text{or}(LC - RS) \to RI$

(3) $(RS - RC)\text{or}(LC - LS) \to MN$

(4) $(RC - RS)\text{or}(LS - LC) \to MX$

Local minima of the subject polygon that lie outside the clip polygon should be treated as contributing local minima.

3.3.6 Greiner-Hormann Polygon Clipping

The last polygon-clipping algorithm we consider is the Greiner-Hormann algorithm . It is very much like Weiler's algorithm but simpler. Like the Weiler and Vatti algorithm it handles any sort of polygons including self-intersecting ones. Furthermore, it, like Vatti's algorithm, can be modified to return the difference and union of polygons, not just their intersections.

Suppose that we want to clip the subject polygon **S** against the clip polygon **C**. What we shall do is find the part of the boundary of **S** in **C**, the part of the boundary of **C** in **S**, and then combine these two parts. See Figure 3.21. Since we allow selfintersecting polygons, one needs to be clear about when a point is considered to be inside a polygon. Greiner-Hormann use the winding number w(**p**,g) of a point **p** with respect to a parameterized curve g. They define a point **p** to be in a polygon **P** if the winding number of the point with respect to the boundary curve of **P** is odd. (The oddness or evenness of the winding number with respect to a curve is independent of how the curve is parameterized.) Polygons are represented by doubly-linked lists of vertices. The algorithm proceeds in three phases. One will find it helpful to compare the steps with those of the Weiler algorithm as one reads.

Phase 1. We compare each edge of the subject polygon with each edge of the clip polygon, looking for intersections. If we find one, we insert it in the appropriate place

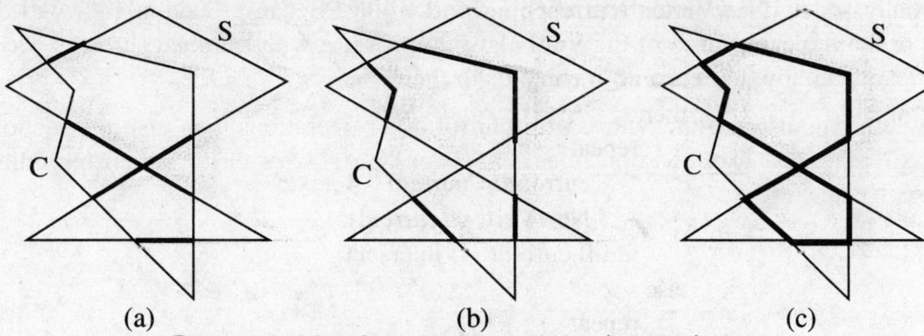

Figure 3.21. Greiner-Hormann polygon clipping.

```
vertex = record
  float           x, y;
  vertex pointer  next, prev;
  boolean         intersect;
  boolean         entry;
  vertex pointer  neighbor;
  float           alpha;
  vertex pointer  nextPoly;
end;
```

Data 3.3.6.1. The Greiner-Hormann vertex structure.

in **both** polygons' vertex lists. If there are no intersections, then either one polygon is contained in the other or they are disjoint. These cases are checked for easily and we then exit the algorithm in this case with our answer.

Phase 2. We traverse each polygon's new vertex lists marking any intersection points as either entry or exit points. This is done by checking whether the first vertex of each polygon lies inside the other polygon or not using the winding number. The rest of the tagging as entry or exit points is then easy.

Phase 3. This stage actually creates the intersection polygons. We start at an intersection point of the subject polygon and then move along its point list either forward or backward depending on its entry-exit flag. If we are at an entry point, then we move forward, otherwise, backward. When we get to another intersection point, we move over to the other polygon's list. The data structure used for vertices is shown in Data 3.3.6.1. In the case of an intersection point, if the **entry** field is false, then the point is an exit point. At an intersection vertex in one of the polygon's vertex lists the field **neighbor** points to the corresponding vertex in the other polygon's vertex list. The field **alpha** for an intersection point specifies the position of the intersection relative to the two endpoints of the edge containing this intersection point.

```
vertex pointer current;

while more unprocessed subject intersection points do
      begin
            current := pointer to first remaining unprocessed subject intersection point;
            NewPolygon (P)
            NewVertex (current);
            repeat
                  if current → entry
                        then
                              repeat
                                    current := current → next;
                                    NewVertex (current);
                              untill current → intersect
                        else
                              repeat
                                    current := current → prev;
                                    NewVertex (current);
                              untill current → intersect
                  current := current → neighbor;
            until Close (P)
      end;
```

Algorithm 3.3.6.1. Algorithm for Greiner-Hormann's Phase 3.

Because the intersection polygon may consist of several polygons, these polygons are linked with this field. The first vertex of each intersection polygon list has its **nextPoly** field point to the first vertex of the next intersection polygon.

The basic steps for Phase 3 are shown in Algorithm 3.3.6.1. The procedure NewPolygon starts a new polygon P and NewVertex creates a new vertex for this polygon and adds it to the end of its vertex list. Figure 3.22 shows the data structure that is created for a simple example.

The algorithm uses an efficient edge intersection algorithm and handles degenerate cases of intersections by perturbing vertices slightly. The advantage of the Greiner-Horman algorithm is that it is relatively simple and the authors claim their algorithm can be more than twice as fast as the Vatti algorithm. The reason for this is that Vatti's algorithm also checks for self-intersections which is not done here. Of course, if one knows that a polygon does not have selfintersections, then the extra work could be avoided in Vatti's algorithm also. The disadvantage of the algorithm is that one does not get any trapezoids but simply the boundary curve of the intersection. In conclusion, the Greiner-Horman algorithm is a good one if all one wants is boundaries of polygons because it is simple and yet fast.

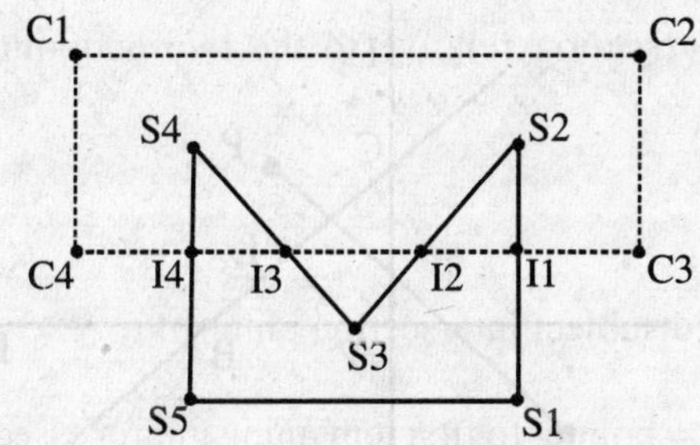

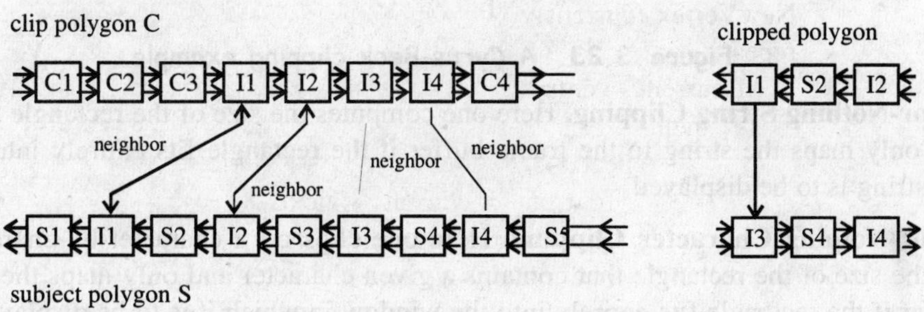

Figure 3.22. The Greiner-Hormann data structures.

3.4 TEXT CLIPPING

The topic of text generation and display is a very complex one. We shall barely scratch the surface here.

Characters can be displayed in many different styles and sizes and each such overall design style is called a *typeface* or *font*. Fonts are defined in one of several ways:

Bit-Mapped Fonts. Each character is represented by a rectangular bitmap. All the characters for a particular font are stored in a special part of the graphics memory and then mapped to the frame buffer when needed.

Vector Fonts. Each character is represented by a collection of line segments.

Outline Fonts. Each character's outline is represented by a collection of straight line segments or spline curves. This is more general than vector fonts. An attractive feature of both vector and outline fonts is that they are device independent and are easily scaled, rotated, and transformed in other ways. In either case, one has the option of scan converting them into the frame buffer on the fly or precomputing them and storing the bitmaps in memory. Defining and scan converting outline fonts gets very complicated if one wants the result to look nice and belongs to what is called *digital typography*.

Two overall strategies that are used to clip text are:

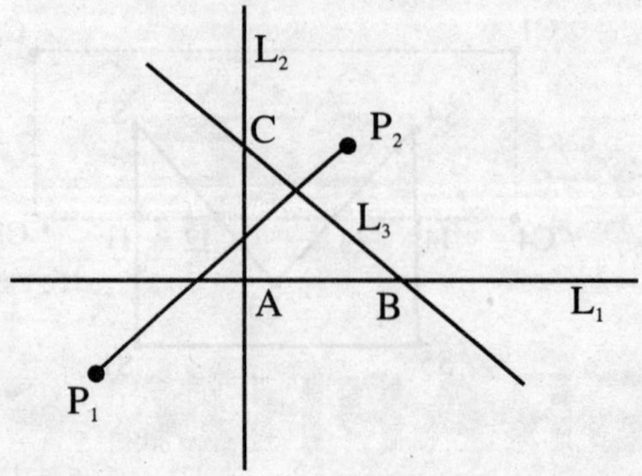

Figure 3.23. A Cyrus-Beck clipping example.

All-or-Nothing String Clipping. Here one computes the size of the rectangle that contains the string and only maps the string to the frame buffer if the rectangle fits entirely into the window in which the string is to be displayed.

All-or-Nothing Character Clipping. Here one clips on a character-by-character basis. One computes the size of the rectangle that contains a given character and only maps the character to the frame buffer if the rectangle fits entirely into the window in which it is to be displayed.

The all-or-nothing approaches are easy to implement because it is easy to check if one rectangle is inside another. The all-or-nothing character clipping approach is often quite satisfactory. A more precise way to clip is to clip on the bit level. What this means in the bit-mapped font case is that one clips the rectangular bitmap of each character against the window rectangle and displays that part which is inside. In the vector or outline font case, one would clip the curve that defines a character against the window using one of the line-clipping algorithms and then scan converts only the part of the character that lies in the window.

EXERCISES

1. Let $\mathbf{p}_1 = (-4, -2)$ and $\mathbf{p}_2 = (2, 3)$. Let $\mathbf{A} = (0,0)$, $\mathbf{B} = (3,0)$, and $\mathbf{C} = (0,3)$. Work out the steps of the Cyrus-Beck clipping algorithm and compute the [ai,bi]s that are generated when clipping the segment $[\mathbf{p}_1, \mathbf{p}_2]$ against triangle **ABC**. See Figure 3.23. Assume that the lines $\mathbf{L}_1$, $\mathbf{L}_2$, and $\mathbf{L}_3$ are defined by equations $y = 0$, $x = 0$, and $x + y = 3$, respectively.
2. Implement either the Vatti or Greiner-Hormann clipping algorithm in such a way so that it handles all three set operations $\cap$, U, and -.

4 TRANSFORMATIONS AND THE GRAPHIC PIPELINE

4.1 INTRODUCTION

In this chapter we combine properties of motions, homogeneous coordinates, projective transformations, and clipping to describe the mathematics behind the three dimensional computer graphics transformation pipeline. With this knowledge one will then know all there is to know about how to display three-dimensional points on a screen. Figure 4.1 shows the main coordinate systems that one needs to deal with in graphics and how they fit into the pipeline. The solid line path includes clipping, the dashed line path does not. Because the concept of a coordinate system is central to this chapter, it is worth making sure that there is no confusion here. The term "coordinate system" for **R**n means nothing but a "frame" in **R**n, that is, a tuple consisting of an orthonormal basis of vectors together with a point that corresponds to the "origin" of the coordinate system. The terms will be used interchangeably. In this context one thinks of **R**n purely as a set of "points" with no reference to coordinates. Given one of these abstract points **p**, one can talk about the coordinates of **p** with respect to one coordinate system or other. If **p** = (x,y,z) OE $\mathbf{R}_3$, then *x, y,* and *z* are of course just the coordinates of **p** with respect to the standard coordinate system or frame ($\mathbf{e}_1$, $\mathbf{e}_2$, $\mathbf{e}_3$, **0**).

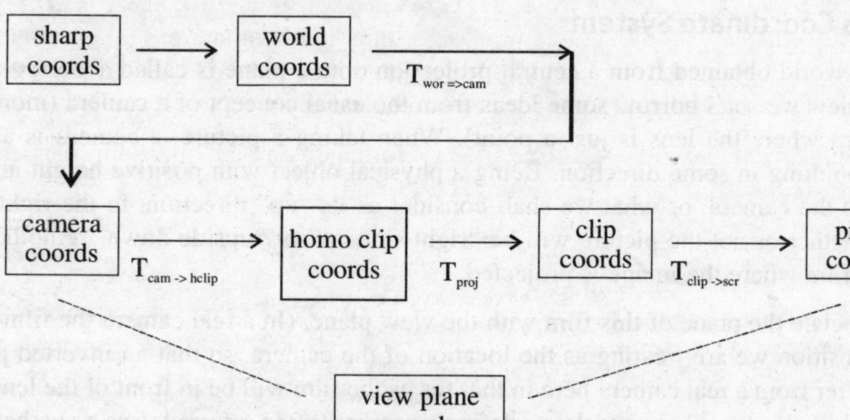

Figure 4.1. The coordinate system pipeline.

4.2 FROM SHAPE TO CAMERA COORDINATES

This section describes the first three coordinate systems in the graphics pipeline. In what follows, we shall use the term "shape" as our generic word for a geometric object independent of any coordinate system.

The World Coordinate System

This is the usual coordinate system with respect to which the **user** defines objects.

The Shape Coordinate System

This is the coordinate system used in the actual definition of a shape. It may very well be different from the world coordinate system. For example, the standard conics centered around the origin are very easy to describe. A good coordinate system for the ellipse in Figure 4.2 is defined by the indicated frame (**u**1,**u**2,**p**). In that coordinate system its equation is simply

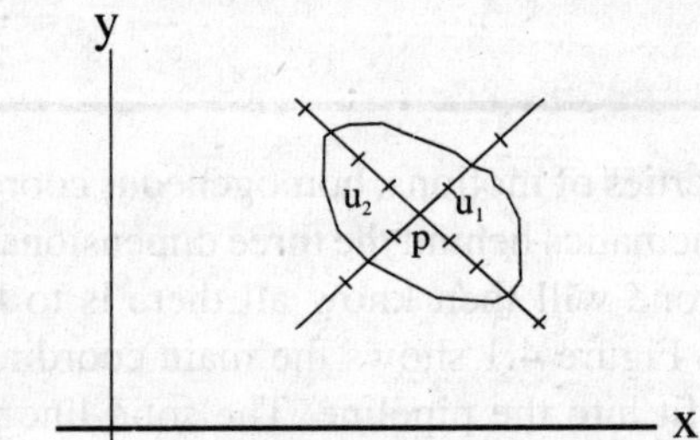

Figure 4.2. *A shape coordinate system.*

$$\frac{x^2}{4}+\frac{y^2}{9}=1$$

The equation of that ellipse with respect to the standard world coordinate system would be much more complicated.

The Camera Coordinate System

A view of the world obtained from a central projection onto a plane is called a *perspective view.* To specify such view we shall borrow some ideas from the usual concept of a camera (more precisely, a *pinhole camera* where the lens is just a point). When taking a picture, a camera is at a particular position and pointing in some direction. Being a physical object with positive height and width, one can also rotate the camera, or what we shall consider as its "up" direction, to the right or left. This determines whether or not the picture will be "right-side up" or "upside down." Another aspect of a camera is the film where the image is projected.

We associate the plane of this film with the view plane. (In a real camera the film is behind the lens, whose position we are treating as the location of the camera, so that an inverted picture is cast onto it. We differ from a real camera here in that for us the film will be in front of the lens.) Therefore, in analogy with such a "real" camera, let us define a *camera* (often referred to as a *synthetic camera*) as something specified by the following data:

- a location **p**
- a "*view*" *direction* **v** (the direction in which the camera is looking)
- an "*up*" *direction* **w** (specifies the two-dimensional orientation for the camera)
- a real number d (the distance that the view plane is in front of the camera)

Clearly, perspective views are defined by such *camera data* and are easily manipulated by means of it. We can view the world from any point **p**, look in any direction **v**, and specify what should be the top of the picture. We shall see later that the parameter d, in addition to specifying the view plane, will also allow us to zoom in or out of views easily.

A camera and its data define a camera coordinate system specifed by a *camera frame* (**u**1,**u2**,**u3**,**p**). See Figure 4.3(a). This is a coordinate system where the camera sits at the origin looking along the positive z-axis and the view plane is a plane parallel to the x-y plane a distance d above it. See Figure 4.3(b). We define this coordinate system from the camera data as follows:

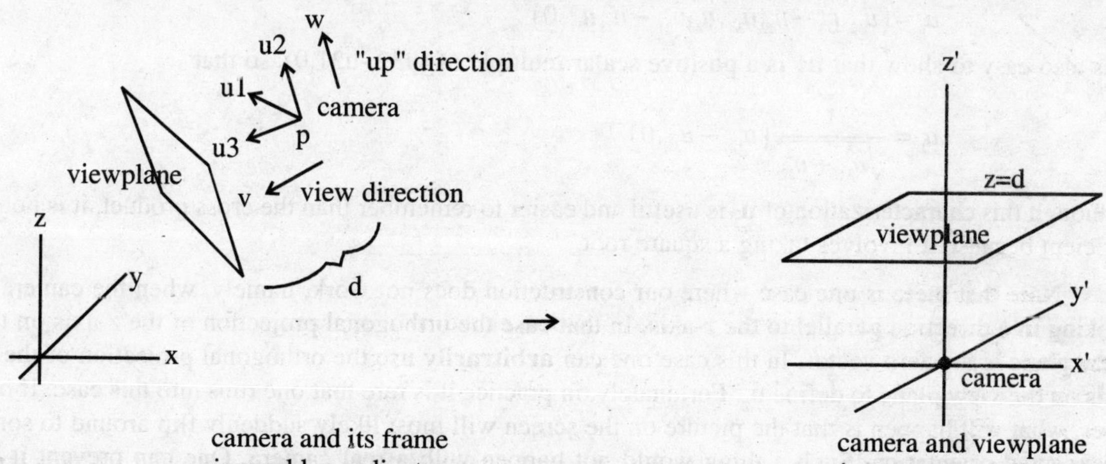

Figure 4.3. The camera coordinate system.

$$u_3 = v/|v|$$

$$u_2 = w/|w|$$

$$u_1 = u_3 \times u_2$$

These last two axes will be the same axes that will be used for the viewport. There were only two possibilities for **u**1 in equations (4.1). Why did we choose **u**3 * **u**2 rather than **u**2 * **u**3? Normally, one would take the latter because a natural reaction is to choose orientation-**preserving** frames; however, to line this x-axis up with the x-axis of the viewport, which one always wants to be directed to the right, we must take the former. (The easiest way to get an orientation-preserving frame here would be to replace **u**3 with -**u**3. However, in the current situation, whether or not the frame is orientation-preserving is not important since we will not be using it as a motion but as a change of coordinates transformation.)

Although an up direction is needed to define the camera coordinate system, it is not always convenient to have to define this direction explicitly. Fortunately, there is a natural default value for it. Since a typical view is from some point looking toward the origin, one can take the z-axis as defining this direction. More precisely, one can use the orthogonal projection of the z-axis on the view plane to define the second axis **u**2 for the camera coordinate system. In other words, one can define the camera frame by

$$u_3 = v/|v|$$

$$u_2 = w/|w|. \qquad \text{where } w = e_3 - (e_3 \cdot u_3)\,u_3$$

$$u_1 = u_3 \times u_2$$

As it happens, we do not need to take the complete cross product to find $\mathbf{u}_1$, because the z-coordinate of $\mathbf{u}_1$ is zero. The reason for this is that $\mathbf{e}_3$ lies in the plane generated by $\mathbf{u}_2$ and $\mathbf{u}_3$ and so $\mathbf{u}_1$ is orthogonal to $\mathbf{e}_3$. It follows that if **u**3 = (u_{31}, u_{32}, u_{33}) and $\mathbf{u}_2 = (u_{21}, u_{22}, u_{23})$, then

$$u_1 = (u_{32}u_{23} - u_{22}u_{33}, u_{33}u_{21} - u_{23}u_{31}, 0)$$

It is also easy to show that **u**1 is a positive scalar multiple of (u32,-u31,0), so that

$$u_1 = \frac{1}{\sqrt{u_{31}^2 + u_{32}^2}}(u_{32,} - u_{31}, 0)$$

Although this characterization of $\mathbf{u}_1$ is useful and easier to remember than the cross product, it is not as efficient because it involves taking a square root.

Note that there is one case where our construction does not work, namely, when the camera is looking in a direction parallel to the z-axis. In that case the orthogonal projection of the z-axis on the view plane is the zero vector. In this case one can **arbitrarily** use the orthogonal projection of the **y-axis** on the view plane to define $\mathbf{u}_2$. Fortunately, in practice it is rare that one runs into this case. If one does, what will happen is that the picture on the screen will most likely suddenly flip around to some unexpected orientation. Such a thing would not happen with a real camera. One can prevent it by keeping track of the frames as the camera moves. Then when the camera moves onto the z-axis one could define the new frame from the frames at previous nearby positions using continuity. This involves a lot of extra work though which is usually not worth it. Of course, if it **is** important to avoid these albeit rare occurrences then one can do the extra work or require that the user specify the desired up direction explicitly.

Finally, given the frame F = ($\mathbf{u}_1$, $\mathbf{u}_2$, $\mathbf{u}_3$, **p**) for the camera, then the world-to-camera coordinate transformation $T_{\text{wor->cam}}$ in Figure 4.1 is the map

$$q \to (q-p)\left(u_1^T u_2^T u_3^T\right) = (q-p)M,$$

where M is the 3 * 3 matrix that has the vectors **ui** as its columns. We begin with a two-dimensional example.

4.2.1 Example. Assume that the camera is located at **p** = (5,5), looking in direction **v** = (-1,-1), and that the view plane is a distance d = 2 in front of the camera. See Figure 4.4. The problem is to find $T_{\text{wor->cam}}$.

Solution. Let $\mathbf{u}_2 = \mathbf{v}/|\mathbf{v}| = \left(-1/\sqrt{2},-1/\sqrt{2}\right)$ ($\mathbf{u}_2$ plays the role of $\mathbf{u}_3$ here). The "up" direction is determined by $\mathbf{e}_2$ in this case, but all we have to do is switch the first and second coordinate of $\mathbf{u}_2$ and change one of the signs, so that $\mathbf{u}_1 = \left(-1/\sqrt{2},1/\sqrt{2}\right)$. We now have the camera frame ($\mathbf{u}_1$,$\mathbf{u}_2$, $\mathbf{p}$). It follows that $T = T_{\mathbf{wor\text{->}cam}}$ is the map

$$(x,y) \to (x-5,y-5)\begin{pmatrix} -\frac{1}{\sqrt{2}} & -\frac{1}{\sqrt{2}} \\ \frac{1}{\sqrt{2}} & -\frac{1}{\sqrt{2}} \end{pmatrix}$$

In other words,

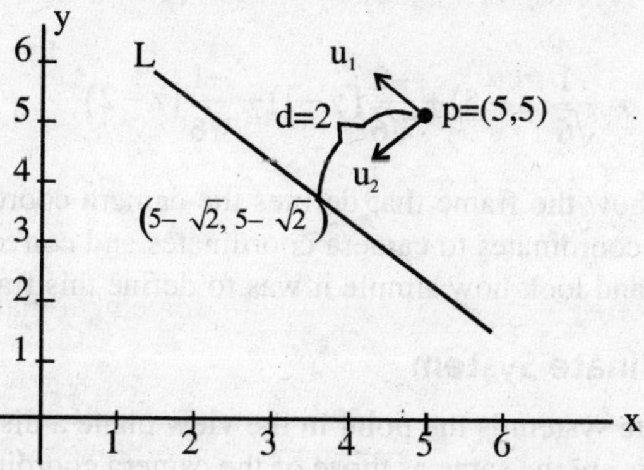

Figure 4.4. Transforming from world to camera coordinates.

$$T_{\text{wor}\to\text{cam}} : x' = -\frac{1}{\sqrt{2}}(x-5) + \frac{1}{\sqrt{2}}(y-5) = -\frac{1}{\sqrt{2}}x + \frac{1}{\sqrt{2}}y$$

$$y' = -\frac{1}{\sqrt{2}}(x-5) - \frac{1}{\sqrt{2}}(y-5) = -\frac{1}{\sqrt{2}}x - \frac{1}{\sqrt{2}}y + 5\sqrt{2}$$

As a quick check we compute T(5,5) = (0,0) and $T\left(5-\sqrt{2},5-\sqrt{2}\right) = (0,2)$, which clearly are the correct values. Next, we work through a three-dimensional example.

4.2.2 Example. Assume that the camera is located at $\mathbf{p}$ = (5,1,2), looking in direction $\mathbf{v}$ = (-1,-2,-1), and that the view plane is a distance d = 3 in front of the camera. The problem again is to find $T_{\mathbf{wor\text{->}cam}}$.

Solution. Using equations (4.2) we get

$$u_3 = \frac{1}{\sqrt{6}}(-1,-2,-1)$$

$$u_2 = w/|w| = \frac{1}{\sqrt{30}}(-1,-2,5), \text{where } w = \frac{1}{6}(-1,-2,5)$$

$$u_1 = u_3 \times u_2 = \frac{1}{\sqrt{5}}(-2,1,0)$$

It follows that

$$T_{wor \to cam} : x' = \frac{-2}{\sqrt{5}}(x-5) + \frac{1}{\sqrt{5}}(y-1)$$

$$y' = \frac{-1}{\sqrt{30}}(x-5) + \frac{-2}{\sqrt{30}}(y-1) + \frac{5}{\sqrt{30}}(z-2)$$

$$z' = \frac{-1}{\sqrt{6}}(x-5) + \frac{-2}{\sqrt{6}}(y-1) + \frac{-1}{\sqrt{6}}(z-2)$$

Note in the two examples how the frame that defines the camera coordinate system also defines the transformation from world coordinates to camera coordinates and conversely. The frame is the whole key to camera coordinates and look how simple it was to define this frame!

The View Plane Coordinate System

The origin of this coordinate system is the point in the view plane a distance d directly in front of the camera and the *x*- and *y*-axis are the same as those of the camera coordinate system. More precisely, if ($\mathbf{u}_1$, $\mathbf{u}_2$, $\mathbf{u}_3$, **p**) is the camera coordinate system, then ($\mathbf{u}_1$, $\mathbf{u}_2$, $\mathbf{p} + d\mathbf{u}_3$) is the view plane coordinate system.

4.3 VANISHING POINTS

If there is no clipping, then after one has the camera coordinates of a point, the next problem is to project to the view plane z = d. The central projection ð of $\mathbf{R}^3$ from the origin to this plane is easy to compute. Using similarity of triangles, we get

$$\pi(x,y,z) = (x',y',z') = (dx/z, dy/z, d) \quad ...(4.5)$$

Let us see what happens when lines are projected to the view plane. Consider a line through a point $\mathbf{p}_0 = (x_0, y_0, z_0)$, with direction vector **v** = (a, b, c), and parameterization

$$p(t) = (x(t), y(t), z(t)) = p_0 + tv$$

This line is projected by π to a curve p'(t) = (x'(t),y'(t),d) in the view plane, where

$$x'(t) = d\frac{x_0 + at}{z_0 + ct} \quad \text{and} \quad y'(t) = d\frac{y_0 + bt}{z_0 + ct}$$

It is easy to check that the slope of the line segment from p'(t1) to p'(t2) is

$$\frac{y'(t_2)-y'(t_1)}{x'(t_2)-x'(t_1)}=\frac{y_0c-bz_0}{x_0c-az_0},$$

which is independent of t_1 and t_2. This shows that the curve p'(t) has constant slope and reconfirms the fact that central projections project lines into lines (but not necessarily onto).

Next, let us see what happens to p'(t) as t goes to infinity. Assume that c "" 0. Then, using equation (4.7), we get that

$$\lim_{t\to\infty}\left(x'(t),y'(t)\right)=\left(da/c,db/c\right)$$

This limit point depends only on the direction vector **v** of the original line. What this means is that all lines with the same direction vector, that is, all lines parallel to the

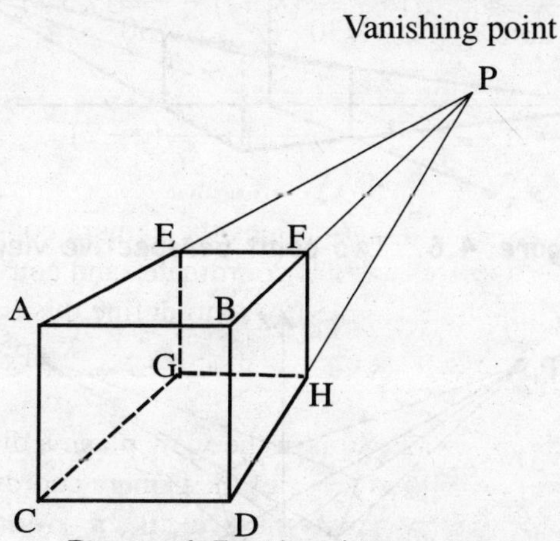

Figure 4.5. Vanishing point.

original line, will project to lines that intersect in a point. If c = 0, then one can check that nothing special happens and parallel lines project into parallel lines. In the context of the world-to-view plane transformation with respect to a given camera, what we have shown is that lines in the world project into lines in the view plane. Furthermore, the projection of some lines gives rise to certain special points in the view plane. Specifically, let **L** be a line in the world and let equation (4.6) be a parameterization for **L** in camera coordinates. We use the notation in the discussion above.

Definition

If the point in the view plane of the camera that corresponds to the point on the right hand side of equation (4.8) exists, then it is called the *vanishing point* for the line **L** with respect to the given camera or view. Clearly, if a line has a vanishing point, then this point is well-defined and unique. Any line parallel to such a line will have the same vanishing point. Figure 4.5 shows a projected cube and its vertices. Notice how the lines through the pairs of vertices **A** and **E**, **B** and **F**, **C** and **G**, and **D** and **H** meet in the vanishing point **P**. If we assume that the view direction of the camera is perpendicular to the front face of the cube, then the lines through vertices such as **A**, **B**, and **E**, **F**, or **A**, **C**, and **B**, **D**, are parallel. (This is the c = 0 case.)

Perspective views are divided into three types depending on the number of vanishing points of the standard unit cube (meaning the number of vanishing points of lines parallel to the edges of the cube).

One-point Perspective View. Here we have one vanishing point, which means that the view plane must be parallel to a face of the cube. Figure 4.5 shows such a perspective view.

Two-point Perspective View. Here we have two vanishing points and is the case where the view plane is parallel to an edge of the cube but not to a face. See Figure 4.6 and the vanishing points $\mathbf{P}_1$ and $\mathbf{P}_2$.

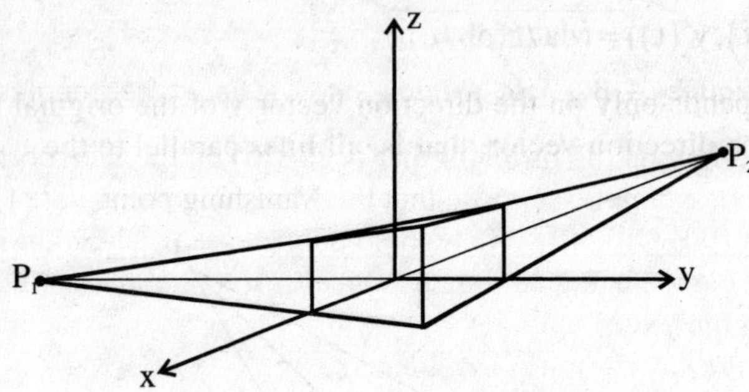

Figure 4.6. Two-point perspective view.

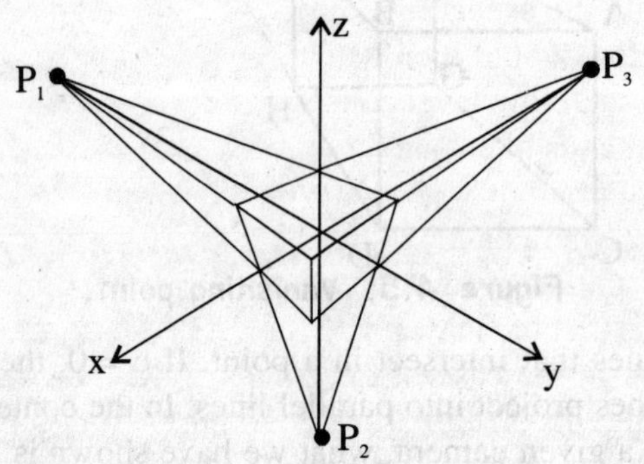

Figure 4.7. Three-point perspective view.

Three-point Perspective View. Here we have three vanishing points and is the case where none of the edges of the cube are parallel to the view plane. See Figure 4.7 and the vanishing points **P**1, **P**2, and **P**3. Two-point perspective views are the ones most commonly used in mechanical drawings. They show the three dimensionality of an object best. Three-point perspective views do not add much

4.4 WINDOWS AND VIEWPORTS REVISITED

Assume that [wxmin,wxmax] * [wymin,wymax] and [vxmin,vxmax] * [vymin,vymax] define the window and viewport rectangles, respectively. See Figure 4.8. We shall not change the basic idea that a window specifies **what** we see and that the viewport specifies **where** we see it, but there was a natural implication that it is by **changing** the window that one sees different parts of the world. Is that not how one would scan a plane by moving a rectangular window around in it?

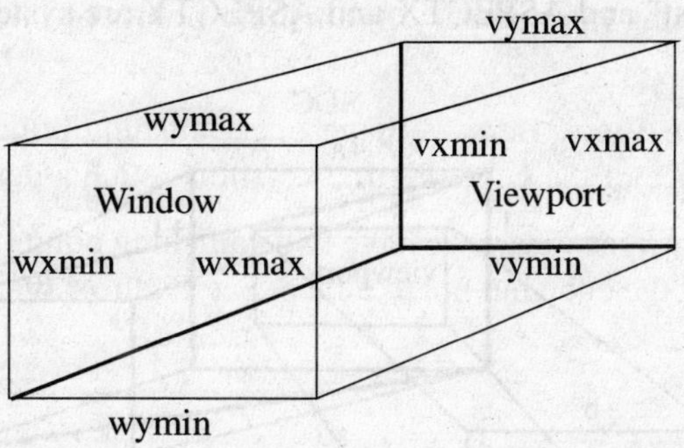

Figure 4.8. The window and viewport rectangles.

What is overlooked here is the problem that occurs when the viewport and the window are not the same size rectangle. For example, suppose that the window is the square [-2,2] * [-2,2] and that the viewport the rectangle [0,100] * [0,50]. What would happen in this situation is that the circle of radius 1 around the origin in the view plane would map to an ellipse centered at (50,25) in the viewport. What we know to be a circle in the world would show up visually as an ellipse on the screen. Would we be happy with that? This is the "aspect ratio" problem.

What can one do to make circles show up as circles?

The best way to deal with the aspect ratio problem would be to let the user change the viewport but not the window. The window would then be chosen to match the viewport appropriately. First of all, users are not interested in such low level concepts anyway and want to manipulate views in more geometric ways by using commands like "pan," "zoom," "move the camera," etc. Secondly, in the case of 3d graphics, from a practical point of view this will in no way affect the program's ability to handle different views. Changing the camera data will have the same effect. In fact, changing the position and direction of the camera gives the program more control of what one sees than simply changing the window. Changing the distance that the view plane is in front of the camera corresponds to zooming. A fixed window would not work in the case of 2d graphics, however. One would have to let the user translate the window and change its size to allow zooming. A translation causes no problem, but the zooming has to be controlled. The size can only be allowed to change by a factor that preserves the height divided by width ratio. There is no reason for a user to know what is going on at this level though. As long as the user is given a command option to zoom in or out, that user will be satisfied and does not need to know any of the underlying technical details.

Returning to the 3d graphics case, given that our default window will be a fixed size, what should this size be? First of all, it will be centered about the origin of the view plane. It should have the same *aspect ratio* (ratio of height to width) as the viewport. Therefore, we shall let the window be the rectangle [-1,1] * [-b,b], where b = (vymax - vymin)/(vxmax - vxmin). Unfortunately, this is not the end of the story. There is also a *hardware aspect ratio* one needs to worry about. This refers to the fact that the dots of the electron beam for the CRT may not be "square." The hardware ratio is usually expressed in the form $a = y_a/x_a$ with the operating system supplying the values x_a and y_a. In Microsoft Windows, one gets these values via the calls

```
xa = GetDeviceCaps (hdc, ASPECTX);
ya = GetDeviceCaps (hdc, ASPECTY);
```

where hdc is a "device context" and ASPECTX and ASPECTY are system-defined constants.

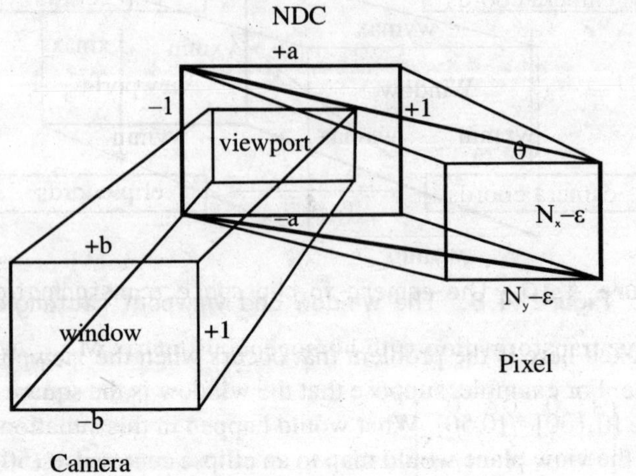

Figure 4.9. Window, normalized viewport,and pixel space.

4.5 THE CLIP COORDINATE SYSTEM

Once one has transformed objects into camera coordinates, our next problem is to clip points in the camera coordinate system to the truncated pyramid defined by the near and far clipping planes and the window. One could do this directly, but we prefer to transform into a coordinate system, called the *clip coordinate system* or *clip space*, where the clipping volume is the unit cube [0,1] *[0,1] * [0,1]. We denote the transformation that does this by $T_{camàclip}$. There are two reasons for using this transformation:

(1) It is clearly simpler to clip against the unit cube.

(2) The clipping algorithm becomes independent of boundary dimensions.

Actually, rather than using these coordinates we shall use the associated homogeneous coordinates. The latter define what we shall call the *homogeneous clip coordinate system* or *homogeneous clip space*. Using homogeneous coordinates will enable us to describe maps via matrices and we will also not have to worry about any divisions by zero on our way to the clip stage. The map $T_{camàclip}$ in Figure 4.1 refers to this camera-to-homogeneous-clip coordinates transformation. Let $T_{camàclip}$ denote the corresponding homogeneous-camera-to-homogeneous-clip coordinates transformation. Figure 4.10 shows the relationships between all these maps. The map T_{proj} is the standard projection from homogeneous to Euclidean coordinates.

Assume that the view plane and near and far clipping planes are a distance d, d_n, and d_f in front of the camera, respectively. To describe $T_{camàclip}$, it will suffice to describe $T_{camàclip}$.First of all, translate the camera to (0,0,-d). This translation is represented by the homogeneous matrix

$$M_{tr} = \begin{pmatrix} 1 & 0 & 0 & 0 \\ 0 & 1 & 0 & 0 \\ 0 & 0 & 1 & 0 \\ 0 & 0 & -d & 1 \end{pmatrix}$$

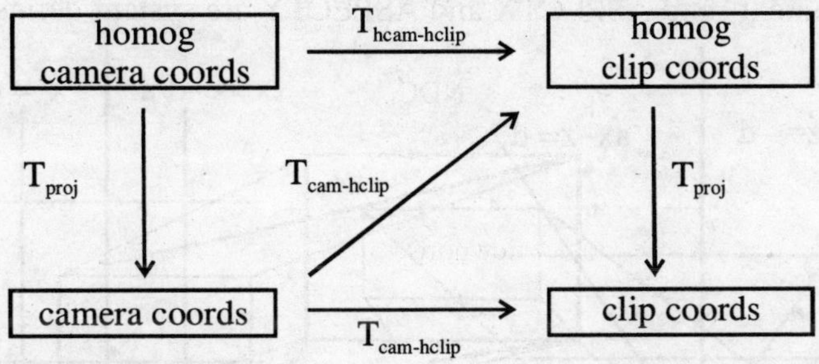

Figure 4.10. The camera-to-clip space transformations.

Next, apply the projective transformation with homogeneous matrix M_{persp}, where

$$M_{persp} = \begin{pmatrix} 1 & 0 & 0 & 0 \\ 0 & 1 & 0 & 0 \\ 0 & 0 & 1 & 1/d \\ 0 & 0 & 0 & 1 \end{pmatrix}$$

To see exactly what the map defined by M_{persp} does geometrically, consider the lines ax + z = -d and ax - z = d in the plane y = 0. Note that $(x,y,z,w)\, M_{persp} = (x,y,z,(z/d)+w)$. In particular,

$$(0,0,-d,1)M_{persp} = (0,0-d,0)$$

$$(x,0,-d-ax,1)M_{persp} = \left(x,0,-d-ax,-\frac{ax}{d}\right) = -\frac{d}{ax}\left(-\frac{d}{a},0,d+\frac{d^2}{ax},1\right)$$

$$(x,0,-d+ax,1)M_{persp} = \left(x,0,-d+ax,\frac{ax}{d}\right) = \frac{d}{ax}\left(\frac{d}{a},0,d-\frac{d^2}{ax},1\right)$$

This shows that the camera at (0,0,-d) has been mapped to "infinity" and the two lines have been mapped to the lines x' = -d/a and x' = d/a, respectively, in the plane y = 0. See Figure 4.11. In general, lines through (0,0,-d) are mapped to vertical lines through their intersection with the x-y plane. Furthermore, what was the central projection from the point (0,0,-d) is now an orthogonal projection of $\mathbf{R}^3$ onto the x-y plane. It follows that the composition of M_{tr} and M_{persp} maps the camera off to "infinity," the near clipping plane to $z = d\,(1 - d/d_n)$, and the far clipping plane to $z = d\,(1 - d/d_f)$. The perspective projection problem has been transformed into a simple orthographic projection problem (we simply project (x,y,z) to (x,y,0)) with the clip volume now being

$$[-1, 1] \times [-b, b] \times [d(1 - d/d_f), d(1 - d/d_n)]$$

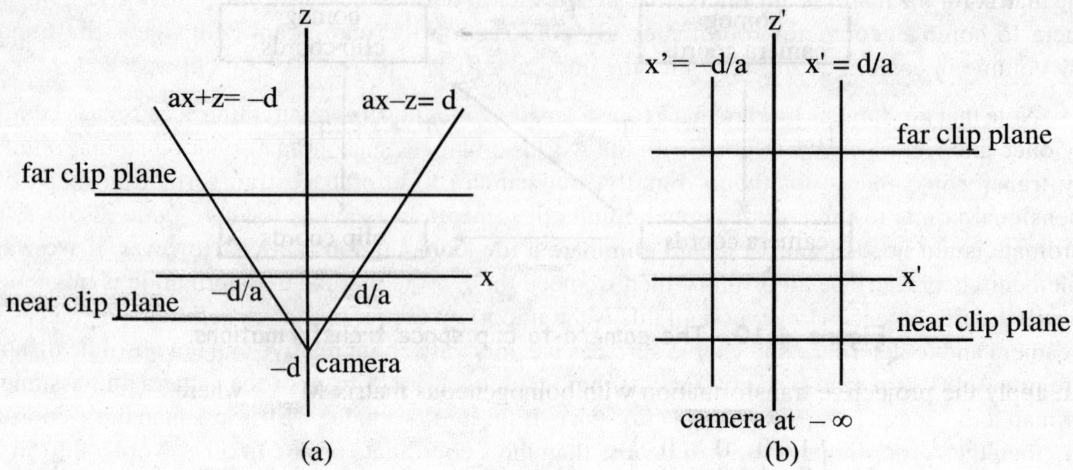

Figure 4.11. Mapping the camera to infinity.

To get this new clip volume into the unit cube, we use the composite of the following maps: first, translate to

$$[0,2]\times[0,2b]\times\left[0, d^2\left(\frac{1}{d_n}-\frac{1}{d_f}\right)\right]$$

and then use the radial transformation which multiplies the x, y, and z-coordinates by

$$\frac{1}{2},\frac{1}{2b},\ and\ \frac{d_n d_f}{d^2\left(d_f-d_n\right)},$$

respectively. If M_{scale} is the homogeneous matrix for the composite of these two maps, then

$$M_{scale}=\begin{pmatrix} 1/2 & 0 & 0 & 0 \\ 0 & 1/2d & 0 & 0 \\ 0 & 0 & \frac{d_n d_f}{d^2\left(d_f-d_n\right)} & 0 \\ \frac{1}{2} & \frac{1}{2} & -\frac{d_n\left(d_f-d\right)}{d\left(d_f-d_n\right)} & 1 \end{pmatrix}$$

so that

$$M_{hcam\to hclip}=M_{tr}M_{persp}M_{scale}=\begin{pmatrix} 1/2 & 0 & 0 & 0 \\ 0 & 1/2d & 0 & 0 \\ \frac{1}{2d} & \frac{1}{2d} & \frac{d_f}{d\left(d_f-d_n\right)} & \frac{1}{d} \\ 0 & 0 & -\frac{d_n d_f}{d\left(d_f-d_n\right)} & 0 \end{pmatrix} \quad ...(4.10)$$

is the matrix for the map ThcamÆhclip that we are after. It defines the transformation from homogeneous camera to homogeneous clip coordinates. By construction the map TcamÆclip sends the truncated view volume in camera coordinates into the unit cube [0,1] * [0,1] * [0,1] in clip space.

Note that the camera-to-clip-space transformation does not cost us anything because it is computed only once and right away combined with the world-to-camera space transformation so that points are only transformed once, not twice. Finally, our camera-to-clip-space transformation maps three-dimensional points to three-dimensional points. In some cases, such as for wireframe displays, the z coordinate is not needed and we could eliminate a few computations above. However, if we want to implement visible surface algorithms, then we need the z. Note that the transformation is not a motion and will deform objects. However, and this is the important fact, it preserves **relative** z-distances from the camera and to determine the visible surfaces we only care about relative and not absolute distances. More precisely, let $\mathbf{p}_1$ and $\mathbf{p}_2$ be two points that lie along a ray in front of the camera and assume that they map to $\mathbf{p}_1'$ and $\mathbf{p}_2'$, respectively, in clip space. If the z-coordinate of **p1** is less than the z-coordinate of $\mathbf{p}_2$, then the z-coordinate of $\mathbf{p}_1'$ will be less than the z coordinate of $\mathbf{p}_2'$. In other words, the "in front of" relation is preserved. To see this, let $\mathbf{p}_i = (t_i x, t_i y, t_i z)$, $0 < t_1 < t_2$, and $\mathbf{p}_i' = (x_i', y_i', z_i')$. It follows from (4.10) that

$$z_1' = \left(1 - \frac{d_n}{t_i z}\right)\frac{d_f}{(d_f - d_n)}$$

from which it is easy to show that $t_1 < t_2$ if and only if $z_1' < z_2'$.

4.6 CLIPPING

In the last section we showed how to transform the clipping problem to a problem of clipping against the unit cube in clip space. The actual clipping against the cube will be done in homogeneous clip space using homogeneous coordinates (*x, y, z, w*). The advantage of homogeneous coordinates was already alluded to: **every** point of camera space is sent to a well-defined point here because values become undefined only when we try to map down to clip space by dividing by w, which may be zero.

Chapter 3 discussed general clipping algorithms for **individual** segments or whole polygons. These have their place, but they are not geared to geometric modelling environments where one often wants to draw **connected** segments. We shall now describe a very efficient clipping algorithm. It uses the "best" parts of the Cohen-Sutherland, Cyrus-Beck, and Liang-Barsky algorithms.

In homogeneous coordinates half planes can be defined as a set of points that have a nonnegative dot product with a fixed vector. For example, the half plane $ax + by + cz + d e \geq 0$, is defined by the vector (*a, b, c, d*) in homogeneous coordinates. Therefore, by lining up vectors appropriately, any convex region bounded by planes can be defined as the set of points that have nonnegative dot products with a fixed finite set of vectors. In our case, we can use the following vectors for the six bounding planes $x = 0$, $x = 1$, $y = 0$, $y = 1$, $z = 0$, and $z = 1$ for the unit cube $\mathbf{I}_3$:

$$\mathbf{B}_1 = (1, 0, 0, 0) \quad \mathbf{B}_3 = (0, 1, 0, 0), \quad \mathbf{B}_5 = (0, 0, 1, 0)$$
$$\mathbf{B}_2 = (-1, 0, 0, 1), \mathbf{B}_4 = (0, -1, 0, 1), \mathbf{B}_6 = (0, 0, -1, 1)$$

If **p** = (x,y,z,w), then let BCi = BCi(**p**) = **p** • **Bi**. We shall call the BCi the *boundary coordinates* of **p**. These coordinates are easy to compute:

$$BC_1 = x, BC_3 = y, BC_5 = z$$

$$BC_2 = w - x, \quad BC_4 = w - y, \quad BC_6 = w - z$$

A point will be inside the clip volume if and only if all of its boundary coordinates are nonnegative. If the ith boundary coordinate of a point is nonnegative, then we shall call the point *i-inside*; otherwise, it is *i-out*. Let BC = BC(**p**) = (BC_1(**p**),BC_2(**p**), . . . ,BC_6(**p**)) denote the vector of boundary coordinates.Next, let $\mathbf{p}_0$ and $\mathbf{p}_1$ be two points and set BC_0 = BC($\mathbf{p}_0$) and BC_1 = BC($\mathbf{p}_1$). The next table shows the relationship of the segment [$\mathbf{p}_0$, $\mathbf{p}_1$] with respect to the ith boundary:

Sign bit $BC0_i$	Sign bit $BC1_i$	Meaning
0	0	Entire segment is i-inside
1	0	Segment straddles boundary, p0 is i-out
0	1	Segment straddles boundary, p1 is i-out
1	1	Entire segment is i-out

It will be convenient to record the sign information of a point **p** into a six-bit word called its *outcode* and denote it by CODE(**p**). More precisely, the ith bit of CODE(**p**) will be the sign bit of BCi(**p**). Let CODE0 = CODE(**p0**) and CODE1 = CODE(**p1**). Simple logical operations on CODE0 and CODE1 now give us a lot of information about the location of the segment. For example, the segment will be inside the clip volume if (CODE0 **or** CODE1) is zero. The segment will be entirely outside the clip volume if (CODE0 **and** CODE1) is nonzero. (Compare this with the Cohen- Sutherland clipping algorithm.)

Whenever the segment crosses the ith clipping plane, we need to find the intersection. This is easy to do if we parameterize the segment, and we have done this sort of thing before. We need to find the t so that

$$\left(p0 + t\left(p1 - p0\right)\right) \cdot B_i = 0$$

Using notation t = $BC0_i/(BC0_i - BC1_i)$.

The segment will intersect the plane only if this t lies in [0,1]. The expression shows that this can only happen if BC0i and BC1i have different signs.

Now, the clipping algorithm we are in the process of describing is intended for situations where we want to do a sequence of "DrawTo" and "MoveTo" commands. The flag parameter in the "Clip" procedure is used to distinguish between the two cases and will save us having to write a separate "Clip" procedure for both. The abstract programs are given in Algorithm 4.6.1 with the ViewPt procedure representing the next stage of the graphics pipeline after clipping, namely, the clip-space-topixel-space map. A more efficient procedure using goto's, assuming that the trivial rejects are the most common cases, is shown in Algorithm 4.6.2. Next, we describe the nontrivial stuff that happens when a segment straddles a boundary. We basically use the Liang-Barsky algorithm here. In Algorithm 4.6.3, the variables a0 and a1 keep track of the still-visible part of a segment. MASK is used to select one boundary at a time. Blinn points out that he does the operation CODE0 **or** CODE1 **again** on the theory that it will not get done often and we save storing an unneeded value earlier.

```
homogeneous point p0, p1;
real      BC0, BC1
6 bit word CODE0, CODE1

Procedure Clip ((move, draw) flag)
{We assume that p0, BC0, and CODE0 have been defined. We clip [p0, p1]}
begin
        Calculate BC1, CODE1;

        case flag of
                move :DoMoveStuff ();
                draw :DoDrawStuff ();
        end;

        {Update globals}
        [p0, BC0, CODE0] := [p1, BC1, CODE1];
end;

Procedure DoMoveStuff ()
if CODE1 = 0 then ViewPt (p1, move);

Procedure DoDrawStuff ()
if (CODE0 and CODE1) =0
        begin
                if (CODE0 or CODE1) = 0
                    then ViewPt (p1, draw)
                    else DoNontrivialStuff ()
        end;
```

Algorithm 4.6.1. Abstract programs for clipping using homogeneous coordinates.

He also made all tests as much as possible into integer comparisons to cut down on floating point operations. There are some limitations to Blinn's clipping algorithm. Although they tend to be more theoretical than practical, one should be aware of them. The problem is that one is clipping to the infinite inverted pyramid in homogeneous coordinate space shown in Figure 4.12(a) when, in fact, one should be clipping to the double pyramid shown in Figure 4.12(b). The points in the negative pyramid will also project to the visible region. On the other hand, the basic graphics pipeline that we have been describing will not introduce any negative w's and so this problem will not arise here. The problem arises only if negative w-coordinates are introduced explicitly or if one wants to represent infinite segments (the complement of a normal segment in a line). If one does want to handle such cases, the quickest way to do it is to draw the world twice, once as described above and then a second time, where the matrix that maps from shape to clip coordinates is multiplied by -1.

```
Procedure Clip ((move, draw) flag)
begin
        label moveit, nontriv, finish;

        Calculate BC1, CODE1;

        if flag = move then goto moveit;
        if (CODE0 and CODE1) ≠ 0 then goto finish;
        if (CODE0 or CODE1) ≠ 0 then goto nontriv;
        ViewPt (p1, draw);

finish:
        [p0, BC0, CODE0] := [p1, BC1, CODE1];
        return;
moveit:
        if CODE ≠ then goto finish;
        ViewPt (p1, move);
        goto finish;
nontriv:
        DoNontrivialStuff ();
        goto finish;
end;
```

Algorithm 4.6.2. More efficient clipping using homogeneous coordinates.

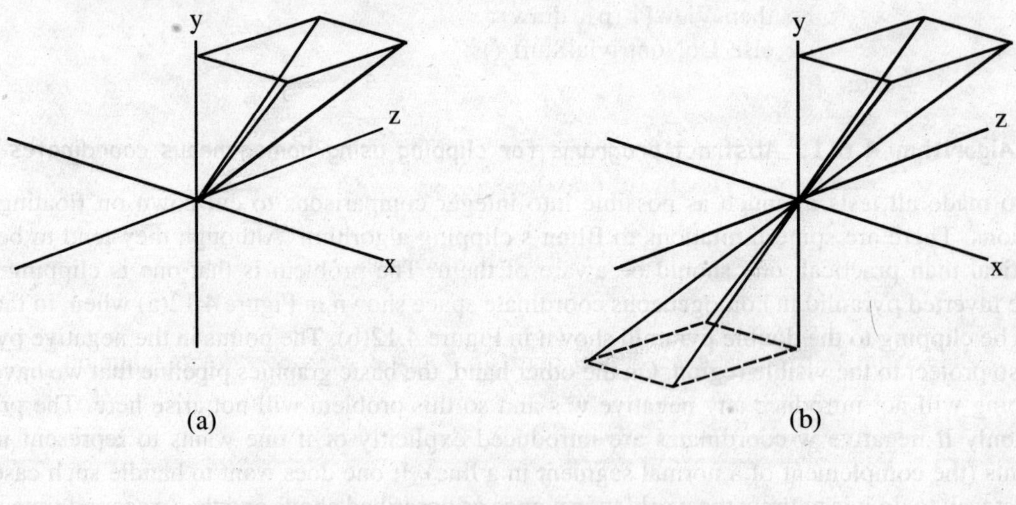

Figure 4.12. Single- and double-clip pyramid.

```
Procedure DoNontrivialStuff ()
begin
        6-bit word BCASE, MASK;
        real    a0, a1, a;
        integer i;
        homogeneous point p;

        BCASE := CODE0 or ODE1;
        a0 := 0.0; a1 := 1.0; MASK := 1;
        for i := 1 to numClipPlanes do
                begin
                    if (BCSE and MASK) ≠ 0 then
                        begin
                            a := BC0[i]/ (BC0[i]–BC1[i]);
                            if (CODE0 and MASK ≠ 0
                                then a0 := max (a0, a)
                                else a1 := min (a1, a);
                            if a1 < a0 then return;         {reject}
                        end;
                    Shift MASK left one bit
                end;
        if CODE0 ≠ 0 then
                begin
                    p := p0+a0*(p1–p0);
                    ViewPt (p, move);
                end;
        if CODE1 ≠ 0
                then
                    begin
                        p := p0+a0*(p1–p0);
                        ViewPt (p, draw);
                    end
                else ViewPt (p1, draw);

end;
```

Algorithm 4.6.3. The nontrivial part of homogeneous coordinate clipping.

4.7 PUTTING IT ALL TOGETHER

We are finally ready to put all the pieces together. See Figure 4.1 again. Starting with some shape we are initially in shape coordinates. We then

(1) transform to world coordinates

(2) transform from world to homogeneous clip coordinates by composing $T_{\text{camàhclip}}$ and $T_{\text{camàhclip}}$

(3) clip

(4) project (x,y,z,w) down to (x/w,y/w,z/w) in the unit cube of clip space with Tproj

(5) map the unit square in the x-y plane of clip space to the viewport

(6) map from the viewport to pixel space

With respect to (4), note that using a front clipping plane does have the advantage that we do not have to worry about a division by zero. Almost, but not quite. There is the very special case of (0,0,0,0) that could occur and hence one needs to check for it. It would be complicated to eliminate this case.

Also, because of the clipping step, Blinn suggests a more complete version of the window-to-pixel map than shown in Figure 4.9. See Figure 4.13. The square [0,1] * [0,1] represents the clipping. This allows one to handle the situation shown in Figure 4.14, where the viewport goes outside the valid NDC range quite easily. One pulls back the clipped viewport

$$[ux_{min}, ux_{max}] \times [uy_{min}, uy_{max}]$$

to the rectangle

$$[wx_{min}, wx_{max}] \times [wy_{min}, wy_{max}]$$

and then uses that rectangle as the window. Only the transformation $T_{camàhclip}$ needs to Le changed, not the clipping algorithm. Blinn's approach is nice, but there may not be any need for this generality. A much simpler scheme that works quite well is to forget about the NDC by incorporating the hardware aspect ratio rh into the window size. Let be the current viewport.

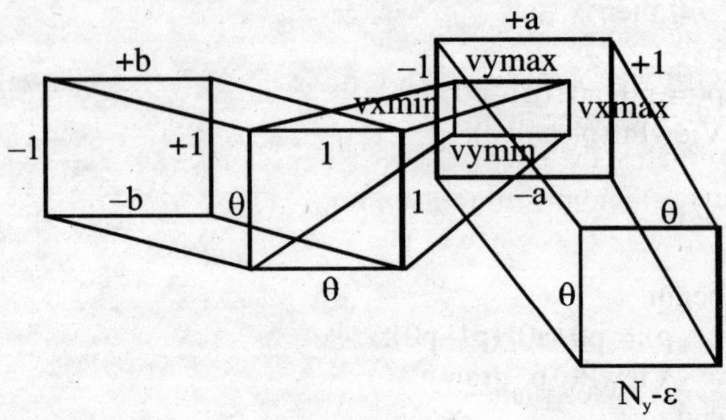

Figure 4.13. From window to pixel coordinates.

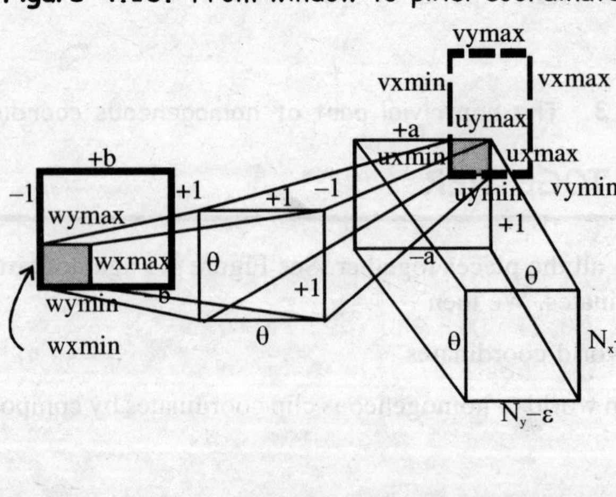

$$[vpx_{min}, vpx_{max}] \times [uvpy_{min}, vpy_{max}]$$

Then **fix** the window to be the rectangle [-1,1] * [-b,b], where

$$b = r_h(y_{max} - y_{min})/[x_{max}, x_{min}]$$

Now map directly from [0,1] * [0,1] to pixel space. With this window and the view transformations discussed in this chapter, circles will look like circles. We close with a final remark on clipping. Clipping is expensive and therefore we would rather not do it! In future chapters we shall discuss ways one can often avoid it (by using bounding boxes, the convex hull property of splines, etc.).

4.8 STEREO VIEWS

Occasionally, it is useful to allow the origin of the view plane to be a point other than the one directly in front of the camera. One such case is where one wants to compute stereo views. This involves computing two views, one for each eye.

The Eye Coordinate System

Given a camera, let ($\mathbf{u}_1$, $\mathbf{u}_2$, $\mathbf{u}_3$, **p**) be the camera coordinate system, where the vectors $\mathbf{u}_1$, $\mathbf{u}_2$, and $\mathbf{u}_3$ are defined by equation (4.1) If we think of one eye as being located at $\mathbf{p} + a\mathbf{u}_1 + b\mathbf{u}_2$, then the eye coordinate system with respect to the given camera and some a, b OE **R** is defined by the frame ($\mathbf{u}_1$, $\mathbf{u}_2$, $\mathbf{u}_3$, $\mathbf{p} + a\mathbf{u}_1 + b\mathbf{u}_2$). If $a = b = 0$, then this is the same as the camera coordinate system.

It is easy to see that if the coordinates of a point **p** in camera coordinates is (x, y, z), then the coordinates of that same point in eye coordinates are $(x - a, y - b, z)$. Furthermore, if **p** projects to (x¢,y¢,d) in eye coordinates, then it projects to $(x' + a, yz' + b, d)$ in camera coordinates. It follows that, using homogeneous coordinates, the only difference in computing the view in camera coordinates to computing it in eye coordinates amounts to replacing the matrix Mpersp in equation (4.9) by

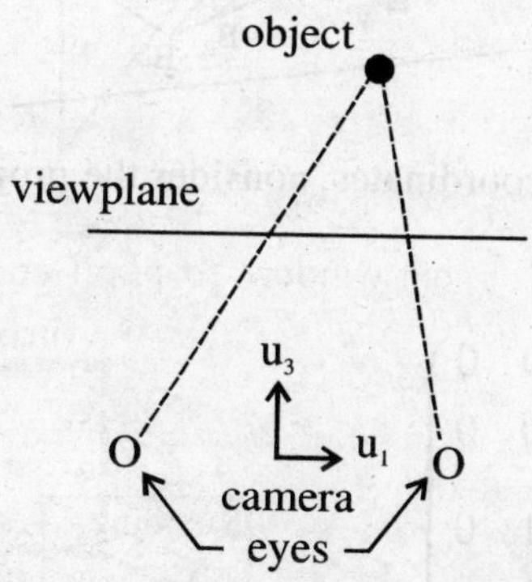

Figure 4.15. Views from two eyes for stereo.

$$M_{eye} = \begin{pmatrix} 1 & 0 & 0 & 0 \\ 0 & 1 & 0 & 0 \\ 0 & 0 & 1 & 0 \\ -a & -b & 0 & 1 \end{pmatrix} \begin{pmatrix} 1 & 0 & 0 & 0 \\ 0 & 1 & 0 & 0 \\ 0 & 0 & 1 & 1/d \\ 0 & 0 & 0 & 1 \end{pmatrix} \begin{pmatrix} 1 & 0 & 0 & 0 \\ 0 & 1 & 0 & 0 \\ 0 & 0 & 1 & 0 \\ a & b & 0 & 1 \end{pmatrix} = \begin{bmatrix} 1 & 0 & 0 & 0 \\ 0 & 1 & 0 & 0 \\ a/d & b/d & 1 & 1/d \\ 0 & 0 & 0 & 1 \end{bmatrix} \quad ...(4.11)$$

To compute stereo views one would compute two views – one with the eye at **p** + **au1** and one with the eye at **p** - **au1** for some suitable a. See Figure 4.15. The two views are then displayed a suitable distance apart in a viewport. Actually, our discussion here is a simplification of what is involved in stereo rendering.

4.9 PARALLEL PROJECTIONS

So far we have dealt solely with perspective views, but there are times when one wants views based on parallel projections. Although this can be thought of as a special case of central projections where the camera is moved to "infinity" along some direction, it is worth considering on its own because one can achieve some simplifications in that case.

Assume that our view plane is the x-y plane and that we are interested in the parallel projection of the world onto that plane using a family of parallel lines. See Figure 4.16.

4.9.1 Proposition

If p is the parallel projection of **R**3 onto **R**2 with respect to a family of parallel lines with direction vector **v** = (v1,v2,v3), then

$$\pi(x, y, z) = (x - z(v_1 / v_3), y - z(v_2 / v_3), 0)$$

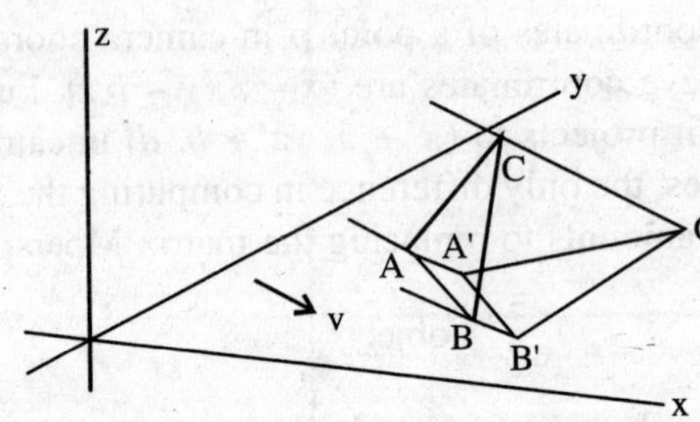

Proof. Passing to homogeneous coordinates, consider the projective transformation T_{par} defined by the matrix

$$M_{par} = \begin{pmatrix} 1 & 0 & 0 & 0 \\ 0 & 1 & 0 & 0 \\ -\dfrac{v_1}{v_3} & -\dfrac{v_2}{v_3} & 1 & 0 \\ 0 & 0 & 0 & 1 \end{pmatrix} \quad ...(4.12)$$

Our parallel projection onto the x-y plane is then nothing but the Cartesian version of Tpar followed by x, y, z) → (x, y, 0). It follows that the matrix Mpar plays the role of the matrix Mpersp in Section 4.5 (equation (4.9)) in that it reduces a general projection problem into a simple orthogonal projection.

Notice that a parallel projection does not depend on the length of the vector *v*. In fact, any multiple of **v** will define the same projection, as is easily seen from its equations. The parallel projection can also be considered the limiting case of a central projection where one places an eye at a position **v** = $(v_1, v_2, v_3) = (a'd, b'd, -d)$ and one lets d go to infinity. This moves the eye off to infinity along a line through the origin with direction vector **v**. The larger d gets, the more parallel are the rays from the eye to the points of an object. The matrix M_{eye} in equation (4.11) (with a = a'd and b = b;d) approaches M_{par} because 1/d goes to zero.

An even simpler case occurs when the vector **v** is orthogonal to the view plane.

Definition

A parallel projection where the lines we are projecting along are orthogonal to the view plane is called an *orthographic* (or *orthogonal*) *projection.* If the lines have a direction vector that is not orthogonal to the view plane, we call it an *oblique (parallel) projection.* A view of the world obtained via an orthographic or oblique projection is called an *orthographic* or *oblique view,* respectively. A single projection of an object is obviously not enough to describe its shape.

Definition

An *axonometric projection* consists of a set of parallel projections that shows at least three adjacent faces. A view of the world obtained via an axonometric projection is called an *axonometric view*

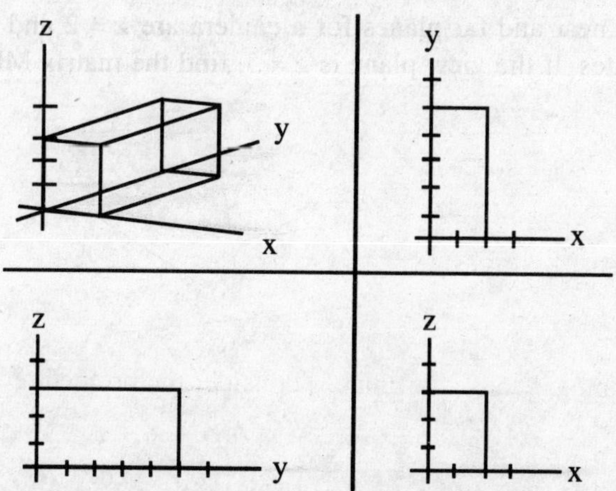

Figure 4.17. Perspective and orthographic views of a 2 * 5 * 3 block.

In engineering drawings one often shows a perspective view along with three orthographic views – a top, front, and side view, corresponding to looking along the z-, y-, and x-axis, respectively. See Figure 4.17.

Finally, in a three-dimensional graphics program one might want to do some 2d graphics. For example, one might want to let a user define curves in the plane. Rather than maintaining a separate 2d structure for these planar objects it would be more convenient to think of them as 3d objects. Using the orthographic projection, one can simulate a 2d world for the user.

EXERCISES

1. Prove equation (4.3).
2. Find the world-to-camera coordinates transformation T in two dimensions given the following data: the camera is at (1,4) looking in direction (–1, –3) with the view "plane" (a line) a distance in front of the camera.
3. Find the world-to-camera coordinates transformation T in three dimensions given that the camera is at (2,3,5) looking in direction (–1, 2, 1) with the view plane a distance 7 in front of the camera.
4. A camera is situated at the origin looking in direction **v**. Find the vanishing points of the view defined by lines parallel to the standard unit cube when
   (a) **v** = (2,0,3)
   (b) **v** = (0,3,0)
   (c) **v** = (3,1,2)
5. With regard to Figure 4.11 show that the regions below are mapped as indicated: Note that *z/w* denotes the "real" *z* coordinate of a projective point (*x, y, z, w*).
6. Assume that the near and far planes for a camera are $z = 2$ and $z = 51$, respectively, in camera coordinates. If the view plane is $z = 5$, find the matrix MhcamÆhclip.

5 TWO-DIMENSIONAL COMPUTER GRAPHICS

Computer graphics involves the use of computers to produce pictures and diagrams. This chapter relates to the production of diagrams made up of lines and curves and which may also be coloured and shaded in various ways.

The most fundamental form of graphical output is the ability to produce a straight line at any required position on whatever output medium is being used. Indeed, if the resolution is sufficiently fine, all other forms of graphics can be produced as a number of straight lines and the human eye will interpret the output as curves or symbols of whatever complexity is required. Since the range of possible results may depend critically on the limits of the available hardware, it is reasonable to start with a discussion of these output devices.

5.1 GRAPHICAL OUTPUT DEVICES

The possible forms of two-dimensional graphical output split into two main types - computer screens of various sizes, colours and resolutions and ***"hard-copy"*** output such as printers and plotters.

There are two possible forms of two-dimensional graphical output

(a) Computer screens of various sizes, colours and resolutions.

(b) Hard-copy output such as printers and plotters.

The so-called ***"three-dimensional"*** output devices are still rare and expensive and so are outside the scope of this chapter - even the virtual reality headsets, which appear three-dimensional, in fact use a separate two-dimensional screen for each eye and rely on the human brain to process the images and produce a three-dimensional result.

5.1.1 Computer Screens

Most computer screens available today are raster terminals. These may be visualised as having a rectangular grid across the screen with a number of equally-spaced lines in each direction. The number of lines determines the accuracy or resolution of the device (1024 x 1024 is quite common).

At each intersection, the screen may be illuminated with a dot of suitably-coloured light, i.e. a ***"pixel"***.

Varying the resolution (space between pixels) and the number of possible colours gives a wide variety of different terminals.

Each raster screen has at least one ***"frame buffer"*** associated with it and alterations to the screen are achieved by changing values in this frame buffer. The current state of the frame buffer is displayed, row by row, on the screen of the terminal and is automatically refreshed several times a second to give a clear steady image.

A monochrome terminal has one frame buffer and points on the screen can be recorded as either "black" or "white" (0 or 1), while colour terminals have several buffers. The number of buffers supplied in the hardware determines the maximum number of colours available at any given moment.

Earlier terminals were of a type known as ***"vector-refresh"*** terminals and had to be programmed rather differently. Much of the terminology used to discuss graphical algorithms still reflects this.

Vector-refresh terminals used the concept of moving a beam of light across the screen and leaving an illuminated line behind it. The disadvantage of the vector-refresh terminal was that refreshing the screen was under the control of the program. If the drawing was output once, it would appear on the screen and then fade away. The program had to loop and re-draw the diagram many times in order to keep it on the screen. Worse than this, if the diagram became too complex, the first lineswould start to fade before the last ones had been drawn and so the whole diagram would flicker most unpleasantly.

Raster terminals make life a great deal easier for the programmer, because they are automatically refreshed and this process takes the same time whatever the colour of the pixels and hence whatever the complexity of the drawing. The limit is now imposed by the number of pixel-positions on the screen.

5.1.2 Hard Copy Devices.

The hard-copy devices include plotters and printers.

The plotters usually contain pens of one or more colour and are designed for graphical output.

The printers were designed for text output, but some types may also be used for graphical output. The daisy-wheel or golf-ball printers, developed from the electric typewriter, cannot be used for graphical output, but these are already sufficiently out-of-date to be rarely met. Dot-matrix, ink-jet and laser printers can be used to copy what is on the screen, whether it be text or graphics. The higher the resolution of the printer, the better the quality of the output.

The pen-plotters use two main mechanisms, either drum plotters with pen movement in one direction and paper movement in the other, or flat bed plotters with pen movement in two directions.

Drum plotters varied from the large Calcomp plotters (with paper up to a metre wide and a resolution of 0.01 mm) at the one extreme, to the small Tandy colour plotter (with a roll of paper about 10 cm wide and 80 plotter steps across) at the other. In each case, movement in one direction was obtained by rotation of the drum resulting in movement of the paper. The pen was moved by a wire in the other direction, and as the loop of wire was rotated so the plotting head was dragged to and fro across the paper. If there was only one pen available, then it was permanently mounted in the plotting head, but if there are several pens of different colours and/or different thicknesses were provided, then the one currently in use was mounted in position in the plotting head and some means of changing pens, either under program control or through operator intervention, was needed.

In the flat bed plotters, the paper lay on a flat surface and there were two wires, one parallel to the x-axis and the other parallel to the y-axis, to control the movement of the pen. The paper supplied to these plotters may be in separate sheets or on a roll, but the paper was not moved during the plotting of a graph.

In either type of plotter, there were two pen positions within the plotting head.

"Pen-up" meant that the pen was raised clear of the paper and left no mark when the plotting head was moved.

"Pen-down" meant that it was in contact with the paper and left a trail as it was dragged across the surface of the paper.

On the screen (or copied to the printer), each pixel may be illuminated or not and this ***"off"*** or ***"on"*** corresponded to the pen-up or pen-down of the plotter.

The smallest distance the pen can move is -1, 0, or +1 units in the x and y directions. This gives the possibility of eight directions in which the pen can move from any given position (the diagonal directions being obtained by simultaneous movement in both x and y) as shown in the figure. All graphs, however complicated, must be broken down into these ***"elementary plotter steps"*** and all graphics packages contain software to calculate these and issue commands to the plotter in the correct form. This mapping from theoretical curve to elementary plotter steps to commands for the appropriate hardware is an essential part of any graphics system.

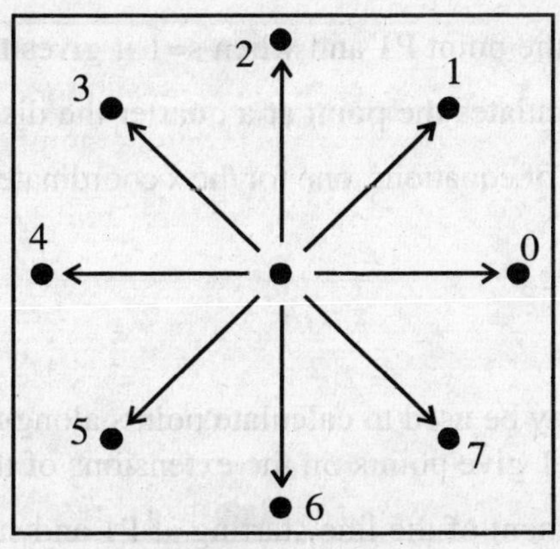

Figure 5.1

The second part of the mapping - from elementary plotter steps to hardware commands is usually supplied in the device-driver software along with the plotter. In addition, the CGI (Computer Graphics Interface) standard has been designed to map from GKS commands such as polyline to a format which the actual plotters can interpret.

5.2 DRAWING STRAIGHT LINES (POLYLINE)

There are actually several stages involved between the idea of a diagram in the mind of its creator and the illumination of a selection of pixels on a computer screen in order to present this diagram to someone else. The additional steps within the human brain required for the recipient to interpret what is seen on the screen will not be discussed here.

Consider the problem of instructing a computer to draw a straight line from A to B, where A and B are points on a computer screen.

To define the position of A and B, we need a coordinate system and the values of the cordinates of A and B in terms of this system.

At the lowest level, the points may be defined in terms of pixel positions on the screen. This uses ***"device coordinates"*** and is the system used by most DDA algorithms to illuminate the actual pixels needed to produce the line.

At a higher level, most problems in graphics work in terms of ***"world coordinates"*** and we shall discuss the equations for straight lines in terms of these. They are Cartesian coordinates with the x-axis horizontally towards the right and the y-axis vertically upwards.

Other coordinate systems, such as polar coordinates, will not be discussed here.

Most graphics systems provide automatic transformations from world coordinates, either directly to device coordinates or via an intermediate set of ***"normalised device coordinates"***.

Equation of a Line

The equation of a straight line joining the points P1 (x1,y1) and P2 (x2,y2) may be written :- $P=(1-s) P_1 + s P_2$

where the parameter s takes values between 0 and 1.

When s=0, the equation gives the point P1 and when s=1 it gives the point P2.

When s=0.25, the equation calculates the point at a quarter the distance from P1 to P2.

This equation gives you the pair of equations, one for the x coordinates and the other for the y coordinates, namely:

$x=(1-s)\ x1 + s\ x2$

$y=(1-s)\ y1 + s\ y2$

Values of s between 0 and 1 may be used to calculate points along the line between P1 and P2. Values of s less than 0 or greater than 1 give points on the extensions of the line beyond P1 or P2.

If you only want the finite segment of the line starting at P1 and stopping at P2, then you must reject any values of s outside the range 0 to 1.

Example: consider the line from (2,2) to (6,4).

This gives the two equations

$x=2(1-s) + 6s$ and $y = 2(1-s) + 4s$

Then s=0.0 gives x=2 and y=2.

s=0.2 gives x=2.8 and y=2.4

s=0.4 gives x=3.6 and y=2.8

s=0.6 gives x=4.4 and y=3.2

s=0.8 gives x=5.2 and y=3.6

s=1.0 gives x=6 and y=4.

These values may be plotted on graph paper to give the required straight line.

Intersection of Two Lines

If the one line has the equation P=(1-s) P1 + s P2

and the other line has the equation P=(1-t) P3 + t P4

then to calculate the point of intersection of these lines, you need to find values of s and t which will give the common point.

i.e. $(1-s)\,x1 + s\,x2 = x = (1-t)\,x3 + t\,x4$

and $(1-s)\,y1 + s\,y2 = y = (1-t)\,y3 + t\,y4$

rearranging this pair of equations gives

$$s=t\,(x_4-x_3)/(x_2-x_1) + (x_3-x_1)/(x_2-x_1)$$

and

$$s=t\,(y_4-y_3)/(y_2-y_1) + (y_3-y_1)/(y_2-y_1)$$

This can be rearranged to give the expression for t, namely:

$$t=\frac{((y_3-y_1)/(y_2-y_1)-(x_3-x_1)/(x_2-x_1))}{((x_4-x_3)/(x_2-x_1)-(y_4-y_3)/(y_2-y_1))}$$

Problems arise if either $x_2=x_1$ or $y_2=y_1$, but in this case the line is parallel to one of the axes and the whole equation becomes very much simpler.

More seriously, if the divisor in the last equation is zero, it is not possible to calculate t.

This occurs when the two lines are parallel so that

$(y_2-y_1)/(x_2-x_1)=(y_4-y_3)/(x_4-x_3)$ and you know that parallel line segments do not have a point of intersection, although the lines through the points may be said to meet at infinity.

Finally you should note that if either the value of t or the corresponding value of s lies outside the range 0 to 1, then the two segments P1P2 and P3P4 do not intersect although the infinite lines through these points may do so.

Mapping on to the Computer Screen

To discuss these algorithms, the coordinates will refer to pixel-positions on the screen of a raster terminal. (For example, an EGA card will have 640 positions along the x-axis and 350 along the y-axis, any one of which is assigned one of the 16 possible colours) To draw a line from a point A (X1,Y1) to the point B (X2,Y2) at some angle across the screen of the terminal, each pixel on the line must be changed from the background colour (usually black) to some other colour (white for example). Any algorithm used to generate this output must satisfy the following requirements:

1) Lines should appear straight and terminate accurately.

Most algorithms draw lines which appear straight. Some allow roundoff errors to build up so that a line from A to B followed by a line from B to C will not meet at B but will either cross or leave a gap. This not only looks bad, but may cause serious problems if you then try to flood-fill a polygon. Also, when attempting to erase a line, it may be found that the line AB does not colour the identical pixels to the line BA.

2) Lines should have constant density, independent of their length.

Most algorithms satisfy this criterion, since it is usual to generate points at a given step-size rather than a given number of points per line.

3) Lines should be drawn rapidly.

Speed of drawing is a very important consideration when comparing algorithms for producing straight lines.

The most widely-used class of algorithms for these methods are the "DDA" or ***"Digital Differential Analyser"*** algorithms which are derived from the expression for the first derivative of the curve in question. (Note that this is constant for a straight line.)

The starting point (X1,Y1) corresponds to the pixel coordinates IX and IY and this pixel is illuminated. To get the next point on the curve, we must add an increment dx to X1 and an increment dy to Y1, and then work out the corresponding pixel coordinates. If these give the same values IX and IY, then the pixel is already illuminated and won't get any brighter so there is no need to do anything. If these give a different value for one or both of the coordinates, then we must illuminate the required pixel. The DDA algorithm gives a method of calculating the dx and dy to obtain the next point.

When we are dealing with a straight line, the DDA algorithm has a particularly simple form. If the line runs from the point (X1,Y1) to (X2,Y2), then the equations are:

$d_y = f * (Y2-Y1)$

and $d_x = f * (X2-X1)$

for some scaling factor f. When f is a very small number, we may find it takes several iterations to get from one pixel position to the next one. On the other hand, when f becomes too large, we find the method skips over several pixel positions and produces an irregular dotted line rather than a continuous one.

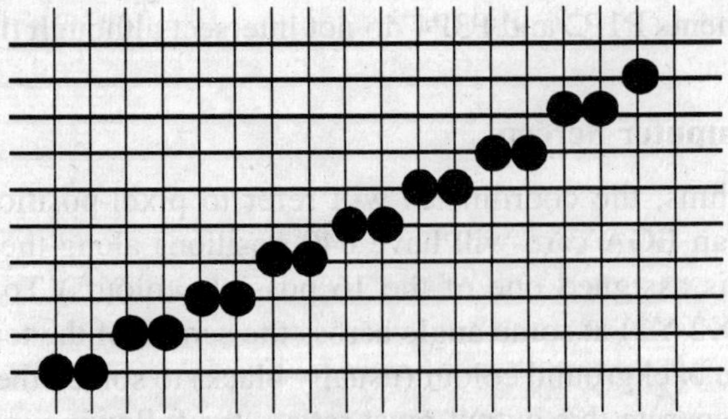

Figure 5.2 Example of DDA Output.

This example corresponds to the **"Simple DDA algorithm."**

Simple DDA Algorithm

Initially this will be discussed in terms of output to a raster terminal. For this algorithm, it is necessary to choose f so that either d_x or d_y is of unit magnitude. The other step size will be less than or equal to one in magnitude, and may be positive or negative in sign. At this level of programming, thc pixcl positions on the raster grid of the screen are indicated by integer numbers, and the coordinates x1, y1, x2 and y2 which are supplied to the algorithm are expressed in terms of these integers. The command **"putpixel(x,y)"** illuminates the pixel at position (x,y) . Then, in Pascal-like notation, the following algorithm may be used.

```
Input data x1,y1,x2,y2
Set dx:=(x2-x1); dy:=(y2-y1)
If abs(dx)>abs(dy)    then f:=1/abs(dx); n:=int(abs(dx))
                      else f:=1/abs(dy); n:=int(abs(dy))
Set dx:=f*dx; dy:=f*dy
Set x:=x1; y:=y1
For i=0 to n
    Putpixel(x,y)
    Set x:=x+dx; y:=y+dy
Repeat
End
```

Since a unit step has been chosen in at least one direction, it is certain that another pixel must be illuminated on each iteration around the loop. The type of output is illustrated in the previous figure, where d_x is larger than d_y and so the next pixel in the x-direction is always illuminated, while in the y-direction there are some cases with several pixels illuminated with the same y-value. There have been many actual implementations of these algorithms, since Bresenham's Algorithm was published in 1965, and although the basic idea remains the same, details of the method vary from one implementation to another.

DDA Output for Curves

Any curve for which the equation can be expressed as increments d_x and d_y added to the previous values of x and y can be used to generate a DDA algorithm. Later in this text, equations in this form can be found for ellipses and other conic sections. Chapter Two of the text by Newman and Sproull discusses several attempts to find a DDA algorithm for a circle, but the problem of roundoff errors which build up during a calculation is particularly severe in this case. Another problem relating to this output occurs when the distance between pixels in the x-direction is not exactly equal to the distance between pixels in the y-direction. In this case, a circle-drawing DDA algorithm which was correctly defined in terms of pixel-steps would produce an ellipse not a circle when it appeared on the screen. The correct algorithm in this case would be an ellipse-drawing algorithm whose eccentricity corrected the ratio of pixel-steps in the x and y directions.

GKS Polyline Output.

The exact form of the subroutine call to polyline is determined by the language binding for the particular language being used. Functionally, the user must supply the number of points and the world coordinates of those points. In FORTRAN for example, the parameters are an integer N containing the number of points followed by two one-dimensional real arrays X and Y containing the world coordinates. In Pascal, on the other hand, the coordinates are expected in an array of records, each record having two components which are the real values x and y.

The polyline output function draws a line from the first point to the second, the second the the third and so on. No attempt is made to produce a closed polygon - this only happens if the first point and the last have identical world coordinates.

Polyline must always have at least two points. Two points will produce a single line joining them.

Resolution and "Jaggies"

The resolution of a terminal is determined by the minimum step-size in x or y, so is either the smallest distance a pen may be moved on the plotter or the distance from one pixel position to the next. A ***"high-resolution"*** terminal has a very small step-size and so is capable of high quality output.

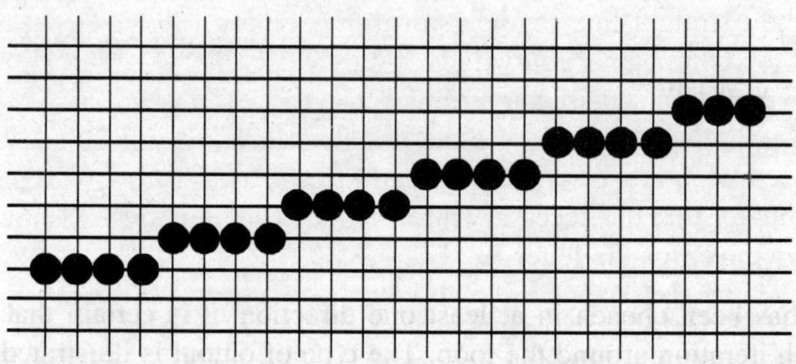

Figure 5.3 DDA Output with Jaggies

The above figure shows an enlargement of a raster screen with a line across it. At each crossing point, the pixel may be illuminated or not and by looking closely at the line, distinct rows of dots may be observed with steps when the output moves to the next row. This effect is referred to as ***"jaggies"*** and is particularly unpleasant on some low-resolution terminals. However even good quality output shows the same behaviour when viewed through a sufficiently powerful magnifying glass.

If the terminal is a monochrome one with only two levels of output, then nothing can be done to remove these jaggies. If it is possible to use a grey-scale terminal, then there are methods to give a better appearance to the output. These rely on the tendency of the human eye to join things up in straight lines.

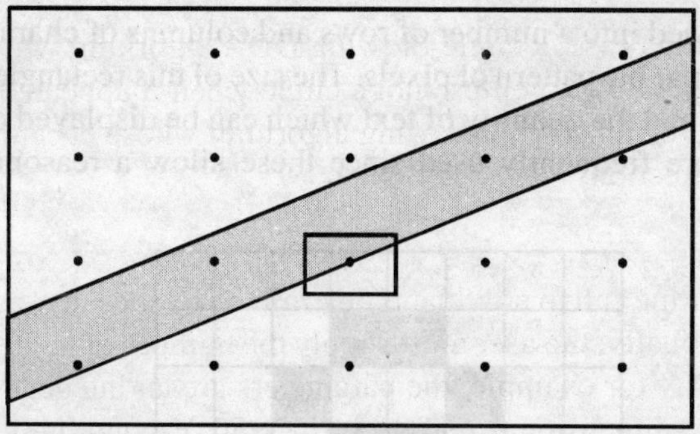

Figure 5.4 Grey-shading algorithm.

In the above figure, the dots indicate the raster positions across the screen and the shaded area is the line we wish to draw. Now imagine that each dot is surrounded by a square large enough to cover the whole area. Many of these squares are intersected by the shaded area and so it is possible to calculate the depth of grey proportional to the amount of the square which is shaded.

5.3 TEXT IN GRAPHICS (POLYMARKER AND TEXT).

There are many occasions on which we require text to be mixed with drawings or images and so need some means of providing text output within a graphics system. This section discusses some general comments and also describes the options provided with the GKS standard.

There are basically two methods of producing text on a computer screen; either the character may be drawn as a series of short straight-line segments or it may be displayed as a pattern of dots. The first may be thought of as the computer's equivalent of handwriting and the second as the equivalent of typing. Most home computers and character terminals use the second ("bit-pattern") approach because it is considerably faster. Plotters generally use the first approach and graphics screens may use either. Both approaches may allow the possibility of additional text fonts, provided the terminal or microcomputer has room to store the necessary information. The figure below shows a greatly enlarged version of these two methods for the letter A.

Figure 5.5 Stroke and Bit-mapped Forms of Letter A

The appearance of this type of text depends on the resolution of the screen and the number of bits used to represent each character, and it is not usually possible to change this. Many computer systems have one buffer for a text screen and another one for a graphics screen, and the extent to which these can be combined in output varies greatly from one type of computer to another. The text screen of the terminal or home computer will be divided into a number of rows and columns of characters, and each character position will contain a rectangular bit-pattern of pixels. The size of this rectangle is usually a compromise between the quality of the text and the quantity of text which can be displayed on the screen. Rectangles of 6x8 pixels or 8x8 pixels are frequently used since these allow a reasonable amount of medium quality text on each screen.

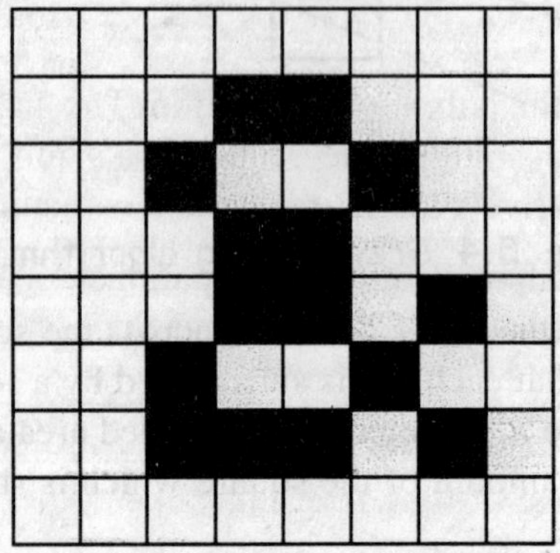

It is usual to leave a border round the character if possible so that it can easily be read in a line of text. Now compare the pattern with the binary representation, shown below:

0 0 0 0 0 0 0 0

0 0 0 1 1 0 0 0

0 0 1 0 0 1 0 0

0 0 0 1 1 0 0 0

0 0 0 1 1 0 1 0

0 0 1 0 0 1 0 0

0 0 1 1 1 0 1 0

0 0 0 0 0 0 0 0

This same method is used on most dot-matrix printers, and again the number of dots in the rectangle used to define the character is responsible for the final appearance of the output. Some printers also provide a "near letter quality" (NLQ) mode where each line is printed twice and is shifted by half the space between dots for the second printing. This fills in the spaces between the dots and gives a much blacker, solider result. Copying any graphics characters on to a dot-matrix printer usually requires a special dump program.

When working in graphics mode, it is possible to access all the pixel positions on the screen. This mode is used for output from G.K.S. and other graphics software. You may also use the stroke characters which have instructions to draw the character in any size and at any position. Such characters may be coded as a series of polyline calls, or they may require some means of calculating smooth curves to give a better representation of curved characters such as "s" or "o". In either case, they are stored as commands to draw the shape of the letter, not as bit-patterns. Consequently they may be shifted, scaled or rotated in the same way as any other drawing.

So far, the discussion has related to monochrome output, but many of the ideas are directly applicable to colour terminals. Text may be output in any color of ink on any color of background and when you are working with a system such as GKS, the choice of these colours is defined using attributes and color tables before the text is output. When dealing with grey-scale devices, some work has been done on choosing the appropriate level of grey for each pixel position in the bit map in order to give a better impression of curved characters.

Text Output in GKS.

One form of Text output in GKS is the polymarker function. This has the same parameters as polyline, but instead of joining the points with straight lines, it draws a symbol at each point. The symbols may be chosen from the selection of the five symmetric characters, namely . * x + o

The other form is the function usually called gtext. Its paramcters are a world coordinate (x,y) and a text string. The relationship between the coordinate and the rectangular box containing the text is controlled by the various setting of the GKS parameters.

One function is provided to set the choice of font and the size of the characters. This is still called "SetTextHeight", but since the choice of font determines the ratio of horizontal to vertical, increasing the height will also increase the overall size.

A second function may be used to set "Character Up Vector". It is assumed that thc text is drawn along an Ox axis and the Up-Vector is the direction of the associated Oy axis. (You will probably find it useful to draw yourself a diagram for this). With stroke text, the characters are rotated as well as the axes. With bit-mapped text, the letters remain upright, but are output along the current direction of the x-axis.

The third function is "Text Path". The default is from left to right along the x-axis. Other possibilities are bottom to top, right to left and top to bottom. The text path determines the relative position of the second character output to the first and so on.

The last function is "Text Alignment". This determines where the coordinate (x,y) appears relative to the rectangle containing the text. The default is the bottom left hand corner. However the alignment can be left, centre or right in the x-direction and bottom, centre or top in the y-direction.

5.4 TWO-DIMENSIONAL TRANSFORMATIONS

5.4.1 Coordinate System

Definition

A coordinate system is a means for defining and stating positions of points in space. The system used in this module is the 2-dimensional Cartesian coordinate system.

5.4.2 Specifying a Point in the Coordinate System

A point in the coordinate system is specified by a (x,y), where x and y are the point's distance, along the x and y axis respectively, from the origin of the system.

Example

The point "A" in the figure on the left is 3 units away along the x-axis from the origin, and is 4 units away along the y-axis from the origin. Thus the coordinates of the point are (3,4).

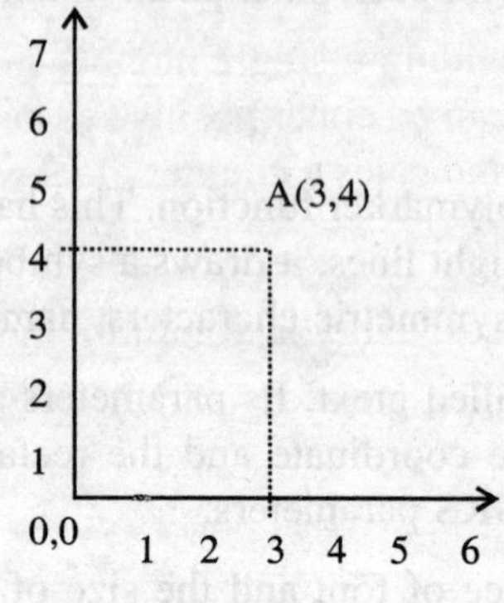

5.4.3 Transformations

A transformation is any operation on a point in space **(x, y)** that maps the point's coordinates into a new set of coordinates $(\mathbf{x_1}, \mathbf{y_1})$. There are several types of basic transformations that are defined:

- Translation
- Rotation
- Scale
- Shear

Any other transformation that needs to be performed can be achieved by performing a sequence of the above transformations. Any such sequence of transformations need not be unique - there can be multiple sequences that would result in the same final transformation.

Translation

Definition

A 2-dimensional translation is a transformation that moves a point a specified distance in the x and/or y directions (i.e. along either or both of the coordinate axes).

Specifying a Translation

A transformation is usually specified by a 2-tuple, such as (2,3). The first number indicates movement along the x-axis, and the second number indicates movement along the y-axis.

Undo'ing a Translation

If you have translated an object by (x,y), and you want to undo this, you need to translate the object again by (-x,-y).

Rotation

Definition

A rotation is a transformation that causes a point p to be moved relative to a central point, without changing the distance of p from the central point. By convention, this central point is the origin of the coordinate system - the point (0,0).

Specifying a Rotation

A rotation is generally specified by providing a single number that indicates how many degrees the point should be rotated by. The number can be either positive or negative. In the coordinate system we are using, a positive number of degrees indicates a counter-clockwise turn.

Undo'ing a Rotation

If you have rotated an object by X degrees, and you want to undo this, you need to rotate the object again by -X degrees.

Scale

Definition

A scaling is a transformation that changes the relative size and possibly the position of the object. Scaling can be performed along either or both of the coordinate axes. A scale by a factor of more than 1 will increase the object's size. A scale by a positive factor of less than 1 will decrease the object's size. A scale by a factor of 1 will not change the object size.

Specifying a Scale

A scale operation is specified by a 2-tuple, such as (0.5, 1). Again, the first number refers to the scale along the x-axis, and the second number refers to the scale along the y-axis.

Undo'ing a Scaled

If you have scaled an object by (x,y), and you want to undo this, you need to scale the object again by (1/x,1/y).

Shear

Definition

A shear is a transformation that distorts the shape of an object along either or both of the axes. Like scale and translate, a shear can be done along just one or along both of the coordinate axes. A shear along one axis (say, the x-axis) is performed in terms of the point's coordinate in the other axis (the y-axis). Thus a shear of 1 in the x-axis will cause the x-coodinate of the point ot distort by 1*(y-coordinate). A shear of 0 along either axis will not change the object along that axis.

Specifying a Shear

A shear is specified by a 2-tuple, such as (1, 0) where the first number is the shear along the x-axis, and the second number is the shear along the y-axis.

Undo'ing a Shear

If you have sheared an object by (x,y), and you want to undo this, you need to shear the object again by (-x,-y).

5.4.4 Transformations in Two-Dimensions

Once a diagram has been defined in terms of straight lines expressed as the values of their end-points (x,y) in some Cartesian coordinate system, you may wish to change its position, size or orientation. All these involve the use of transformations to map from the old values of the coordinates to the new ones, after which the diagram is redrawn in its new position.

Shift Transformation or Translation.

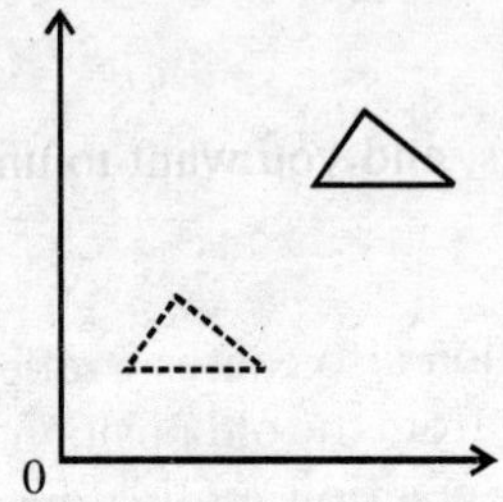

Figure 5.6 Shift Transformation

This is the easiest transformation to visualise. It involves shifting the whole diagram to a new position while leaving its size and orientation unchanged. The above figure shows the shift transformation applied to a triangle to move it from its old position (shown by solid lines) to its new position (shown by dashed lines).

This involves a recalculation of each pair of (x,y) values using the formulae connecting the old values (x,y) and the new values (x',y').

$x' = x - x_t$

$y' = y - y_t$

These may also be written as the single matrix equation

$$\begin{vmatrix} x' \\ y' \\ 1 \end{vmatrix} = \begin{vmatrix} 1 & 0 & -x_t \\ 0 & 1 & -y_t \\ 0 & 0 & 1 \end{vmatrix} \begin{vmatrix} x \\ y \\ 1 \end{vmatrix}$$

When this is expanded using the normal rules of matrix multiplication,

you get the following equations.

$$x' = 1*x + 0*y + 1*(-x_t) = x - x_t$$

$$y' = 0*x + 1*y + 1*(-y_t) = y - y_t$$

$$1 = 0*x + 0*y + 1*1 = 1$$

which reduce to the first pair of equations. The third equation (1=1) is a useful check that the transformation has been remembered correctly. If you are not happy with matrix arithmetic, then you may apply each transformation in turn using the equations quoted above. This is slightly less efficient than building up one overall transformation matrix and applying it once, but so long as you are careful to apply the transformations in the correct order, the final result will be the same.

Scale Transformation

This may be used to change the size of a diagram, by using the following pair of equations.

$x' = S_x * x$

$y' = S_y * y$

However, if Sx is negative, this transformation also causes a reflection in the y-axis and similarly if Sy is negative. The figure below shows scaling from the old position (solid lines) to a new position (dotted lines) when $S_x = S_y = 1/2$ and from the old position (solid lines) to a new position (dashed lines) corresponding to $S_x = +1$, $S_y = -1$.

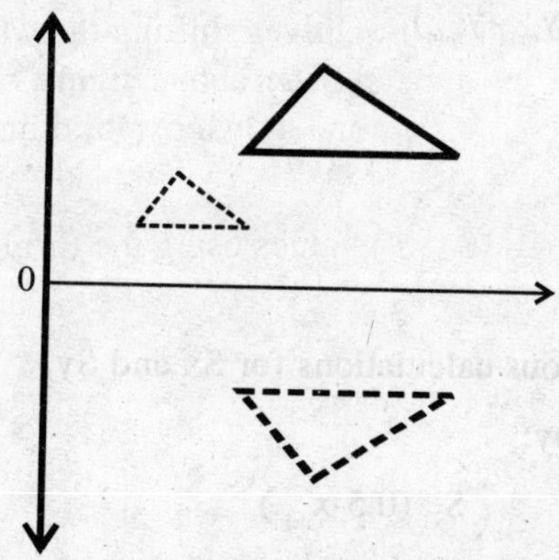

Figure 5.7 Scale Transformations

Examples of Transformations

Example One: World Coordinates to Normalized Device Coordinates.

The area x_{min} to x_{max} and y_{min} to y_{max} on to the area 0 to 1 and 0 to 1.

First shift the point (x_{min}, y_{min}) to (0,0).

$x' = x - x_{min}$

$y' = y - y_{min}$

Secondly scale the lengths $(x_{max} - x_{min})$ and $(y_{max} - y_{min})$ to unity.

$S_x = 1/(x_{max} - x_{min})$

$S_y = 1/(y_{max} - y_{min})$

and then

$x'' = S_x * x'$

$y'' = S_y * y'$

Applying this to all the points will carry out the transformation.

Example Two: World Coordinates on to part of the unit square.

The area x_{min} to x_{max} and y_{min} to y_{max} on to the area 0.5 to 1.0 and 0.0 to 0.5.

First shift (x_{min}, y_{min}) to (0.5,0.0).

$x' = x - (x_{min} - 0.5)$

$y' = y - (y_{min} - 0.0)$

Secondly calculate the scaling factors.

$S_x = (1.0-0.5)/(x_{max} - x_{min}) = 0.5/(x_{max} - x_{min})$

$S_y = (0.5-0.0)/(y_{max} - y_{min}) = 0.5/(y_{max} - y_{min})$

Finally scale the coordinate values.

$x'' = S_x * x'$

$y'' = S_y * y'$

It is easy to show that with the previous calculations for Sx and Sy,

the Transformation matrix is given by:

$$T = \begin{matrix} S_x & 0 & S_x*(0.5-x_{min}) \\ 0 & S_y & S_y*(-y_{min}) \\ 0 & 0 & 1 \end{matrix}$$

Rotate Transformation

This allows the whole diagram to be rotated through an angle A about the origin of the coordinate system. The next figure shows a diagram rotated through a small positive angle A from the old position (solid lines) to the new position (dashed lines).

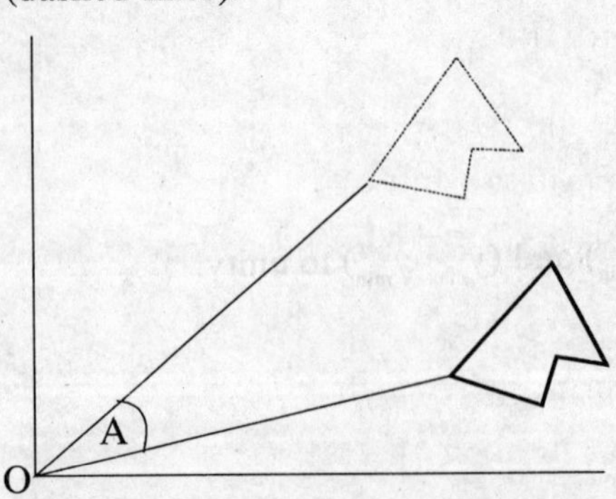

Figure 5.8 Rotation of Diagram

To derive the equations for this, let us consider a single point P(x,y) and use the figure below to study the geometry.

The point P is moved to P' when the diagram is rotated through an angle A about the origin O. This means that the lengths OP and OP' are equal. If this length is denoted by d, then

d*d = x*x + y*y = x'*x' + y'*y'

and

x=d cos B and y = d sin B

Similarly

x'=d cos (A+B) and y' = d sin(A+B)

x' =d cos (A+B)

=d cos A cos B - d sin A sin B

=x cos A - y sin A

y' =d sin (A+B)

=d sin A cos B + d cos A sin B

=x sin a + y cos A

These equations have to be applied to every pair of coordinates and then the new points must be joined up in the required order to redraw the diagram in its new position. As usual, this may also be expressed in matrix form :

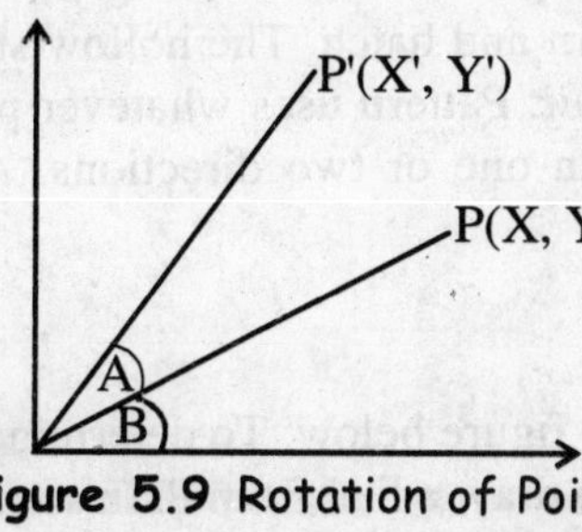

Figure 5.9 Rotation of Point P

Example Three: Rotate the diagram through an angle A about a point P which is not at the origin. This requires three stages:

1. Move P to the origin. (shift by -px,-py).
2. Rotate about the origin.(rotate through angle A).
3. Move P back to its original position (shift by px,py).

Now calculate the transformation matrix T from these three transformations.

$$T=\begin{vmatrix}1 & 0 & px\\0 & 1 & py\\0 & 0 & 1\end{vmatrix}\begin{vmatrix}\cos A & -\sin A & 0\\\sin A & \cos A & 0\\0 & 0 & 1\end{vmatrix}\begin{vmatrix}1 & 0 & -px\\0 & 1 & -py\\0 & 0 & 1\end{vmatrix}$$

```
      |1   0   px|        |cosA   -sinA    -px*cosA+py*sinA|
  =   |0   1   py|        |sinA    cosA    -px*sinA-py*cosA|
      |0   0   1 |        | 0       0        1             |

      |cosA      - sinA                 px -px*cosA + py*sinA |
  =   |sinA      cosA                   py -px*sinA - py*cosA |
      | 0        0                              1             |
```

Having evaluated the matrix T, you can multiply all coordinate pairs by the matrix and then redraw the diagram in its new position.

5.5 SHADING OF POLYGONS (FILL-AREA)

A polygon is an area enclosed by a sequence of linear segments. There is no restriction on the complexity of the shape produced by these segments, but the last point must always be connected to the first one giving a closed boundary. This differs from Polyline which may produce an open curve with the first and last points being any distance apart. Since a polygon defines an area, then it is possible to decide whether any other point is inside or outside the polygon and there are two very simple tests to determine this.

The GKS Fillarea function has the same parameters as polyline, but will always produce a closed polygon. The filling of this polygon depends on the setting of the appropriate GKS parameter. The FillAreaStyles are hollow, solid, pattern and hatch. The hollow style produces a closed polygon with no filling. Solid fills with a solid colour. Pattern uses whatever patterns are offered by the particular system. Hatch will fill it with lines in one or two directions. Algorithms for hatching and cross-hatching are described in this section.

5.5.1 Intersection Test

Consider the situation illustrated in the figure below. To determine which of the points Pi, (i=1,2 or 3) lie inside the polygon, it is necessary to draw a line from Pi in some direction and project it beyond the area covered by the polygon. If the number of intersections of the line from Pi with the sides of the polygon is an even number, then the point lies outside the polygon. (Note that the line must start at Pi and may not extend back behind Pi - it is an half-infinite line from Pi). This means that the triangle to the right of the line Q4 Q5 in the figure counts as outside the polygon. If you wished to make it doubly inside, you would have to introduce a parameter equal to the minimum number of intersections of all half-infinite lines through Pi.

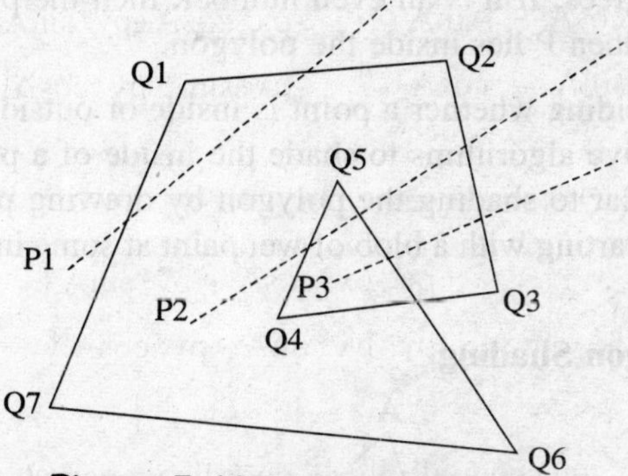

Figure 5.10 Intersection Test

It is then easy to see that the figure gives values of 0, 2 or 4 for lines through P1 with a minimum of 0. For P2, there are values of 1 or 3 with the minimum=1. All lines from P3 have a value 2.

One possible problem arises when lines pass through a vertex. The line P2 Q5 must count the vertex Q5 as two intersections while P2 Q2 must only count Q2 once. The easy way to avoid this problem is to omit all lines which pass through vertices. This still leaves plenty of lines to test the position.

Angle Test

Here the point Pi is joined to all the vertices and the sum of the angles Qk Pi Q(k+1) is calculated. If counter-clockwise angles are positive and clockwise ones are negative, then for a point Pi outside the polygon there will be some positive angles and some negative and the resulting sum will be zero.

For a point Pi inside the polygon, the points will be either all positive or all negative and the sum will have a magnitude of 360 degrees. The next figure illustrates this for the same polygon as figure 3.1the previous figure and a point P inside the triangle (but outside the polygon).

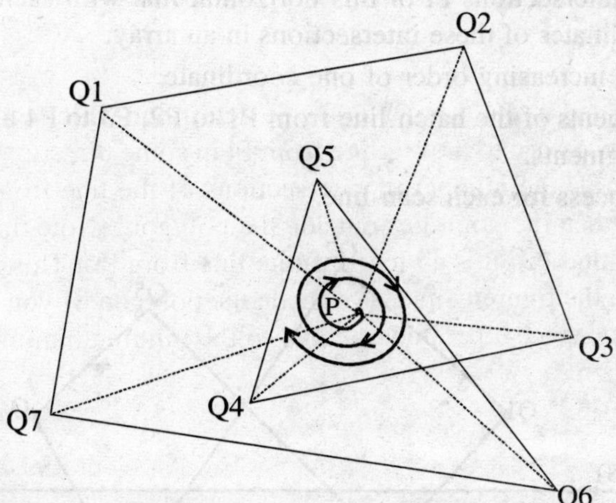

Figure 5.11 Angle Test

Here the sum of angles is 2 * 360 degrees, thus implying that it is doubly inside the polygon. To give consistency with the Intersection Test, this test must be carefully worded. Having evaluated the sum of angles, it will be n * 360 degrees. If n is an even number, then the point P lies outside the polygon, while if n is an odd number, then P lies inside the polygon.

Once a unique method of deciding whether a point is inside or outside a polygon has been agreed, it then becomes possible to derive algorithms to shade the inside of a polygon. The two main methods here are linear, which is similar to shading the polygon by drawing parallel lines with a crayon, and floodfill, which is similar to starting with a blob of wet paint at some interior point and spreading it out to fill the polygon.

Linear Algorithm for Polygon Shading

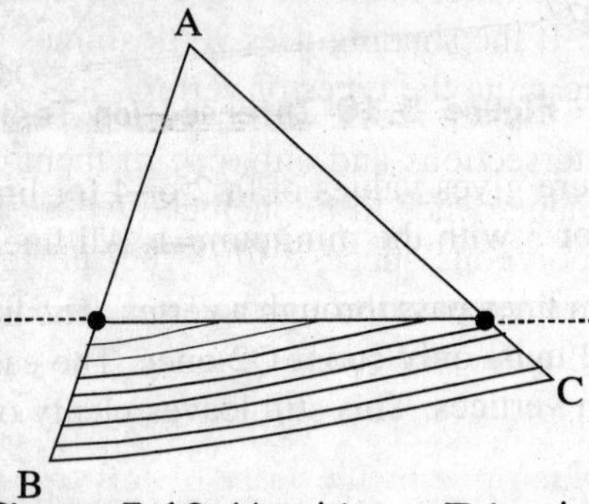

Figure 5.12 Hatching a Triangle

This involves shading the polygon by drawing a series of parallel lines throughout the interior. The lines may be close enough to touch, giving a solid fill or they may be a noticeable distance apart, giving a hatched fill. If you have two sets of hatched lines at right angles to each other, this gives a "cross-hatched" result. The figure shows a triangle in the process of being hatch-filled with horizontal lines. For each horizontal scan-line, the following process must be applied.

1. Assume (or check) that the edge of the screen is outside the polygon.
2. Calculate the intersections Pi of this horizontal line with each edge of the polygon and store the coordinates of these intersections in an array.
3. Sort them into increasing order of one coordinate.
4. Draw the segments of the hatch-line from P1 to P2, P3 to P4 and so on. Do not draw the intervening segments.
5. Repeat this process for each scan-line.

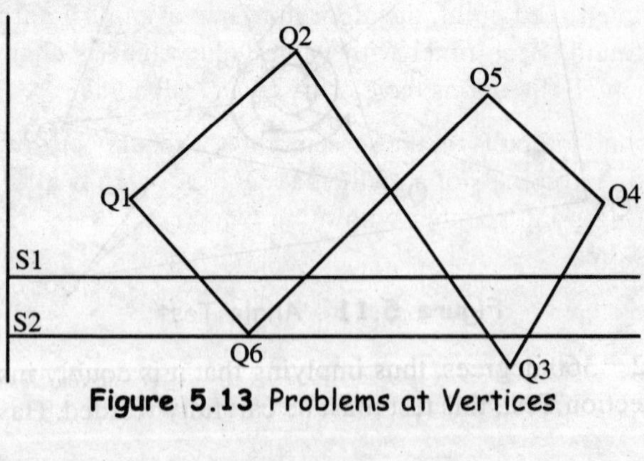

Figure 5.13 Problems at Vertices

(Note that this does not rely on the lines being horizontal, although scan-lines parallel to one of the axes makes the calculation of the intersection points very much easier). The figure shows one problem with this approach. The scan-line s1 will work correctly since it has four distinct intersections, but the scan-line s2 has two coincident intersection points at the vertex Q6. This is detectable since the number of intersection points will be an odd number.

Looking at the vertices, you can see that moving from Q5 to Q6, y decreases as x decreases and from Q6 to Q1, y increases as x decreases. In this case, the hatch lines have the equation y=constant and so this reversal in the direction of y indicates a vertex which must be included twice and consequently known as a Type 2 vertex. Q1 on the other hand is a Type 1 vertex since y continues to increase when going from Q6 through Q1 to Q2. If the shading uses vertical lines (x = constant) then it is necessary to study the behaviour of x to determine the types of vertex.

If you have an odd number of intersections and only one of them coincides with a vertex, then it is usually safe to assume that this value needs to be included twice. This may save some time in your algorithm, and will shade most polygons successfully. The full method, testing the type of vertex whenever a vertex is included in the intersection list, will successfully shade even the few cases when two Type Two vertices appear in the intersection list thus giving an even number of points and at least one segment incorrectly drawn.

The other problem case occurs when one of the sides of the polygon is parallel to the direction of shading. Mathematically this has an infinite number of intersection points, but computationally only the two end points should be entered in the array so that the whole line is shaded as part of the interior.

Floodfill Algorithm for Polygon Shading

This works in terms of pixels and is applied after the lines forming the boundary have been converted into pixels by a DDA algorithm. The background of the screen has one pixel-value, called "old value" and the points forming the boundary have another, called "edge-value". The aim of the algorithm is to change all interior pixels from "old-value" to "new-value". (e.g. from black to red) Assume the following software is available:

(a) A function Read-Pixel(x,y) which takes device coordinates (x,y) and returns the value of the pixel at this position.

(b) A routine Write-Pixel(x,y,p) which sets the new value p to the pixel at the position (x,y) in device coordinates.

Then, starting at the designated seed point, the algorithm, moves out from it in all directions, stopping when an "edge value" is found. Each pixel with value "old value" is changed to "new-value". The recursive method stops when all directions have come to an "edge value".

Because this method is applied to pixels on the screen or in the display buffer, it may run into problems arising from the quantisation into pixels of a mathematical line which is infinitely thin and recorded to the full accuracy of a floating-point number within the computer.

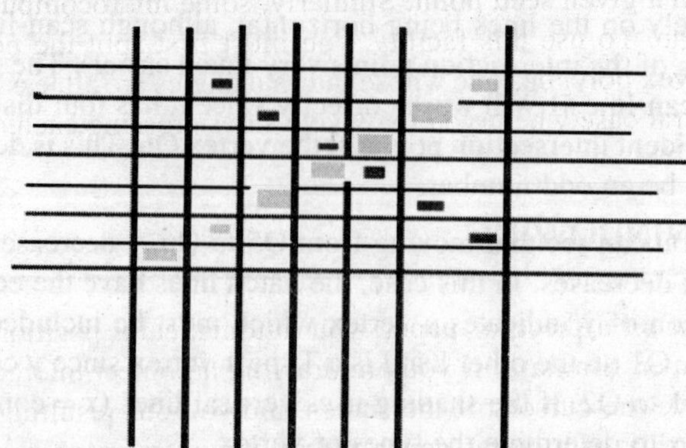

Figure 5.14 Intersecting Lines

One such problem concerns the method of identifying an intersection of two lines. If you calculate it mathematically, then the equation will give a correct result unless the lines are parallel or nearly parallel. On the other hand, on some hardware it may be quicker to check whether the two lines have any pixels in common and this can be dangerously misleading in some cases. The previous figure shows two lines, one at an angle of 45° and the other at an angle of 135° which cross near the centre of the diagram without having any pixels in common. This type of problem is unlikely to affect the Floodfill routine given above, since the scan-lines move parallel to the x and y axes and the DDA algorithm described earlier ensures that every line has at least one pixel illuminated on each scan-line.

However the next figure illustrates another possible problem. Note that in a complex polygon with sides crossing each other, you will need one seed point in each section of the interior to floodfill the whole area. This also occurs in a polygon as shown in below, even though it does not have any of its sides, indicated by the lines in the figure, crossing each other.

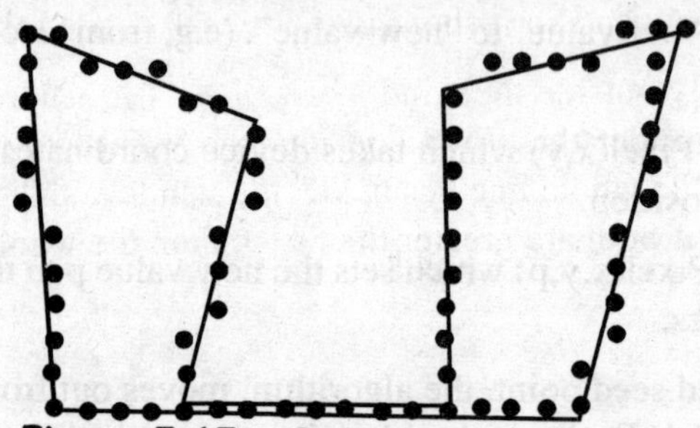

Figure 5.15 Quantisation of Pixels

Mathematically it is all one contiguous area and any tests on the equations of the sides for intersections will confirm this. However two of the lines are nearly parallel and very close together and consequently although both lines are quite separate and distinct in their mathematical equations, they lead to the same row of pixels after quantisation. The scale of this figure has been enlarged so that the quantisation into pixels appears very coarse in order to emphasize this problem. This polygon will require two seed points in order to shade it completely using the Floodfill algorithm. A little thought will allow you to produce many other similar examples and these can readily be studied by drawing the polygons on squared paper and then marking in the pixel patterns which result.

This approach remains of interest in spite of its problems because some terminals provide a very fast hardware polygon fill from a given seed point. Similarly, some microcomputers provide a function to fill the interior of a triangle. To use this facility, you must first split the polygon into triangles and while this is easy for a convex polygon (one whose internal angles are all less than 180°) it is very much more difficult for the general case where you may have sides crossing each other and holes inside the polygon

5.6 CLIPPING AND WINDOWING.

When you draw a diagram on a piece of paper, you automatically position and scale it so that the drawing remains on the paper. Similarly if you are drawing an object interactively on the screen of a terminal, you will not move the cursor off the screen and so your resulting drawing will be wholly visible. However, the majority of pictures generated in computer graphics do not have these visual checks on the size and position of the resulting output. Usually the coordinates will themselves be the result of lengthy calculations, and it is difficult if not impossible to predict the size of the resulting numbers. Some graphics devices cause the program to crash if you try to access a point outside the permitted area, while others detect this and merely present you with a blank drawing. In either case you will wish to avoid this problem.

In place of the piece of paper, you need to specify a window in world coordinates. This means that only x values between x_{min} and x_{max} and only y values between y_{min} and y_{max} will be plotted. Because these values are specified by the program in the world coordinates in which the problem is defined, the software can test them and if necessary shift the output to ensure that it is visible. To clip the drawing against this window, you could include extra tests within the DDA algorithm to check each pixel and only illuminate those which lie inside the window. This requires an additional four tests for every pixel and makes the whole process very slow. A little thought makes it clear that this amount of work is quite unnecessary when you are dealing with straight line segments and a rectangular window. If both end points of the line lie within the window, then both mathematics and common sense tell you that the whole line lies within the window and so it should be drawn without any further tests.

Lines which are wholly or partly outside the window require a little more work, and you will need to refer to the figure below to consider this. First consider the y values of the two end points. If both values are less than ymin, then the whole line lies below the window and the entire line is invisible and should not be drawn. Similarly if both are greater than y_{max}, then the whole line lies above the window and should not be drawn.

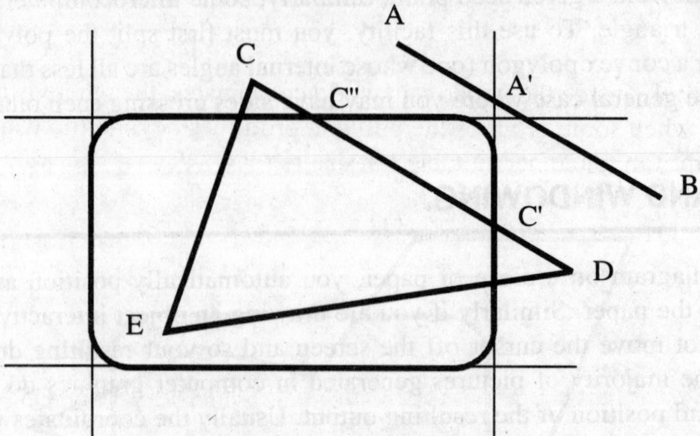

Figure 5.16 *Clipping against a Window*

Lines with both x values less than xmin lie to the left of the window while those with both values greater than x_{max} lie to the right of it. In neither of these cases should the lines be drawn. Once these tests have been applied, you will usually find that large sections of the drawing have now been dealt with and you are left with the comparatively small number of lines, such as AB and CD in the figure, which require further processing. At this stage it is not possible to distinguish between AB which is wholly invisible and CD which has a small visible segment.

To process these lines and draw the visible segments, you must calculate the intersection of each edge of the window in turn with those of the remaining lines which cross it. Consider the edge $x=x_{max}$ and the points A', C' and D' where it intersects the lines AB, CD and DE. AB is now split into the two segments AA' whose y values are both greater than y_{max} and A'B whose x values are both greater than x_{max}. Hence you can now see that it consists of two segments, which are both invisible for different reasons. CD is now split into CC' which requires further processing and C'D which is invisible. DE is now split into the invisible segment DD' and the visible one D'E. A final comparison with the edge $y=y_{max}$ now splits CC' into the invisible segment CC'' and the visible one C''C' and this picture is complete.

There are a number of ways in which these ideas can be implemented. The text by Angell associates parameters IX and IY with each end point and then applies tests to IX and IY which are equivalent to the discussion above. The text by Newman and Sproull is probably designed for low-level programming since it assigns bit patterns to each end point and applies logical operations to them. If x is less than xmin, the first 2 bits are set to 10, if x lies between x_{min} and x_{max} then they are set to 00 and of x is greater than x_{max}, then they are set to 01. The second 2 bits are set according to the value of in the same way. They may then be tested as follows:

If the logical OR of the codes for the two end points is zero, then the codes must both be 0000 and so the line is wholly on the screen. If the logical AND of the codes for the two end points is non-zero, then the line is wholly off the screen and should not be drawn. Otherwise it must be clipped and tested again.

These methods give fast, correct results for diagrams and drawings made up of many individual lines. However when we are dealing with an area such as the interior of a polygon, a slightly different approach is needed.

Polygon Clipping.

If the polygon lies entirely inside the window in world coordinates, then there is no problem. However there are many cases when some or all of the polygon protrudes beyond the window and then care is needed in order to clip it in a manner suitable for shading.

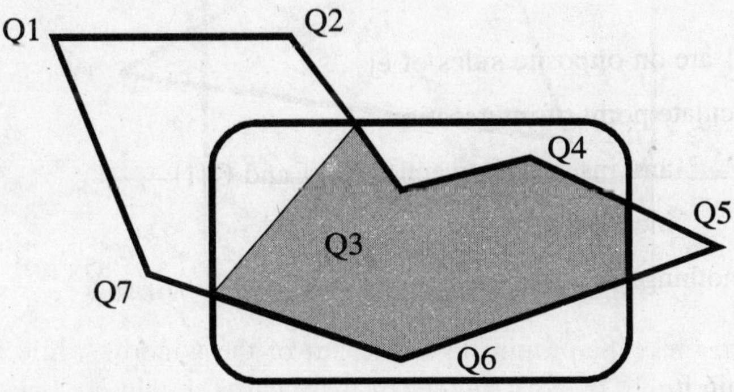

Figure 5.17 Incorrect Polygon Clipping

Using the previous algorithm for line-clipping, it might seem reasonable to clip each side of the polygon in turn against the window, resulting in the example shown in the figure below. These points could then be joined up in order to give the clipped polygon. This would include the dotted line, which is certainly not part of the original polygon and shading this would fail to fill an area in the top left hand corner of the screen. So this method is satisfactory to produce those linear segments of the polygon sides which lie on the screen, but is not suitable to produce the area of intersection of polygon and screen.

It is possible to check whether a corner of the screen lies between two intersection points and inside the polygon and insert this in the array for the new perimeter of the clipped polygon, but it is usually neater and more efficient to use the 'Sutherland-Hodgeman Algorithm', described below. In this case, instead of clipping each side of the polygon in turn against the rectangular window, the algorithm is applied four times and each time the sides of the polygon are clipped against one edge of the window. The next figure shows the first application of this where the polygon used in the previous figure is clipped against the edge e1 (x=xmin).Those parts of the polygon on the shaded side of e1 are outside the window and therefore invisible while those on the other side are visible and must be retained.

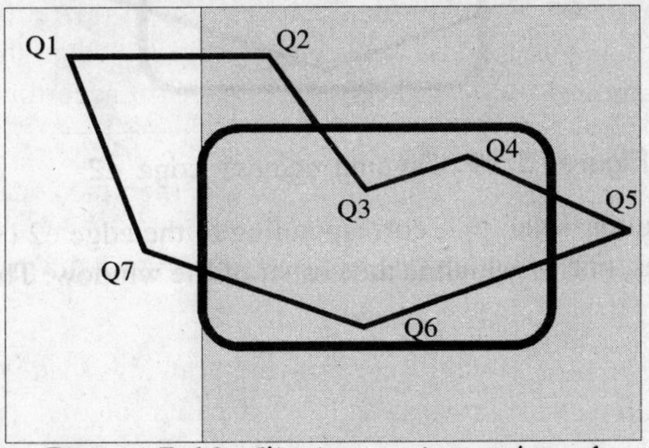

Figure 5.18 Clipping against edge e1

The algorithm can be described as follows:

Set Q{1}=Q{n+1}

For j=1 to 4

For i=2 to n+1

If Q{i-1} and Q{i} are on opposite sides of ej

then calculate point of intersection

and insert it between Q{i-1} and Q{i}

increase n by 1.

else do nothing

If Q{i} is visible

then retain it

else reject it, move all points

and reduce n by 1.

Repeat

Repeat

End

In the above figure, for j=1 you have the situation where Q1 is replaced by a new vertex, Q2 to Q6 are visible and unchanged and Q7 is replaced by a new vertex. In this case, the number of vertices remains the same.

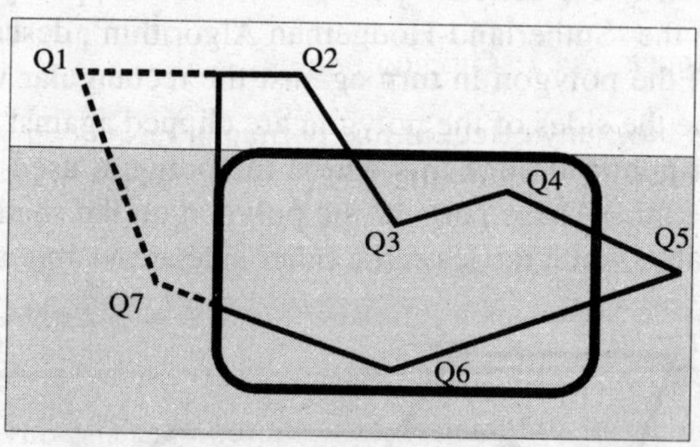

Figure 5.19 Clipping against edge e2

The next figure shows the situation when j=2, corresponding to the edge e2 (y = ymax). Here Q1 and Q2 are replaced by new vertices, one of which is the corner of the window. The remaining vertices are unchanged.

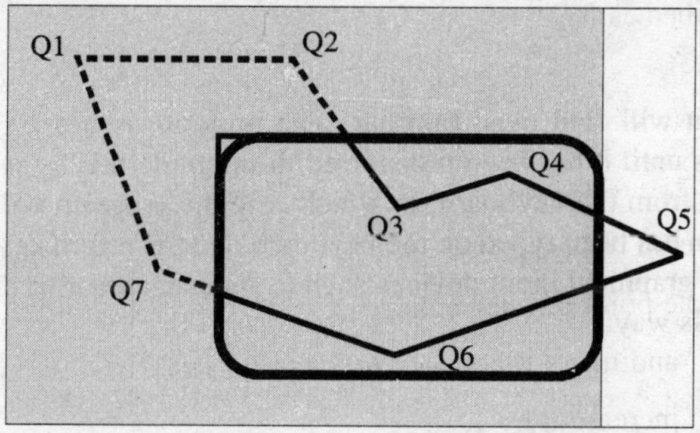

Figure 5.20 *Clipping against edge e3*

When j=3, the clipping is against edge e3. In this case, Q5 has to be replaced by two new vertices, thus increasing the total number of vertices by one.

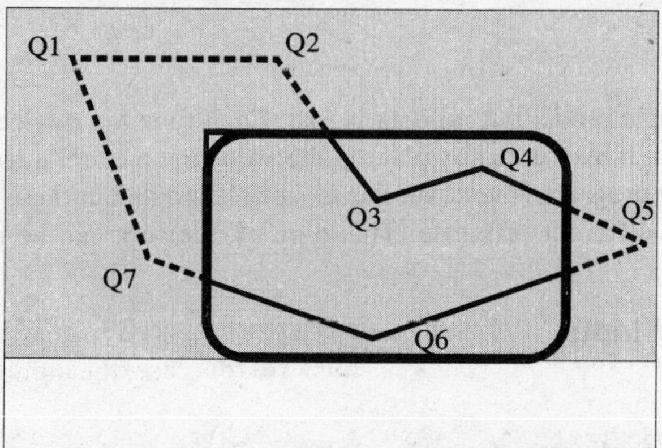

Figure 5.21 *Clipping against edge e4*

The final case when j=4 does not have any effect in this particular case. You should also supply some extra examples for yourselves and work through them to ensure that you have the correct idea.

5.7 INTERACTIVE GRAPHICS.

Most of the programs written today are interactive to some extent. The days when programs were punched on cards and left in a tray to be collected and run by the computer operators, who then returned cards and printout to the users' pigeonholes several hours later, are now past. 'Batch-processing', as this rather slow and tedious process was called, may be a very efficient use of machine time but it is very wasteful of programmers' time, and as the cost of hardware falls and that of personnel rises so installations move from batch to interactive use. Interactive use generally results in a less efficient use of the mainframe computer, but gives the programmer a much faster response time, and so speeds up the development of software.

5.7.1 Modes of Input

1. **Request Mode**

   This is the mode you will find most familiar. The program issues a request for data from a device and then waits until it has been transferred. It might do this by using a 'Read' statement to transfer characters from the keyboard, in which case the program will pause in its execution and wait until the data has been typed on the keyboard and the return key pressed to indicate the end of the input. The graphical input devices such as mouse, cursor or digitising tablet can also be programmed in this way.

2. **Sample Mode**

   In this case the input device sends a constant stream of data to the computer and the program samples these values as and when it is ready. The excess data is overwritten and lost. A digitising tablet may be used in this way - it will continually send the latest coordinates of its puck position to the buffer of the serial port and the program may copy values from this port as often as needed.

3. **Event Mode**

   This is similar to sample mode, but no data is lost. Each time the device transmits a value, the program must respond. It may do so by placing the value in an event queue for later processing, so that the logic of the program is very similar to sample mode, but there may also be some data values which cause a different response. This type of interrupt can be used to provide a very powerful facility.

5.7.2 Classes of Logical Input

1. **Locator**

   This inputs the (x,y) coordinates of a position. It usually comes from a cursor, controlled either by keys or by a mouse, and has to be transferred from Device Coordinates to Normalised Device Coordinates to World Coordinates. If you have several overlapping viewports, they must be ordered so that the one with the highest priority can be used to calculate these transformations. Each pixel position on the screen must correspond to a unique value in world coordinates. It need not remain the same throughout the running of the program, since the priorities of the viewports may be changed. At every moment there must be a single unambiguous path from cursor position to world coordinates.

2. **Pick**

   This allows the user to identify a particular object or segment from all those displayed on the screen. It is usually indicated by moving the cursor until it coincides with the required object, and then performing some other action such as pressing a mouse button or a key on the keyboard to indicate that the required object is now identified. The value transferred to this program is usually a segment identifier.

3. **Choice**

   This works in a very similar manner to the pick input. You now have a limited set of choices, as might be displayed in a menu, and some means of indicating your choice. Only one of the limited list of choices is acceptable as input, any attempt to choose some other segment displayed on the screen will be ignored.

4. **Valuator**

This inputs a single real number by some means, the simplest method being typing it in from the keyboard.

5. **String**

This inputs a string of characters, again the simplest method is to type them in from the keyboard.

6. **Stroke**

This inputs a series of pairs of (x,y) coordinates. The combination of Stroke, Input and Sample Mode from a digitising tablet is a very fast method of input.

Most of the terminals or microcomputers you will meet will have some form of cursor control for graphic input. You can write your programs using which ever combination of logical input class and mode is most convenient. Alternatively, you could ignore all forms of graphic input and merely rely on 'Read' statements and data typed from the keyboard. The choice is yours.

5.7.3 Software Techniques

1. **Locating**

Probably you have all used software in which the cursor is moved around the screen by means of keys or a mouse. The program may well give the impression that the cursor and mouse are linked together so that any movement of the mouse is automatically indicated by movement of the cursor on the screen. In fact, this effect is achieved by means of a graphics program which has to read in the new coordinates indicated by the mouse, delete the previous drawing of the cursor and then redraw it at the new position. This small program runs very quickly and gives the impression of a continuous process.

Usually this software also contains a test for input from the keyboard and when a suitable key is pressed, the current position of the cursor is recorded. This allows fast input of a number of points to form a picture or diagram on the screen. Some means of storing the data and terminating the program is also required.

Such points are recorded to the full accuracy of the screen, which has both advantages and disadvantages. If you are using a digitising tablet instead of a mouse, then the accuracy is even greater and the resulting problems even more extreme. You very seldom want to record information to the nearest 0.1mm, usually to the nearest millimetre is quite sufficient. Problems arise when you want to select the same point a second time. Whatever accuracy you have chosen, you must be able to indicate the point to this accuracy in order to reselect it, as you might need to do if you had several lines meeting at a point. To achieve this more easily, software involving the use of various types of constraint may be used to speed up the input process.

2. **Modular Constraints**

In this case, you should imagine a grid, which may be visible or invisible, placed across the screen. Now, whenever you indicate a position with the cursor, the actual coordinates are replaced by the coordinates of the nearest point on the grid. So to indicate the same point a second time, you merely have to get sufficiently close to the same grid point. Provided the grid allows enough flexibility to choose the shapes required in the diagram, this gives much faster input.

3. **Directional Constraints**

These can be useful when you want some lines to be in a particular direction, such as horizontal or vertical. You can write software to recalculate the coordinates so that a line close to vertical becomes exactly vertical. You can choose whether this is done automatically for every line within a few degrees of vertical or only applied when requested by the user. If the constraint is applied automatically, then you can choose how close the line must be to the required direction before it is moved and how the recalculation is computed. You may wish to move both vertices by a small amount, or one vertex by a larger amount, and if you are only moving one, you must specify some rule or rules to decide which one.

4. **Gravity Field Effect**

The name implies that the line should be visualised as lying at the bottom of a gravity well and points close to the line slide down on to it. As each line is added to the diagram, a small area is defined which surrounds it. When a new point is defined which lies inside the area, its actual coordinates are replaced by the coordinates of the nearest point on the line.

There are two commonly used shapes for this area. In each case, along most of the line, two parallel lines are drawn, one each side of the line and a small distance t from it. In the one shape, each vertex at the end of the line is surrounded by a semi-circle of radius t. In the other shape, each vertex is surrounded by a circle of radius greater than t, giving a dumb-bell shape to the entire area. This second case expresses the philosophy that users are much more likely to want to connect other lines to the vertices than to points along the line.

5. **Scales and Guidelines**

Just as you may use a ruler when measuring distances on a piece of paper, so you may wish to include software to calculate and display a ruler on the screen. The choice of scales and the way in which the ruler is positioned on the screen must be decided when the software is written.

6. **Rubber-banding**

This is name given to the technique where a line connects the previous point to the present cursor position. This line expands or contracts like a rubber band as the cursor is moved. To produce this effect, the lines must be deleted and re-drawn whenever the cursor is moved.

7. **Menus**

Many programs display a menu of choices somewhere on the screen and allow the user to indicate a choice of option by placing the cursor over the desired symbol. Alternatively, the options could be numbered and the choice could be indicated by typing a number on the keyboard. In either case, the resulting action will depend on the program.

8. **Dragging**

Many software packages provide a selection of commonly used shapes, and allow the user to select a shape and use the cursor to drag a copy of the shape to any required position in the drawing. Some packages continually delete and redraw the shape as it is dragged, others only redraw it when the cursor halts or pauses.

9. Inking-in

Another type of software imitates the use of pen or paintbrush in leaving a track as it is drawn across the paper. These routines allow the user to set the width and colour of the pen and some also allow patterned 'inks' in two or more colours. Then as the cursor is moved across the screen, a large number of coordinates are recorded and the lines joining these points are drawn as required.

All these techniques may be coded, using a combination of graphical input and output. The success of such software depends very much on the user-interface. If it is difficult or inconvenient to use, then as soon as something better comes along, the previous software will be ignored. When designing your own graphical packages, you need to have a clear idea of the purpose for which your package is designed and also the habits and experience of the users for whom it is intended.

Exercise

1. If 0 indicates a step of +1 in the x-direction, 1 a step of +1 in both x and y directions and so on, what diagram is produced by the following sequence of plotter-steps ?

   0 6 6 0 0 6 4 4 6 6 4 2 2 4 4 2 0 0 2 2

   The use of these chain-codes to represent line drawings has been used in many applications. In some cases it may be the most efficient way to store diagrams (note that the numbers 0 to 7 can be represented by 3 bits and packed several values per computer word when it is necessary to store them).

References

1. *Rogers and Adams* chapter 1, *Foley et al* section 1.2 and chapter 4, *Hearn and Baker* chapter 2.
2. *Rogers and Adams* section 2-5, *Foley et al* Sections 3.2, 3.3 and 3.14, *Hearn and Baker* chapter 3.
3. *Foley et al* section 3.12.
4. *Rogers and Adams* chapter 2, *Foley et al* sections 5.1 to 5.6, *Hearn and Baker* chapter 5.
5. *Foley et al* sections 3.4 to 3.6, *Hearn and Baker* section 3.11.
6. *Rogers and Adams* section 1-4, *Foley et al* sections 3.8 to 3.11.
7. *Rogers and Adams* section 1-5, *Foley et al* sections 1.3, 4.5, and chapter 8.
8. *Rogers and Adams* chapter 4, *Foley et al* chapter 9, *Hearn and Baker* section 3.7.

6

3D-TRANSFORMATIONS

6.1 POINTS AND LINES

This section covers mathematical tools used in Three Dimensional Computer Graphics (3D Graphics). A 3D graphics program builds a scene composed of three dimensional objects in three dimensional space. Then two dimensional images are produced from the 3D scene. The scene is represented as a data structure in computer memory. The 2D image is typically the picture on the face of a computer monitor.

The 3D objects are composed of points, lines, and polygons. You know what these are, but so that we can start from a common ground, this section reviews these concepts and introduces some of the vocabulary of computer graphics.

Topics:

- Points
- Lines
- Triangles
- Vectors
- Representing points, lines, and vectors

Picture of a Point

A geometrical **point** is a location in space. It has no other characteristics. It has no length, width, or thickness. It is pure location.

The above answer would not help you if you somehow did not already understand the concept of "point". The phrase "location in space" designates the same concept as the word "point". The definition cannot convey a concept you do not already have.

In geometry texts the word *point* is usually not defined. It is regarded as one of the undefined primitives that are used to define other objects. Instead of defining "point" books give examples and hope that you somehow build up the concept from them.

At right is a picture that I hope will clarify this. The picture shows two spires atop a building. The picture is 2D, but think about the actual 3D building. Focus on the spike at the top of the closest spire.

What is the location of the very top of the spike? On the scale of the building, the end of the spike defines an exact location. We can conceptualize that location as a point.

Physical Points

A point is an idealization. On the scale of a building, the end of a spike is small enough to be considered an exact location, a point. But on the scale of your desktop, its end does not exactly define one location. For the scale of a desktop, the spike would have to taper to a pin point. Then, perhaps, you could consider its end to define a point.

But if you put that pin point under a microscope, then for that scale it is again too blunt. It would have to taper further, perhaps to the thickness of a bacterium, before the end could define a point. But now, on the scale of bacteria, the end of the spike is again too thick to exactly define a location.

So, points in 3D space are an idealization. For a computer model of a building, the sharp end of a spike is exact enough to be a point. The edges, planes, and other shapes that make up the building do not need to be specified to any greater accuracy.

Points in Space

In the physical world (the "real world"), the endpoints of the two spikes are at definite locations. Later on, locations will be specified using a coordinate frame. But for now let's just think of points in space. In 3D graphics programs you put points in space, and lines in space, and other things in space. And then project them into a 2D picture.

This mimics what has happened when the picture was produced with a camera. The ends of the spikes in the physical world define two 3D points. The whole scene was projected by a lens onto a 2D sheet of film. The ends of the spikes in the 2D picture define two 2D points.

Lines

In a 2D picture it is often hard to judge depth. When a 2D picture is produced from a 3D scene (either a real scene or a scene in a computer), a great deal of information is lost.

A line segment is the straight path between two points. It has no thickness. There is only one line segment between the two points.

Again, if you did not already have the concept of "line" the above definition would not be enough to learn it. The phrase "straight path" designates the concept that is being defined. In 3D graphics you mostly deal with line segments. In geometry, lines continue without end. A line segment is the part of a line between two points.

In geometry books the world *line* is usually not defined. It (like *point*) is an undefined concept used to define other objects. Books give pictures and examples of lines and hope that somehow you will come to understand what a line is by looking at them.

Often people say "line" when properly they should say "line segment." These notes will do that also, since line segments are so common.

Very Thin Wire

At the scale of the building, a thin wire stretched between the two spikes is a close approximation to a line segment.

Again, this is a matter of scale. The wire is likely to be thicker than a line drawn by a pencil. On your desk the wire is too thick to be considered a line segment. Perhaps a thin, straight pencil line is thin enough to be considered a geometrical line. If that is too thick, then a length of spider silk stretched between two points might work.

But on an architectural level, taught wires can be considered line segments. You could build a geometrical model of the building using line segments to represent edges.

Try This: *The bird is gliding perhaps 50 feet above the building. Mentally draw a triangle that connects the two spikes and the left tip of the bird's wing.*

Triangles

A **triangle** is made by connecting three points in 3D space with line segments. Unless the three points all lie on the same line, three points in space define a unique triangle. Triangles in space are very important in 3D graphics. The 3D objects that make up the scene are constructed out of triangles and other flat polygons.

The triangle in the 2D picture is a projection of the 3D triangle in the scene. The projection distorts the 3D triangle. The 3D triangle is much larger than the 2D triangle, and the angles are different.

Say that a 3D object in the scene is constructed of several triangles. Now project each triangle into a 2D picture. The result is the projected version of the 3D object. The white lattice work on the building is made up of many triangles. The image of the lattice in the picture shows all these triangles projected (by the lens and camera).

Representation

You can think about the points, lines, and plane figures that compose the 3D scene without using a coordinate system. In fact, that is what we have been doing. But in computer graphics we need to represent these objects, somehow, and to manipulate them. To do this, we need a method to represent such objects.

Pick a convenient point in the 3D scene and call it the **origin**. Now define three lines called X, Y, and Z that go through the origin. Usually the three lines are perpendicular to each other. Each line is called an **axis**.

Pick a positive direction for each line. There are several choices here, but let's make the choice shown in the picture.

Now each point of the X axis is a unique distance (positive, negative, or zero) from the origin. For example, the corner of the building that lies on the X axis is at a distance of 8.0 feet (or so) from the origin.

Coordinates

Or you could say that for the endpoint of the spike, y=12.0.

Any point in our 3D scene can be assigned a representation by measuring its distance along the three axes. For these notes (and for many computer graphics books), these three distances are put into a column matrix as follows.

$$\begin{bmatrix} x \\ y \\ z \end{bmatrix}$$

You are probably accustomed to putting the three coordinates into a triple such as (x, y, z). But it will turn out that for computer graphics it is more conventient to put them into a column, as above.

For example, the coordinates of the corner of the building that lies along the X axis are (about):

$$\begin{bmatrix} 8.0 \\ 0.0 \\ 0.0 \end{bmatrix}$$

Little Boxes

In determining coordinates, measure distance along lines that are parallel to the coordinate axes. The lines you use will form a rectangle or the sides of a box.

For example, in the figure, the black dotted lines used for point Q0 form a rectangle. Measuring the sides of the rectangle leads to the coordinates:

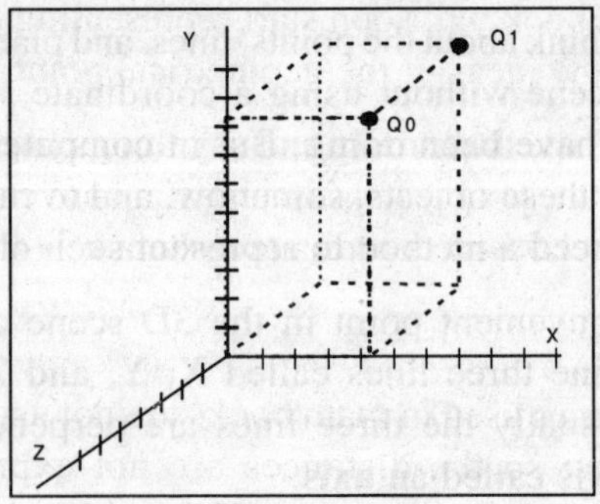

$$\begin{bmatrix} 4.0 \\ 8.0 \\ 0.0 \end{bmatrix}$$

It is harder to figure out the coordinates of Q1. The picture is 2D, but the scene it shows is 3D, so the Z axis is distorted. The dotted lines in the 3D scene form a box. All the angles are 90 degrees.

More Points

Now back to our real-world scene. The white lattice is eight feet long on each side.

Try it: *Make a reasonable guess about the coordinates of the end of the closest spike:*

$$\begin{bmatrix} ? \\ ? \\ ? \end{bmatrix}$$

The Point and its Representation

The column matrix is a mathematical object that **represents** the point using our choosen coordinate frame. The column matrix <u>is not</u> the point. The column matrix and the point are different things. One is used to represent the other, just as your name is used to represent you.

I hope this is obvious, but students who try to skip lightly through he mathematics of computer graphics sometimes are vague about this, to their eventual grief. Your computer graphics book will soon start representing the same point in several different ways. It is vital o keep separated the ideas of the geometrical point, and the several ways it might be represented.

Note: often people speak casually and say things like, "the point (4, 12, -4)," as if the triple of numbers were identical to the point. This is just for convenience. They really should say "the point that is epresented in our choosen coordinate system by (4, 12, -4)."

Another Frame

The coordinate frames used in math books are not usually placed in a real world scene, so the distances are not expressed in any particular unit. When you create your 3D world inside a computer you need to decide on the units you are using.

The picture shows our 3D world with a different coordinate frame placed in it. The points in the world are the same points as before. But now, with a different coordinate frame, they will have different epresentations.

n the previous frame, the point labeled P1 was given the epresentation:

$$\begin{bmatrix} 4.0 \\ 12.0 \\ -4.0 \end{bmatrix}$$

Now, the distances along the axes in the new (green) frame are different. The column matrix that epresents P1 in the new frame is roughly:

$$\begin{bmatrix} -2.0 \\ 16.0 \\ -8.0 \end{bmatrix}$$

The same point has a different representation in each frame. When you represent a point with a column matrix you have to know what frame is being used.

Try this: *Estimate the coordinates of the point P0, on the top edge of the lattice:*

$$\begin{bmatrix} ? \\ ? \\ ? \end{bmatrix}$$

Sunlight

Look at the picture of the building again. The scene is being illuminated by the sun, which is not in the picture. In the scene, sunlight is coming in diagonally from off scene to the left.

Try This: *Mentally sketch some lines in the picture that show light from the sun.*

Vector

As you look at the building, Light is flooding in from the upper left. The picture represents this sunlight as arrows. Although the picture is 2D, try to think of the 3D scene. The direction in which the light is travelling is shown by an arrow. The length of the arrow (let us say) represents the intensity of the light. Although there are several arrows in the picture, any one arrow is enough to represent the light and its intensity.

The direction of the light and its intensity can be represented as a **vector**. A vector is a geometrical object that has two properties: length and direction. Light from the sun has two properties: brightness and direction (we are disregarding color information.) The length of the vector proportional to the brightness of the light.

Wind, also, can be represented as a vector. Wind has direction and speed. A particle of dust travels in the direction of the wind. The length of the vector is proportional to the speed of the dust particle.

A vector does not have a position. The picture shows several arrows that represent the flood of light coming in from the sun. But the arrows could have been drawn anywhere as long as their direction and length was the same.

Representing a Vector

Vectors are used for several purposes in 3D computer graphics. So they need to be represented in a way that programs can manipulate. And, just as you feared, this is done with numbers. The picture now includes our coordinate frame.

A vector is represented with a column matrix (as are points). It is somewhat confusing that both points and vectors are represented with the same thing. But this will prove to be convenient for computer manipulation.

To represent a vector as a column matrix:

1. Choose a coordinate frame.
2. Calculate the X length (positive or negative) from the tail of the vector to the tip.
3. Calculate the Y length (positive or negative) from the tail of the vector to the tip.
4. Calculate the Z length (positive or negative) from the tail of the vector to the tip.
5. Put those three numbers into a column.

A convenient way to do this is to position the tail of the vector at the origin, and then just read off the x, y, z values at the tip.

Try to do this with the picture.

1. For the arrows in the picture, how many feet in the X direction is the tip from the tail? ______
2. How many feet in the Y direction is the tip from the tail? ______
3. How many feet in the Z direction is the tip from the tail? ______

Vectors and Frames

So the vector that gives the intensity and direction of sunlight in the picture is:

$$\begin{bmatrix} 3.0 \\ -4.0 \\ 3.0 \end{bmatrix}$$

The column matrix **represents** the vector using our choosen coordinate frame. The column matrix is not the vector. If we had picked a different coordinate frame, the vector in the physical scene would be the same, but its representation using the new frame would change.

6.2 TRANSFORMATIONS IN 3D

6.2.1 Introduction

Any geometric primitive can be subjected to certain "changes" when inserted into a coordinate system where the primitive will keep its underlying structure but will be moved, scaled and rotated with matrices derived in this document. Those changes are called *transformations* and are quite easy to understand and implement.

Here the three common transformations which is: translation (moving), scaling and rotating will be discussed. I will introduce the 3D versions using 3x3 matrices to begin with and move up to 4x4 matrices when I'm sure the 3x3 versions are understood.

6.2. 2 Transformations

6.2.2.1. Translation

When you move an object in 3D space it's called "translation". If we forget about matrices for a time translation is very simple. If you have a point (x,y) and want to move it dx in the x-axis and dy in the y-axis you do this (which should be no suprise):

$$x' = x + dx \qquad (6.1)$$

$$y' = y + dy \qquad (6.2)$$

The procedure is shown if the following figure:

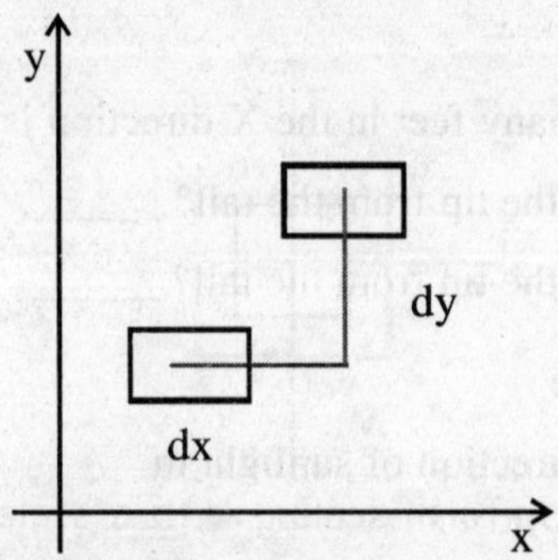

Figure 6.1 : Translation by dx and dy.

Expanding this into 3 dimensions should be straightforward. Now to put those numbers into a standard matrix is quite easy too, its just to 4x1 matrices representing column vectors:

$$\begin{bmatrix} dx \\ dy \\ dz \end{bmatrix} + \begin{bmatrix} x \\ y \\ z \end{bmatrix} = \begin{bmatrix} x+dx \\ y+dy \\ z+dz \end{bmatrix} = \begin{bmatrix} x' \\ y' \\ z' \end{bmatrix} \qquad (6.3)$$

The above formula is not used by many programmers however. This has a very logical reason which I'll explain later when the other transformations has been explained.

Composing Translations

Now, what happens if you move an object in one direction and move it in another direction afterwards, That would be expressed in matrices like this:

$$\begin{bmatrix} x \\ y \\ z \end{bmatrix} + \begin{bmatrix} d_x \\ d_y \\ d_z \end{bmatrix} + \begin{bmatrix} d_{x1} \\ d_{y1} \\ d_{z1} \end{bmatrix} = \begin{bmatrix} x+d_x+d_{x1} \\ y+d_y+d_{y1} \\ z+d_z+d_{z1} \end{bmatrix} \qquad (6.4)$$

The two translations can be composed into a single matrix looking like this:

$$\begin{bmatrix} d_x \\ d_y \\ d_z \end{bmatrix} + \begin{bmatrix} d_{x1} \\ d_{y1} \\ d_{z1} \end{bmatrix} = \begin{bmatrix} d_x+d_{x1} \\ d_y+d_{y1} \\ d_z+d_{z1} \end{bmatrix} \qquad (6.5)$$

If you a point the that matrix you will get the same result as we got before. So if you have several translations you can combine them into one single matrix, that proves to be very usefull!

6.2.2.2. Scaling

Scaling is to increase or decrease the size of an object. For example, if you have the unit cube (length = depth = height = 1) and you take one corner and pull it until the lengt, depth and height is 2 you have succesfully scaled the unit cube by a factor 2 for every axis. This is shown in this figure:

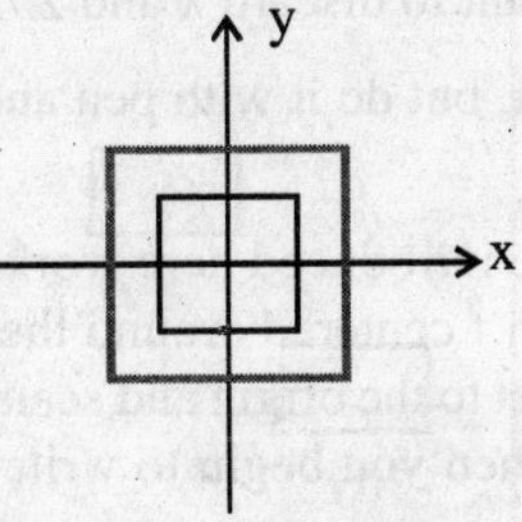

Figure 6.2: Uniform scaling with a scale factor of 2.

If we have a line segment with a length of 1 and want's to make it n times as long we multiply the length with n. That applies to all the axes and gives us the followind equation for scaling:

$$x' = x \cdot n \tag{6.6}$$

$$y' = y \cdot n \tag{6.7}$$

This can also be expressed using matrix math - this time just a litlle trickier. One of the things I found most difficult when learning matrix transformations was where to put the numbers to achive the desired effect. I'll start by showing you the scaling matrix and then I'll descripe how you can determine why the numbers are put that way: The scaling matrix is:

$$\begin{bmatrix} s_x & 0 & 0 \\ 0 & s_y & 0 \\ 0 & 0 & x_z \end{bmatrix} \tag{6.8}$$

An important thing you should note is that I've substituted my previus scale factor 'n' by seperate scale factors for each axis. That way you can make your scaling non-uniform - that is, different for each axis.

Now how can I derive that matrix? It's actually pretty basic if you can memorize the multiplication algorithm for matrices. The following formula shows the math;

$$\begin{bmatrix} s_x & 0 & 0 \\ 0 & s_y & 0 \\ 0 & 0 & x_z \end{bmatrix} \times \begin{bmatrix} x \\ y \\ z \end{bmatrix} = \begin{bmatrix} x.s_x + y.0 + z.0 \\ x.0 + y.s_y + z.0 \\ x.0 + y.0 + z.s_z \end{bmatrix} = \begin{bmatrix} x.s_x \\ y.s_y \\ z.s_z \end{bmatrix} \tag{6.9}$$

The result is excactly as we expected it to be right? It's a bit hard to explain how that could increase you understanding on how matrices work but I'll try anyway. If you don't get my point I strongly advice you to sit down with pen and paper and perform the multiplication yourself! If you want to calculate the x scale you must perform the matrix multiplication which results in:

$$x \cdot s_x + y \cdot 0 + z \cdot 0 = x \cdot s_x \tag{6.10}$$

So you have to include the y and z coordinates as well, but since you only want to scale the x axis you set the other values to zero. When you wan't to calculate the new y value you must include x and z too, but as we did with y and z we want to discard x and z. That's acomplished by making the values zero.

I don't know if you got my point, but do it with pen and paper if you have problems getting it right in your head :)

One more thing. The scaling I've introduced here works relative to the origin, that may or may not be what you want. If your object isn't centered around the origin, and you wan't a scaling as though you were, you must translate the object to the origin and scale it. You could also use a local coordinatesystem which Is what you want to do when you begin to write more advanced 3D programs.

Composing Scales

Scaling matrices can be composed just like the translation matrices, let's look at a situation where we scale a point my a matrix and then scale it with another:

$$\begin{bmatrix} s_{x1} & 0 & 0 \\ 0 & s_{y1} & 0 \\ 0 & 0 & s_{z1} \end{bmatrix} \times \left(\begin{bmatrix} s_x & 0 & 0 \\ 0 & s_y & 0 \\ 0 & 0 & s_z \end{bmatrix} \times \begin{bmatrix} x \\ y \\ z \end{bmatrix} \right) = \begin{bmatrix} x \cdot s_x \cdot s_{x1} \\ y \cdot s_y \cdot s_{y1} \\ z \cdot s_z \cdot s_{z1} \end{bmatrix} \qquad (6.11)$$

Now let's see if we can combine the two scaling matrices before multiplying with the point.

$$\begin{bmatrix} s_{x1} & 0 & 0 \\ 0 & s_{y1} & 0 \\ 0 & 0 & s_{z1} \end{bmatrix} \times \begin{bmatrix} s_x & 0 & 0 \\ 0 & s_y & 0 \\ 0 & 0 & s_z \end{bmatrix} = \begin{bmatrix} s_x \cdot s_{x1} & 0 & 0 \\ 0 & s_y \cdot s_{y1} & 0 \\ 0 & 0 & s_x \cdot s_{z1} \end{bmatrix} \qquad (6.12)$$

If you multiply this matrix with a point you get the same result as the one we began with.

6.2.2.3. Rotation

The last of the three transformations which I'll explain here is rotation. The mathematical definition is this:

$$x' = x \cdot \cos(V) - y \cdot \sin(V) \qquad (6.13)$$

$$y' = x \cdot \sin(V) - y \cdot \cos(V) \qquad (6.14)$$

Expanding to 3D is easy, but I will wait until I introduce the matrices to show the full 3D rotation formula.

About the z axis

The matrix for rotating about the z-axis can be thought of as a basic 2D rotation, the z value for the object never changes. (Think it through!). Deriving the matrix is then done easely using the matrix knowledge introduced in the scaling section. We see that in computing the x-coordinate we must multiply x with the cosine to the angle and substract y multiplied by the sine to the angle. this can be shown as:

$$x' = (x \cdot \cos(V)) + (-y \cdot \sin(V)) + 0 \cdot z \qquad (6.15)$$

You should now be able to see the connection to the matrix multiplication algorithm and derive the matrix. The same is applied to the y coordinate giving the following matrix for rotation about the z-axis.

$$R_z = \begin{bmatrix} \cos(V) & -\sin(V) & 0 \\ \sin(V) & \cos(V) & 0 \\ 0 & 0 & 1 \end{bmatrix} \quad (6.16)$$

Now that wasn't so hard was it?

About the y axis

When you wan't to rotate about the y axis you do virtually the same as you did when rotating about the z axis. This this you discard the y coordinates and look at the z axis like is was the y axis. The rotation matrix is:

$$R_y = \begin{bmatrix} \cos(V) & 0 & \sin(V) \\ 0 & 1 & 0 \\ -\sin(V) & 0 & \cos(V) \end{bmatrix} \quad (6.17)$$

About the x axis

Again you look at the rotation about the z axis, this time the x coordinates are discarded resulting in the following matrix:

$$R_x = \begin{bmatrix} 1 & 0 & 0 \\ 0 & \cos(V) & -\sin(V) \\ 0 & \sin(V) & \cos(V) \end{bmatrix} \quad (6.18)$$

That should do the job.

Dependency of Position

You probably all know what It'll look like if we rotate an object centered about the origin with, let's say 45 degrees - but if we rotate an object about the z axis using the derived matrix and the object is translated away from the origin we get a result similar to this figure.

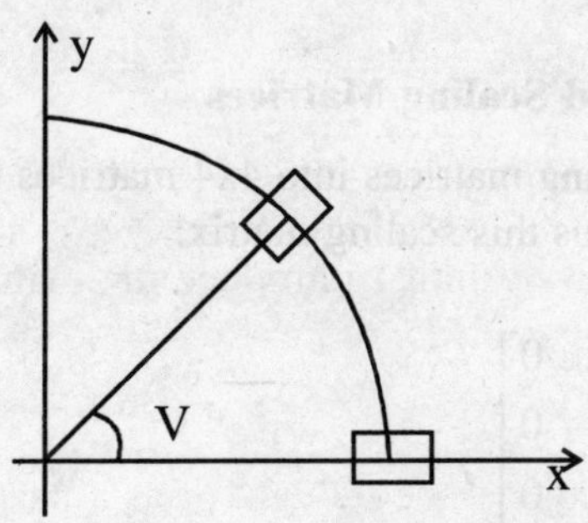

Figure 6.3: Rotating an object not cantered at the origin.

The result may not be the one we expected and it's important to remember that the position of the object relative to the coordinate systems origin plays an important role in the rotation procedure. Just like the scaling problem you will have to translate the object to the origin or use some sort of local coordinatesystem.

Composing Rotations

Several rotations can be composed into a single matrix like scaling and translation, I'll give you an example. First I'll rotate a point V degrees about the z axis and the V_1 degrees about the y axis. Using several matrices we get this result:

$$\begin{bmatrix} \cos(V_1) & 0 & \sin(V_1) \\ 0 & 1 & 0 \\ -\sin(V_1) & 0 & \cos(V_1) \end{bmatrix} \times \left(\begin{bmatrix} \cos(V) & -\sin(V) & 0 \\ \sin(V) & \cos(V) & 0 \\ 0 & 0 & 1 \end{bmatrix} \times \begin{bmatrix} x \\ y \\ z \end{bmatrix} \right)$$

$$= \begin{bmatrix} \cos(V_1) & 0 & \sin(V_1) \\ 0 & 1 & 0 \\ -\sin(V_1) & 0 & \cos(V_1) \end{bmatrix} \times \begin{bmatrix} x \cdot \cos(V) - y \cdot \sin(V) \\ x \cdot \sin(V) + y \cdot \cos(V) \\ 1 \end{bmatrix}$$

$$= \begin{bmatrix} (x \cdot \cos(V) - y \cdot \sin(V)) \cdot \cos(V_1) + \sin(V_1) \\ x \cdot \sin(V) + y \cdot \cos(V) \\ (x \cdot \cos(V) - y \cdot \sin(V)) \cdot (-\sin(V_1)) + \cos(V_1) \end{bmatrix} \quad (6.19)$$

That was extremely messy. Now if you compose the two rotation matrices you should end up with the same result.

6.2.3 Homogeneus Coordinate System

We know that a translation matrix can be combined with a translation matrix, a scaling matrix with a scaling matrix and a rotation matrix with a rotation matrix. Since scaling and rotation matrices both are 3x3 matrices they can be combined as well, that is you can combine several scaling matrices with several rotation matrices. That's very useful since you can precalculate very advanced transformation and just use a single matrix to perform them at runtime. But it would be even more usefull if we could combine translation matrices with them too. But since translation matrices are added together it's a no can-do. The solution to this is *homogeneous* coordinates. The trick is to make all the transformation into 4x4 matrices instead.

Expanding the Rotation and Scaling Matrices

Making the rotation and scaling matrices into 4x4 matrices is very easy, you just add another column and another row. That gives us this scaling matrix:

$$\begin{bmatrix} s_x & 0 & 0 & 0 \\ 0 & s_y & 0 & 0 \\ 0 & 0 & s_z & 0 \\ 0 & 0 & 0 & 1 \end{bmatrix} \quad (6.20)$$

and the following rotation matrices. (It's easy to add another row and column so I'll only show the matric for a rotation about the x axis).

$$\begin{bmatrix} 1 & 0 & 0 & 0 \\ 0 & \cos(V) & -\sin(V) & 0 \\ 0 & \sin(V) & \cos(V) & 0 \\ 0 & 0 & 0 & 1 \end{bmatrix} \tag{6.21}$$

If you use 4x4 matrices you must store a point in a 4x1 matrix too, our new point looks like this:

$$\begin{bmatrix} x \\ y \\ z \\ W \end{bmatrix} \tag{6.22}$$

As you can see the fourth coordinate (called W) is preserved in both the rotation and the scaling matrix, we don't use it here.

The Translation Matrix Expanded

Expanding the translation matrix to our new 4x4 size is a bit tricky but if you have a good understanding of the matrices you can figure it out. We don't want to multiply our point with a scalar, we wan't to add something to it. So we must preserve the (x,y,z,W) components. That's done by adding 1's in a diagonal. Next we want to add a scalar to the coordinates. Since we have to multiply the matrices together in a (xa+yb+zc+Wd) fashion we can use the fourth row. Making W one in our point we get the correct result (x+d). If you didn't understand it you should do alot of translations on paper then you'll see the light :). The translation matrix in homogeneus coordinates is:

$$\begin{bmatrix} 1 & 0 & 0 & d_x \\ 0 & 1 & 0 & d_y \\ 0 & 0 & 1 & d_z \\ 0 & 0 & 0 & 1 \end{bmatrix} \tag{6.23}$$

It's really quite simple don't you think?.

Exercises

1. Two fundamental objects in geometry are points and lines. What are they?
2. What is a point?
3. If you had the spike lying in front of you on your desk, would you consider its end to be a point?
4. Where, in space, is the end of the more distant spike?
5. What is the distance between the two points at the ends of the spikes?
6. Could you stretch a length of wire between the two points?
7. Do you need a coordinate frame (a system of labeling points with x, y, and z coordinates)

to talk about points, lines, and plane figures?

8. The origin is at a height of zero. About how high is the end point of the closest spike?

9. Are the distances measured along the coordinate axes in feet or in meters?

10. Do you suspect that a computer graphics program needs to represent light intensity and direction?

7 COMPUTER GRAPHICS USING C LANGUAGE

We will restrict our discussion on Graphics in C Language to 16 bit C programming and MS DOS environment. In a C Program first of all you need to initialize the graphics drivers on the computer. This is done using the initgraph method provided in graphics.h library. In the next few pages we will discuss graphics.h library in details. Important functions in graphic.h library will be discuees in details and samples programmes will be provided to show the power of C programming language.

7.1 GRAPHICS MODE INITIALIZATION

First of all wc have to call the initgraph function that will intialize the graphics mode on the computer. initigraph have the following prototype.

void initgraph(int far *graphdriver, int far *graphmode, char far *pathtodriver);

Initgraph initializes the graphics system by loading a graphics driver from disk (or validating a registered driver) then putting the system into

graphics mode.Initgraph also resets all graphics settings (color, palette, current position, viewport, etc.) to their defaults, then resets graphresult to 0.

*graphdriver

Integer that specifies the graphics driver to be used. You can give graphdriver a value using a constant of the graphics_drivers enumeration type.

*graphmode

Integer that specifies the initial graphics mode (unless *graphdriver = DETECT). If *graphdriver = DETECT, initgraph sets *graphmode to the highest resolution available for the detected driver. You can give *graphmode a value using a constant of the graphics_modes enumeration type.

*pathtodriver

Specifies the directory path where initgraph looks for graphics drivers (*.BGI) first.

1. If they're not there, initgraph looks in the current directory.

2. If pathtodriver is null, the driver files must be in the current directory.

*graphdriver and *graphmode must be set to valid graphics_drivers and graphics_mode values or you'll get unpredictable results. (The exception is graphdriver = DETECT.)

After a call to initgraph, *graphdriver is set to the current graphics driver, and *graphmode is set to the current graphics mode. You can tell initgraph to use a particular graphics driver and mode, or to autodetect the attached video adapter at run time and pick the corresponding driver. If you tell initgraph to autodetect, it calls detectgraph to select a graphics driver and mode.

Normally, initgraph loads a graphics driver by allocating memory for the driver (through _graphgetmem), then loading the appropriate .BGI file from disk.As an alternative to this dynamic loading scheme, you can link a graphics driver file (or several of them) directly into your executable program file.

Here is a sample program that initializes the graphics mode in C Language.

```
#include <graphics.h>
#include <stdlib.h>
#include <stdio.h>
#include <conio.h>
int main(void)
{
/* request auto detection */
  int gdriver = DETECT, gmode, errorcode;
/* initialize graphics mode */
  initgraph(&gdriver, &gmode, "");
/* read result of initialization */
  errorcode = graphresult();
if (errorcode != grOk) /* an error occurred */
  {
    printf("Graphics error: %s\n", grapherrormsg(errorcode));
    printf("Press any key to halt:");
    getch();
    exit(1); /* return with error code */
  }
/* draw a line */
  line(0, 0, getmaxx(), getmaxy());
/* clean up */
  getch();
  closegraph();
  return 0;
}
```

The graphics programming in C language is discussed in brief to provide an over view to the beginner.

```
/* Sample program to draw a circle*/
#include<graphics.h>
#include<conio.h>
main()
{
 int gd=DETECT,gm;
 initgraph(&gd,&gm,""); /* initialization of graphic mode */
 circle(150,150,100);
 getch();
 closegraph(); /* Restore orignal screen mode */
}
/* End of program */
```

Normally the screen which u view in DOS is in the text mode which means it is meant for text. And for graphics u need to initialize graphics mode. And for this to happen u need to include graphics.h?.

```
circle(x coordinate ,y coordinate , radius);
```

The circle command takes a X coordinate which means Vertical axis and Y coordinate which means Horizontal axis. And the last one is the radius of the circle. closegraph();

With out this function the screen mode will still remain in graphic mode and when u come out, to DOS u will see a different screen, which is not in the text mode.

```
/*A program to draw a space with stars*/
#include<graphics.h>
main()
{
  int gd=DETECT,gm;
  int i,x,y;
  initgraph(&gd,&gm,"");
  line(0,0,640,0);
  line(0,0,0,480);
  line(639,0,639,480);
  line(639,479,0,479);
  for(i=0;i<=1000;i++)
  {
   x=rand()%639;
   y=rand()%480;
   putpixel(x,y,15);
  }
  getch();
  closegraph();
```

```
}
/* End of program */
/*Here a sample program to illustrate how to use BARS which are used for visual statistics */
#include<graphics.h>
main() {
  int gd=DETECT,gm,maxx,maxy,x,y,button;
  initgraph(&gd,&gm,"");
  line(80,150,200,150);
  line(80,150,80,50);
  settextstyle(1,HORIZ_DIR,1);
  outtextxy(100,153,"<-X axis");
  settextstyle(1,VERT_DIR,1);
  outtextxy(60,50,"<-Y axis");
  bar(100,100,120,150);
  bar(130,120,150,150);
  getch();
  closegraph();
}
```

7.2 MINIMUM DISTANCE BETWEEN A POINT AND A LINE

This note describes the technique and gives the solution to finding the shortest distance from a point to a line or line segment. The equation of a line defined through two points **P1** (x1,y1) and **P2** (x2,y2) is

P = P1 + u (P2 - P1)

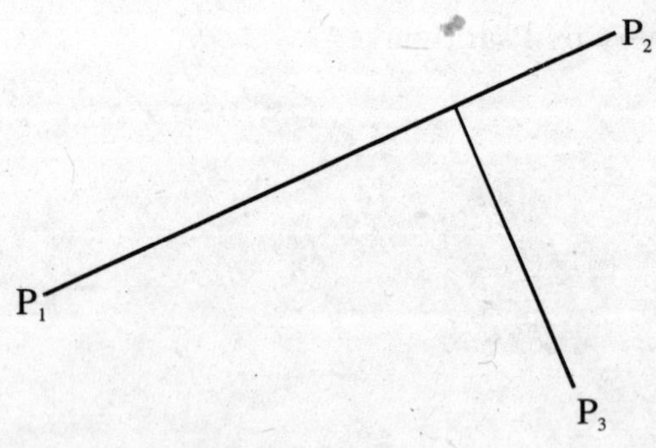

The point **P3** (x3,y3) is closest to the line at the tangent to the line which passes through **P3**, that is, the dot product of the tangent and line is 0, thus

(P3 - P) dot **(P2 - P1)** = 0

Substituting the equation of the line gives

[**P3** - **P1** - u(**P2** - **P1**)] dot (**P2** - **P1**) = 0

Solving this gives the value of u

$$u = \frac{(x3 - x1)(x2 - x1) + (y3 - y1)(y2 - y1)}{\|p2 - p1\|^2}$$

Substituting this into the equation of the line gives the point of intersection (x,y) of the tangent as

x = x1 + u (x2 - x1)

y = y1 + u (y2 - y1)

The distance therefore between the point **P3** and the line is the distance between (x,y) above and **P3**.

Notes

- The only special testing for a software implementation is to ensure that **P1** and **P2** are not coincident (denominator in the equation for u is 0)
- If the distance of the point to a line segment is required then it is only necessary to test that u lies between 0 and 1.
- The solution is similar in higher dimensions.

Source code

```
//================
//
// DistancePointLine Unit Test
// Copyright (c) 2002, All rights reserved
//
// Damian Coventry
// Tuesday, 16 July 2002
//
// Implementation of theory by Paul Bourke
//
//================
#include <stdio.h>
#include <math.h>
typedef struct tagXYZ
{
 float X, Y, Z;
}
XYZ;
float Magnitude( XYZ *Point1, XYZ *Point2 )
{
 XYZ Vector;
 Vector.X = Point2->X - Point1->X;
 Vector.Y = Point2->Y - Point1->Y;
 Vector.Z = Point2->Z - Point1->Z;
 return (float)sqrt( Vector.X * Vector.X + Vector.Y * Vector.Y + Vector.Z * Vector.Z );
}
```

```
int DistancePointLine( XYZ *Point, XYZ *LineStart, XYZ *LineEnd, float *Distance )
{
 float LineMag;
 float U;
 XYZ Intersection;
 LineMag = Magnitude( LineEnd, LineStart );
 U = ( ( ( Point->X - LineStart->X ) * ( LineEnd->X - LineStart->X ) ) +
 ( ( Point->Y - LineStart->Y ) * ( LineEnd->Y - LineStart->Y ) ) +
 ( ( Point->Z - LineStart->Z ) * ( LineEnd->Z - LineStart->Z ) ) ) /
 ( LineMag * LineMag );

 if( U < 0.0f || U > 1.0f )
 return 0; // closest point does not fall within the line segment
 Intersection.X = LineStart->X + U * ( LineEnd->X - LineStart->X );
 Intersection.Y = LineStart->Y + U * ( LineEnd->Y - LineStart->Y );
 Intersection.Z = LineStart->Z + U * ( LineEnd->Z - LineStart->Z );
 *Distance = Magnitude( Point, &Intersection );
 return 1;
}
void main( void )
{
 XYZ LineStart, LineEnd, Point;
 float Distance;
 LineStart.X = 50.0f; LineStart.Y = 80.0f; LineStart.Z = 300.0f;
 LineEnd.X = 50.0f; LineEnd.Y = -800.0f; LineEnd.Z = 1000.0f;
 Point.X = 20.0f; Point.Y = 1000.0f; Point.Z = 400.0f;
 if( DistancePointLine( &Point, &LineStart, &LineEnd, &Distance ) )
 printf( "closest point falls within line segment, distance = %f\n", Distance );
 else
 printf( "closest point does not fall within line segment\n" );
 LineStart.X = 0.0f; LineStart.Y = 0.0f; LineStart.Z = 50.0f;
 LineEnd.X = 0.0f; LineEnd.Y = 0.0f; LineEnd.Z = -50.0f;
 Point.X = 10.0f; Point.Y = 50.0f; Point.Z = 10.0f;
 if( DistancePointLine( &Point, &LineStart, &LineEnd, &Distance ) )
 printf( "closest point falls within line segment, distance = %f\n", Distance );
 else
 printf( "closest point does not fall within line segment\n" );
}
```

7.3 THE SHORTEST LINE BETWEEN TWO LINES IN 3D

Two lines in 3 dimensions generally don't intersect at a point, they may be parallel (no intersections) or they may be coincident (infinite intersections) but most often only their projection onto a plane intersect.. When they don't exactly intersect at a point they can be connected by a line segment, the shortest line segment is unique and is often considered to be their intersection in 3D.

The following will show how to compute this shortest line segment that joins two lines in 3D, it will as a biproduct identify parrallel lines. In what follows a line will be defined by two points lying on it, a point on line "a" defined by points P_1 and P_2 has an equation $P_a = P_1 + mu_a (P_2 - P_1)$ similarly a point on a second line "b" defined by points P_4 and P_4 will be written as $P_b = P_3 + mu_b (P_4 - P_3)$.

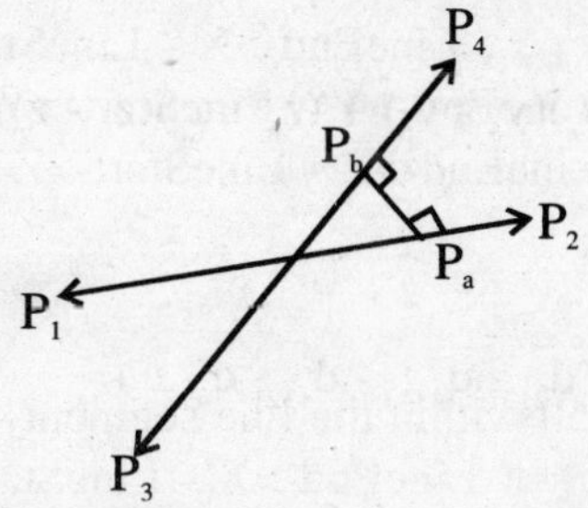

The values of mu_a and mu_b range from negative to positive infinity. The line segments between P_1 P_2 and P_3 P_4 have their corresponding mu between 0 and 1.

There are two approaches to finding the shortest line segment between lines "a" and "b". The first is to write down the length of the line segment joining the two lines and then find the minimum. That is, minimise the following

$$\| P_b - P_a \|^2$$

Substituting the equations of the lines gives

$$\| P_1 - P_3 + mu_a (P_2 -P_1) - mu_b (P_4 - P_3) \|^2$$

The above can then be expanded out in the (x,y,z) components. There are conditions to be met at the minimum, the derivative with respect to mu_a and mu_b must be zero. Note: it is easy to convince oneself that the above function only has one minima and no other minima or maxima. These two equations can then be solved for mu_a and mu_b, the actual intersection points found by substituting the values of mu into the original equations of the line.

An alternative approach but one that gives the exact same equations is to realise that the shortest line segment between the two lines will be perpendicular to the two lines. This allows us to write two equations for the dot product as

$$(P_a - P_b) \text{ dot } (P_2 - P_1) = 0$$

$$(P_a - P_b) \text{ dot } (P_4 - P_3) = 0$$

Expanding these given the equation of the lines

$$(P_1 - P_3 + mu_a (P_2 -P_1) - mu_b (P_4 - P_3)) \text{ dot }$$
$$(P_2 - P_1) = 0$$

$$(P_1 - P_3 + mu_a (P_2 -P_1) - mu_b (P_4 - P_3)) \text{ dot }$$
$$(P_4 - P_3) = 0$$

Expanding these in terms of the coordinates (x,y,z) is a nightmare but the result is as follows

$d_{1321} + mu_a\, d_{2121} - mu_b$

$d_{4321} = 0$

$d_{1343} + mu_a\, d_{4321} - mu_b$

$d_{4343} = 0$

where

$$d_{mnop} = (x_m - x_n)(x_o - x_p) + (y_m - y_n)(y_o - y_p) + (z_m - z_n)(z_o - z_p)$$

Note that $d_{mnop} = d_{opmn}$

Finally, solving for mu_a gives

$$mu_a = (\, d_{1343}\, d_{4321} - d_{1321}\, d_{4343}\,) \,/\, (\, d_{2121}\, d_{4343} - d_{4321}\, d_{4321}\,)$$

and backsubstituting gives mu_b

$$mu_b = (\, d_{1343} + mu_a\, d_{4321}\,) \,/\, d_{4343}$$

```
typedef struct {
   double x,y,z;
} XYZ;
```

```
/*
   Calculate the line segment PaPb that is the shortest route between
   two lines P1P2 and P3P4. Calculate also the values of mua and mub where
      Pa = P1 + mua (P2 - P1)
      Pb = P3 + mub (P4 - P3)
   Return FALSE if no solution exists.
*/
int LineLineIntersect(
   XYZ p1,XYZ p2,XYZ p3,XYZ p4,XYZ *pa,XYZ *pb,
   double *mua, double *mub)
{
   XYZ p13,p43,p21;
   double d1343,d4321,d1321,d4343,d2121;
   double numer,denom;

   p13.x = p1.x - p3.x;
   p13.y = p1.y - p3.y;
   p13.z = p1.z - p3.z;
   p43.x = p4.x - p3.x;
   p43.y = p4.y - p3.y;
   p43.z = p4.z - p3.z;
   if (ABS(p43.x) < EPS && ABS(p43.y) < EPS && ABS(p43.z) < EPS)
      return(FALSE);
   p21.x = p2.x - p1.x;
```

```
    p21.y = p2.y - p1.y;
    p21.z = p2.z - p1.z;
    if (ABS(p21.x) < EPS && ABS(p21.y) < EPS && ABS(p21.z) < EPS)
       return(FALSE);

    d1343 = p13.x * p43.x + p13.y * p43.y + p13.z * p43.z;
    d4321 = p43.x * p21.x + p43.y * p21.y + p43.z * p21.z;
    d1321 = p13.x * p21.x + p13.y * p21.y + p13.z * p21.z;
    d4343 = p43.x * p43.x + p43.y * p43.y + p43.z * p43.z;
    d2121 = p21.x * p21.x + p21.y * p21.y + p21.z * p21.z;

    denom = d2121 * d4343 - d4321 * d4321;
    if (ABS(denom) < EPS)
       return(FALSE);
    numer = d1343 * d4321 - d1321 * d4343;

    *mua = numer / denom;
    *mub = (d1343 + d4321 * (*mua)) / d4343;

    pa->x = p1.x + *mua * p21.x;
    pa->y = p1.y + *mua * p21.y;
    pa->z = p1.z + *mua * p21.z;
    pb->x = p3.x + *mub * p43.x;
    pb->y = p3.y + *mub * p43.y;
    pb->z = p3.z + *mub * p43.z;

    return(TRUE);
}
```

7.4 GRAPHICS LIBRARAY IN C/C++ PROGRAMMING

Graphics library provided by borland C is most widely used library for graphics programming. Mostly this graphics library is restricted to be used under 16 bit C programming and MS DOS environment. As discussed earlier that first of all you need to initialize the graphics drivers on the computer. This is done using the initgraph() method provided in graphics.h library. graphics.h is used to include the reference to the graphics library, but actual graphics library can be found in lib directory with the name of graphics.lib. In Dev C++ there is no default graphics library, but there are some third party graphics libraries to be used with Dev C++. You can download this library here, after downloading the library you can read through the manual and copy all the files at their desired locations. Also you will have to add reference to this graphics library in your projects or programs.

Adding the graphics.h in your C programs

If you are using borland C/C++ compiler to program, then you will have to follow these simple steps in orderd to get your C or C++ program running in graphics mode.

- First you will need to add #include <graphics.h> reference at the top of you C/C++ program.
- Next step is to initialize the graphics environment. This can be achieved using the function

  void far initgraph(int far *driver, int far *mode, char far *path)

- Here path is the actual path to the graphics library. You can give the path to this library by giving the complete path, like "C:\\TC\\BGI", where BGI is the graphics library directory.
- Afeter initializing the graphics mode you can check for any error which may happen while initializing the graphics mode. The function used to find out any errors is int errorcode = graphresult() which returns the error code for the specific error.
- If you pass this errorcode to grapherrormsg() function the, it will return the complete description of the error message. And if the errorcode==grOk the you are on the way to develop your first graphics program using C/C++.

If you are using Dev C++ compiler for your graphcis programs then you can follow these simple steps to configure your environment for graphics programming.

7.5 SIMPLE GRAPHICS FUNCTIONS

I am providing few functions here with some description to make you start with graphcis programming.

Function circle

Draws the circle on the screen using a point(x,y) and the radius for the circle.

void far circle(int x, int y, int radius)

Function line

This function draws a line in the graphics mode.

void far line(int startx, int starty, int endx, int endy)

Function outtext

Displays a text string on the grpahics screen.

void far outtext(char far *str)

Function outtextxy

Displays the text at a specified position in graphics mode.

void far outtext(int x, int y, char *str)

Function rectangle

Draws a rectangular box on the screen using the points given in the parameters.

void far rectangle(int left, int top, int right, int bottom)

8 QUESTIONS

QUESTION BANK

Very Short Type Questions

1. What, in outline, are the main types of scan conversion.
2. Briefly, in conceptual terms, how can raster ops enable fast scrolling?
3. For each of the two types of multiplication of two vectors, give examples of important applications of them in computer graphics
4. What is Gouraud shading, and what does it achieve (in the context of assuming diffuse reflection)?
5. What is specular reflection, and how is it usually modeled?
6. What does ray tracing involve?
7. Outline what ray tracing achieves, and its limitations?
8. Vector scaling is multiplication of a vector by a scalar. Using vector scaling, give a formula for a vector **s** which is a weighted average of three vectors **p**, **q** and **r**.
9. An image contains a regular hexagon with length of side 1. Note that you can divide a regular hexagon into six equilateral triangles each with length of side 1.
10. Show reasoning not involving trigonometry which derives a formula for the distance between two opposite sides of the hexagon
11. Name, draw or describe two well-known polyhedrons of cubic symmetry which, from some viewpoints, have a hexagonal outline
12. How could you model polyhedron P in a computer graphics program, using an iteration corresponding to its symmetry to avoid unnecessary repetition?
13. Outline the different types of method for scan-conversion of filled areas

14. What main factors affect the time taken to scan-convert a filled area?
15. Outline EITHER raster-ops or 3D graphics hardware
16. Briefly, in conceptual terms, how can raster ops enable fast scrolling.
17. What is the resolution of an image?
18. Compute the size of a 640*480 image at 240 pixels per inch.
19. Compute the resolution of a 2*2 inch image that has 512*512 pixels.
20. What is an image,s aspect ratio?
21. What is persistence?
22. What is the function of the control electrode in a CRT?
23. Name the two methods by which an electron beam can be sent?
24. What do you call the path the electron beam takes when returning to the left side of the CRT screen?
25. What do you call the path the electron beam takes at the end of each refresh cycle?
26. What is the pitch of a color CRT?
27. Why do many color printers use black pigment?
28. What is RLE?
29. The endpoints of a given line are(0,0) and (6,18).Compute each value of y as x stepa from 0 to 6 and plot the results.
30. What steps are required to plot a line whose slope is between deg. and 45 deg. Using slope intercept equation?
31. Indicate which raster locations would be chosen by Bresenham's algorithm when scan-converting a line from pixel coordinate (1,1) to pixel coordinate(8,5).
32. What steps are required to generate a circle?
33. What steps are required to generate a circle using Bresenham's algorithm?
34. How would a flood-fill algorithm fill the region?
35. What are the three major adverse side defects of scan conversion?
36. What steps are required to fill a region if it is filled with a pattern?
37. How can we eliminate overstrike?
38. Derive the transformation that rotates an object point with an angle about origin.Write the matrix representation for this rotation.
39. Find the matrix that represents rotation of an object by 30 deg. About the origin.
40. What are the new coordinates of the point p(2,-4) after the rotation?
41. Write the general form of the matrix for rotation about a point(h,k).

42. Perform a 45 deg. Rotation of triangle a(0,0) b(1,1) c(5,2)

43. a.)about the origin

44. b.)about p(-1,-1)

45. Magnify the triangle with vertices a(0,0) b(1,1) And c(5,2) to twice its size while keeping c(5,2) fixed.

46. Is a simultaneous shearing the same as a shearing in one direction followed by shearing in another direction? why?

47. Find the condition under which we can switch the order of a rotation and a simultaneous shearing and still get the same result.

48. Express a simultaneous shearing in terms of rotation and scaling transformations.

49. How can we determine whether a point p(x,y) lies to the left or to the right of a line segment joining the points a(x1,y1) and b(x2,y2).?

50. Illustrate the logic of the Sutherland –Hodgeman algorithm.

51. Find the transformation for mirror reflection with respect to a given plane.

52. How can scaling with respect to a point p0(x0,y0,z0) be defined in terms of scaling with respect to the origin?

53. Derive the general equation of parallel projection on to a given view plane in the direction of a given projector V.

54. Implement the DDA line drawing algorithm.

55. Implement the Bresenham's line drawing algorithm.

56. Write a function to draw a rectangle

57. Write a function to draw a polyline

58. Write a function to draw a polygon.

59. Implement the Bresenham's circle drawing algorithm.

60. Implement the Midpoint circle drawing algorithm

61. Implement the Midpoint ellipse drawing algorithm.

62. Implement the Scanline algorithm to fill a polygon.

63. Modify the Scanline algorithm to draw patterned fills.

64. Write a program to display your name in Hindi

65. Modifications to the above interface may be made as required.

66. Write a program to demonstrate the following transformations Translation, Rotation, Scaling.

67. Modify the above program to use homogenous coordinates.

68. Demonstrate the various transformations with a suitable program

69. Implement the Midpoint Subdivision Line Clipping Algorithm
70. Implement the Cohen-Sutherland Line Clipping Algorithm.
71. Implement the Liang-Barsky Line Clipping Algorithm.
72. Implement the Sutherland-Hodgman Polygon Clipping Algorithm.
73. Design an algorithm for clipping circles, ellipses and arcs.
74. Write functions to store and retrieve the data structure created in the previous problem to/from secondary storage.
75. Write a program to demonstrate the Reflection and Shear transformations.
76. Modify Bresenham's line drawing algorithm to draw lines of various styles and thickness.
77. Express window-to-viewport mapping in the form of a composite transformation matrix.
78. Use the Cohen–sutherland algorithm to clip the line segments give example.
79. Suppose that a triangle is clipped to a rectangular window. After being clipped against the window, what is the maximum number of sides that the resulting clipped polygon might have? Draw an example to illustrate the worst case.
80. What is the difference between a left-handed and a right-handed 3-dimensional coordinate system?
81. What is the reflection property that characterizes a pure diffuse reflector (also called a *Lambertian reflector*)?
82. What is *Lambert's law* of diffuse reflection?
83. What is the *inverse texture wrapping function*, and why is it more relevant to the rendering process than the *texture wrapping function*?
84. What is *back-face culling*? For an average view, what fraction of the faces of a scene would be expected to be eliminated by this method? Explain briefly.
85. You want to know whether a point *P* lies on a given surface. From which representation of the surface is this question easier to answer: *implicit* or *parametric*?
86. Let *P* be a point on a B´ezier curve of degree 3. True or false: The curve has *C*4 parametric continuity at this point.
87. Fill in the blank: "The complex point *c* = *a* + *bi* lies in the Mandelbrot set if and only if the Julia set generated by *c* is .
88. State clearly which properties of the B´ezier blending functions, *bi;d*(*u*), guarantee that the B´ezier curve lies within the convex hull of the control points.
89. Name two different events or actions that could trigger a call to your *display callback* function. (This is the function passed to glutDisplayFunc()).
90. Given two nonzero vectors ~*u* and ~*v* in 3-dimensional space, the operation ~*u* _ ~*v* will produce a nonzero vector that is perpendicular to both, *except* under what circumstances? (Be as general as possible.)

LONG QUESTIONS

1. Explain what seculars and di_use reflection are in the real world. State and explain equations for calculating approximations to both in a computer.

2 Explain why homogeneous coordinates are used for handling geometric Transformations.

3. Prove that, from the viewer's perspective the points *D*, *S*, and *C* are collinear? In the figure we show that *S* lies between *D* and *C*. Explain why this is so.

4 Describe, in detail, an algorithm that will draw a one-pixel wide outline of a Circle of integer radius centered on the origin.

5. Derive the value of the (normalized) normal vector ~*n* at this intersection point. There is no notion of outside hit or inside hit, but the normal should be directed to the same side of the surface from which the ray approaches.

6. Formulate transformation matrices for the following :

   * Rotation about any pivot point (xp, yp) not just origin
   * Scaling relative to any fixed point (xf, yf) not just origin
   * Scaling along any arbitrary axis, not just the standard x and y axes

7. Derive a linear interpolation function *C*(*x*; *y*) that maps a point *Q*= (*x*; *y*) in the triangle to an RGB color vector by blending these three colors together. You may express your answer either as a formula (using affine geometry) or using pseudo-code. The final color should be a function of *x* and *y* and *C*0, *C*1, and *C*2.

8. An image processing package allows the user to design 3 × 3 convolution filters. Design 3 × 3 filters to perform the following tasks:

   (a) blurring

   (b) edge detection of vertical edges

9. Consider a hyperboloid in 3-space defined by the following equation:

   z + *x*2

   *a*2 - *y*2

   *b*2 = 1

   (for some nonzero constants *a* and *b*). Given a point *P*0 = (*x*0; *y*0; *z*0) *T* on the surface of this hyperboloid, derive a normal vector for such a point. You do not need to normalize your vector to unit length. (If the constants *a* and *b* confuse you, you may assume that *a* = *b* = 1 for partial credit.) Show how your derived your answer.

10. Describe an algorithm to draw a straight line using only integer arithmetic. You may assume that the line is in the first octant, that the line starts and ends at integer coordinates, and that the function setpixel (x, y) turns on the pixel at location (x, y).

17. Describe Douglas and Peucker's algorithm for removing superfluous points.

18 (a) Explain how straight lines can be used to draw Bezier cubic curves.

   (b) Describe the z-bu_er polygon scan conversion algorithm

19. In ray tracing a large computational cost is associated with determining ray–object intersections. Explain how the use of bounding volumes and space subdivision methods may reduce this cost.

20. A certain image contains a number Q of differently colored pixels. There are not enough di_erent pixel values available to represent these and so a method of approximation is needed. Describe an approach and comment on its performance.

21. (a) Explain the difference in how smooth shading is performed in *Phong shading* and *Gouraud shading*. Which method does OpenGL use?

(b) The Phong lighting model, as implemented in OpenGL, models light as a combination of four different effects. Name them.

22. (a) Define the *angle of incidence* between a ray and a surface to be the acute angle between the ray's direction and the surface normal at the point of contact. As a ray goes from a medium of higher index of refraction to one of lower index of refraction does the angle of incidence tend to increase or decrease? Justify your answer.

(b) Explain the meaning of a *regularized boolean operation.*

(c) Among the following surfaces, which (if any) is the hardest to apply a 3-dimensional procedural texture: plane, sphere, torus? Briefly explain. You may assume that the contact point and normal vector are given.

23. Compare object-space and image-space visibility tests in synthesizing an image for display. Describe one visibility test in detail.

24. Why the solids are sectioned?

(a) How is the isometric view of an object obtained?

(b) Distinguish between single curved surface and double curved surface.

(c) Define apparent section and true section.

(d) What are applications of the intersection of surfaces?

25. Derive the value of the (normalized) normal vector ~*n* at this intersection point. There is no notion of outside hit or inside hit, but the normal should be directed to the same side of the surface from which the ray approaches.

26 Describe the method of Douglas & P¨ucker for approximating one line chain by another to within some tolerance. Are there any special cases?

30. Discuss transformations applied to 3D wireframe objects.Discuss the use of homogeneous coordinate representations

(a) for presenting concepts

(b) within programs

QUESTION BANK WITH SOLUTIONS

1. Define Computer Graphics.

Computer graphics remains one of the most existing and rapidly growing computer fields. Computer graphics may be defined as a pictorial representation or graphical representation of objects in a computer.

2. What is meant by scan code?

When a key is pressed on the keyboard, the keyboard controller places a code carry to the key pressed into a part of the memory called as the keyboard buffer. This code is called as the scan code.

3. What is meant by refreshing of the screen?

Some method is needed for maintaining the picture on the screen. Refreshing of screen is done by keeping the phosphorus glowing to redraw the picture repeatedly. (i.e.)By quickly directing the electronic beam back to the same points.

4. Define Random scan/Raster scan displays.

Random scan is a method in which the display is made by the electronic beam which is directed only to the points or part of the screen where the picture is to be drawn. The Raster scan system is a scanning technique in which the electrons sweep from top to bottom and from left to right. The intensity is turned on or off to light and unlight the pixel.

5. List out the merits and demerits of Penetration techniques.

The merits and demerits of the Penetration techniques are as follows

- It is an inexpensive technique
- It has only four colors
- The quality of the picture is not good when it is compared to other Techniques
- It can display color scans in monitors
- Poor limitation etc.

6. List out the merits and demerits of DVST.

The merits and demerits of direct view storage tubes [DVST] are as follows

- It has a flat screen Refreshing of screen is not required
- Selective or part erasing of screen is not possible
- It has poor contrast
- Performance is inferior to the refresh CRT.

7. What do you mean by emissive and non-emissive displays.

The emissive display converts electrical energy into light energy. The plasma Panels, thin film electro-luminescent displays are the examples. The Non emissive are optical effects to convert the sunlight or light from any other source to graphic form. Liquid crystal display is an example.

8. **List out the merits and demerits of Plasma panel display.**

Merits

Refreshing is not required

- Produce a very steady image free of Flicker Less bulky than a CRT.

Demerits

- Poor resolution of up to 60 d.p.i It requires complex addressing and wiring
- It is costlier than CRT.

9. **What is persistence?**

The time it takes the emitted light from the screen to decay one tenth of its original intensity is called as persistence.

10. **What is resolution?**

The maximum number of points that can be displayed without an overlap on a CRT is called as resolution.

11. **What is Aspect ratio?**

The ratio of vertical points to the horizontal points necessary to produce length of lines in both directions of the screen is called the Aspect ratio. Usually the aspect ratio is ¾.

12. **What is meant by Addressability?**

The Addressability is the number of individual dots per inch (d.p.i) that can be created. If the address of the current dot is (x, y) then the next dot will be (x+y), (x+y+1) etc.

13. **What is a dot size?**

Dot size may be defined as the diameter of a single dot on the devices output. Dot size is also called as the Spot size.

14. **What is interdot distance?**

Interdot distance is the reciprocal of addressability. If the addressability is large, the interdot distance will be less. The interdot distance should be less to get smooth shapes.

15. **What is the difference between impact and non-impact printers?**

Impact printer press formed character faces against an inked ribbon on to the paper. A line printer and dot-matrix printer are examples. Non-impact printer and plotters use Laser techniques, inkjet sprays, Xerographic process, electrostatic methods and electro thermal methods to get images onto the papers.

Examples are: Inkjet/Laser printers.

16. **What are the features of Inkjet printers?**

They can print 2 to 4 pages/minutes. Resolution is about 360d.p.i. Therefore better print quality is achieved.

- The operating cost is very low. The only part that requires replacement is ink cartridge.
- 4 colors cyane, yellow, majenta, black are available.

17. What are the advantages of laser printer?

- High speed, precision and economy.
- Cheap to maintain. Quality printers, Lasts for longer time.
- Toner power is very cheap.

18. What are the advantages of electrostatic plotters?

They are faster than pen plotters and very high quality printers.

- Recent electrostatic plotters include a scan-conversion capability.
- Color electrostatic plotters are available. They make multiple passes over the paper to plot color pictures.

19. Define pixel?

Pixel is shortened forms of picture element. Each screen point is referred to as pixel or pel.

20. What is frame buffer?

Picture definition is stored in a memory area called frame buffer or refresh buffer.

21. What is bitmap and what is pixmap?

The frame buffer used in the black and white system is known as bitmap which take one bit per pixel. For systems with multiple bits per pixel, the frame buffer is often referred to as a pixmap.

22. What is a Vector display or stroke writing or calligraphic display?

Random scan monitors draw a picture one line at a time and for this reason are also referred as vector displays.

23. Where the video controller is used?

A special purpose processor, which is used to control the operation of the display device, is known as video controller or display controller.

24. What do you mean by scan conversion?

A major task of the display processor is digitizing a picture definition given in an application program into a set of pixel-intensity values for storage in the frame buffer. This digitization process is called scan conversion.

25. What is run length encoding?

Run length encoding is a compression technique used to store the intensity values in the frame buffer, which stores each scan line as a set of integer pairs. One number each pair indicates an intensity value, and second number specifies the number of adjacent pixels on the scan line that are to have that intensity value

26. What is an output primitive?

Graphics programming packages provide function to describe a scene in terms of these basic geometric structures, referred to as output primitives.

27. What do you mean by 'jaggies'?

Line with stair step appearance is known as jaggies.

28. What is point in the computer graphics system?

The point is a most basic graphical element & is completely defined by a pair of user coordinates (x , y).

29. Write short notes on lines?

A line is of infinite extent can be defined by an angle of slope ??and one point on the line P=P(x,y). This can also be defined as Y=mx+C where C is the Y- intercept.

30. Define Circle?

Circle is defined by its center xc, yc and its radius in user coordinate units. The equation of the circle is (x-xc) + (y-yc) = r2.

31. Define Ellipse?

An ellipse can use the same parameters xc, yc ,r as a circle, in addition to the eccentricity e. the eqn of an ellipse is: (x-xc)2/a2 + (y-yc)2/b2 = 1

32 Define polygon?

A polygon is any closed continues sequence of line segments ie, a polyline whose last node point is same as that of its first node point. The line segments form the sides of the polygon and their intersecting points form the vertices of the polygon.

33. Distinguish between convex and concave polygons.

If the line joining any two points in the polygon lies completely inside the polygon then, they are known as convex polygons. If the line joining any two points in the polygon lies outside the polygon then, they are known as concave polygons.

34. What is seed fill?

One way to fill a polygon is to start from a given point (seed) known to be inside the polygon and highlight outward from this point i.e neighboring pixels until encounter the boundary pixels, this approach is called seed fill.

35. What is scan line algorithm?

One way to fill the polygon is to apply the inside test. i.e to check whether the pixel is inside the polygon or outside the polygon and then highlight the pixel which lie inside the polygon. This approach is known as scan-line algorithm.

36. Define coherence properties.

A coherence property of a scene is apart of a scene by which relate one part of the scene with the other parts of the scene.

37. What is an active edge list in the scan line algorithm?

The active edge list for a scan line contains all edges crossed by that scan line.

38. What is a winding number?

Winding number method is used to check whether a given point is inside or out side the polygon. In this method give a direction number to all the edges which cross the scan line. If the edge starts below the line and ends above scan line give direction as -1 . otherwise1. Fr polygons or two dimensional objects, the point is said to be inside when the value of winding number is nonzero.

39. What is cell array?

The cell array is a primitive that allows uscrs to display an arbitrary shape defined as a two dimensional grid pattern.

40. What is type face?

Letters, numbers and other characters can be displayed in a variety of sizes and styles. The overall design style for a set of characters is called a type face.

41. What do you mean by font?

The term font referred to a set of cast metal character forms in a particular size and format, such as 10-point courier italic.

42. What is a bitmapped font?

A simple method for representing the character shapes in a particular typeface is to use rectangular grid patterns. The set of characters are then referred to as a bitmap font.

43. What is an outline font?

A flexible scheme is to describe character shapes using straight-line and curve sections. In this case, the set of character is called an out line font.

44. What is an attribute parameter?

Any parameter that affects the way a primitive is to be displayed is referred to as an attribute parameter.

45. What are the various attributes of a line?

The line type, width and color are the attributes of the line. The line type include solid line, dashed lines, and dotted lines.

45. What is pixel mask?

Pixel mask is a string containing the digits 1 and 0 to indicate which positions to plot along the line path. The mask 1111000, could be used to display a dashed line with a dash length of 4 and inter dot spacing of three.

46. What is a Line cap?

Line caps can be used to adjust the shape of the line ends to give a better appearance. There are three types of line caps. Butt cap which has a square end, round cap which has a semi circle end, projecting square cap which has one half of the line width beyond the specified end points.

47. What is Color Look up table?

In color displays, 24 bits per pixel are commonly used, where 8 bits represent 256 level for each color. It is necessary to read 24- bit for each pixel from frame buffer. This is very time consuming. To avoid this video controller uses look up table to store many entries to pixel values in RGB format. This look up table is commonly known as colour table.

48. What is tiling patterns?

The process of filling an area with rectangular pattern is called tiling and rectangular fill patterns are sometimes referred to as tiling patterns.

49. What is soft fill?

Soft fill is a filling method in which fill color is combined with the background colors.

50. What is kerned character?

The characters which extend beyond the character body limits is known as kerned character. Example f and j.

51. What is character up vector?

The orientation for a displayed character string is set according to the direction of the character up vector.

52. Define bundled attributes.

Individual attribute commands provide a simple and direct method for specifying attributes when a single output device is used. When several kinds of output device are available at a graphics installation, it is convenient to set up a table for each output device that lists set of attribute values that are to be used on that device to display each primitive type. Attribute specified in this manner is known as bundled attribute.

53. What is aliasing?

In the line drawing algorithms, all rasterzed locations do not match with the true line and have to represent a straight line. This problem is severe in low resolution screens. In such screens line appears like a stair-step. This effect is known as aliasing.

54. What is antialiasing?

The process of adjusting intensities of the pixels along the line to minimize the effect of aliasing is called antialiasing.

55. What is pixel phasing?

Pixel phasing is an antialiasing technique, stair steps are smoothed out by moving the electron beam to more nearly approximate positions specified by the object geometry.

56. What is Transformation?

Transformation is the process of introducing changes in the shape size and orientation of the object using scaling rotation reflection shearing & translation etc.

57. Write short notes on active and passive transformations?

In the active transformation the points x and x??represent different coordinates of the same coordinate system. Here all the points are acted upon by the same transformation and hence the shape of the object is not distorted. In a passive transformation the points x and x??represent same points in the space but in a different coordinate system. Here the change in the coordinates is merely due to the change in the type of the user coordinate system.

58. What is translation?

Translation is the process of changing the position of an object in a straight-line path from one coordinate location to another. Every point (x , y) in the object must under go a displacement to (x?,y?). the transformation is: x??= x + tx ; y??= y+ty

59. What is scaling?

The scaling transformations changes the shape of an object and can be carried out by multiplying each vertex (x,y) by scaling factor Sx,Sy where Sx is the scaling factor of x and Sy is the scaling factor of y.

60. What is shearing?

The shearing transformation actually slants the object along the X direction or the Y direction as required.ie; this transformation slants the shape of an object along a required plane.

67. What is reflection?

The reflection is actually the transformation that produces a mirror image of an object. For this use some angles and lines of reflection.

68. Distinguish between window port & view port.

A portion of a picture that is to be displayed by a window is known as window port. The display area of the part selected or the form in which the selected part is viewed is known as view port.

69. Define clipping.

Clipping is the method of cutting a graphics display to neatly fit a predefined graphics region or the view port.

70. What is covering (exterior clipping)?

This is just opposite to clipping. This removes the lines coming inside the windows and displays the remaining. Covering is mainly used to make labels on the complex pictures.

71. What is the need of homogeneous coordinates?

To perform more than one transformation at a time, use homogeneous coordinates or matrixes. They reduce unwanted calculations intermediate steps saves time and memory and produce a sequence of transformations.

72. Distinguish between uniform scaling and differential scaling?

When the scaling factors sx and sy are assigned to the same value, a uniform scaling is produced that maintains relative object proportions. Unequal values for sx and sy result in a differential scaling that is often used in design application.

73. What is fixed point scaling?

The location of a scaled object can be controlled by a position called the fixed point that is to remain unchanged after the scaling transformation.

74. Distinguish between bitBlt and pixBlt?

Raster functions that manipulate rectangular pixel arrays are generally referred to as raster ops. Moving a block of pixels from one location to another is also called a block transfer of pixel values. On a bilevel system, this operation is called a bitBlt (bit-block transfer), on multilevel

75. What is Bezier Basis Function?

Bezier Basis functions are a set of polynomials, which can be used instead of the primitive polynomial basis, and have some useful properties for interactive curve design.

76. What is surface patch?

A single surface element can be defined as the surface traced out as two parameters (u, v) take all possible values between 0 and 1 in a two-parameter representation. Such a single surface element is known as a surface patch.

77. Write short notes on rendering bi-cubic surface patches of constant u and v method?

The simple way is to draw the iso-parmetric lines of the surface. Discrete approximations to curves on the surface are produced by holding one parameter constant and allowing the other to vary at discrete intervals over its whole range. This produce curves of constant u and constant v.

78. What are the advantages of rendering polygons by scan line method?

i. The max and min values of the scan were easily found.

ii. The intersection of scan lines with edges is easily calculated by a simple incremental method.

iii. The depth of the polygon at each pixel is easily calculated by an incremental method.

79. What are the advantages of rendering by patch splitting?

i. It is fast- especially on workstations with a hardware polygon-rendering pipeline.

ii. It's speed can be varied by altering the depth of sub-division.

80. Define B-Spline curve?

A B-Spline curve is a set of piecewise(usually cubic) polynomial segments that pass close to a set of control points. However the curve does not pass through these control points, it only passes close to them.

81. What is a spline?

To produce a smooth curve through a designed set of points, a flexible strip called spline is used. Such a spline curve can be mathematically described with a piecewise cubic polynomial function whose first and second derivatives are continuous across various curve section.

82. What is the use of control points?

Spline curve can be specified by giving a set of coordinate positions called control points, which indicates the general shape of the curve, can specify spline curve.

83. What are the different ways of specifying spline curve?

- Using a set of boundary conditions that are imposed on the spline.
- Using the state matrix that characteristics the spline
- Using a set of blending functions that calculate the positions along the curve path by specifying combination of geometric constraints on the curve

84. What are the important properties of Bezier Curve?

It needs only four control points?

It always passes through the first and last control points The curve lies entirely within the convex half formed by four control points.

85. Differentiate between interpolation spline and approximation spline?

When the spline curve passes through all the control points then it is called interpolate. When the curve is not passing through all the control points then that curve is called approximation spline.

86. What do you mean by parabolic splines?

For parabolic splines a parabola is fitted through the first three points p1,p2,p3 of the data array of kot points. Then a second parabolic arc is found to fit the sequence of points p2, p3, p4. This continues in this way until a parabolic arc is found to fit through points pn-2, pn-1 and pn. The final plotted curve is a meshing together of all these parabolic arcs.

87. What is cubic spline?

Cubic splines are a straight forward extension of the concepts underlying parabolic spline. The total curve in this case is a sequence of arcs of cubic rather than parabolic curves

Each cubic satisfies :ax3 + bx 2+ cx + d

88. What is a Blobby object?

Some objects do not maintain a fixed shape, but change their surface characteristics in certain motions or when in proximity to other objects. That is known as blobby objects. Example – molecular structures, water droplets.

89. Define Octrees?

Hierarchical tree structures called octrees, are used to represent solid objects in some graphics systems. Medical imaging and other applications that require displays of object cross sections commonly use octree representation.

90. Define Projection?

The process of displaying 3D into a 2D display unit is known as projection. The projection transforms 3D objects into a 2D projection plane.

91. What are the steps involved in 3D transformation?

- Modeling Transformation
- Viewing Transformation

- Projection Transformation
- Workstation Transformation

92. What do you mean by view plane?

A view plane is nothing but the film plane in camera which is positioned and oriented for a particular shot of the scene.

93. What is view-plane normal vector?

This normal vector is the direction perpendicular to the view plane and it is called as [DXN DYN DZN]

94. What is view distance?

The view plane normal vector is a directed line segment from the view plane to the view reference point. The length of this directed line segment is referred to as view distance

95. Define projection?

The process of converting the description of objects from world coordinates to viewing coordinates is known as projection

96. What you mean by parallel projection?

Parallel projection is one in which z coordinates is discarded and parallel lines from each vertex on the object are extended until they intersect the view plane.

97. What do you mean by Perspective projection?

Perspective projection is one in which the lines of projection are not parallel. Instead, they all converge at a single point called the center of projection.

98. What is Projection reference point?

In Perspective projection, the lines of projection are not parallel. Instead, they all converge at a single point called Projection reference point.

99. What is the use of Projection reference point?

In Perspective projection, the object positions are transformed to the view plane along these converged projection line and the projected view of an object is determined by calculating the intersection of the converged projection lines with the view plane.

100. What are the different types of parallel projections?

The parallel projections are basically categorized into two types, depending on the relation between the direction of projection and the normal to the view plane. They are orthographic parallel projection and oblique projection.

101. What is orthographic parallel projection?

When the direction of the projection is normal (perpendicular) to the view plane then the projection is known as orthographic parallel projection

102. What is orthographic oblique projection?

When the direction of the projection is not normal (not perpendicular) to the view plane then the projection is known as oblique projection.

103. What is an axonometric orthographic projection?

The orthographic projection can display more than one face of an object. Such an orthographic projection is called axonometric orthographic projection.

104. What is cavalier projection?

The cavalier projection is one type of oblique projection, in which the direction of projection makes a 45-degree angle with the view plane.

105. What is cabinet projection?

The cabinet projection is one type of oblique projection, in which the direction of projection makes a n angle of arctan (2)=63.4- with the view plane.

106. What is vanishing point?

The perspective projections of any set of parallel lines that are not parallel to the projection plane converge to appoint known as vanishing point.

107. What do you mean by principle vanishing point.

The vanishing point of any set of lines that are parallel to one of the three principle axes of an object is referred to as a principle vanishing point or axis vanishing point.

108. What is view reference point?

The view reference point is the center of the viewing coordinate system. It is often chosen to be close to or on the surface of the some object in the scene.

109. Define computer graphics animation?

Computer graphics animation is the use of computer graphics equipment where the graphics output presentation dynamically changes in real time. This is often also called real time animation.

110. What is tweening?

It is the process, which is applicable to animation objects defined by a sequence of points, and that change shape from frame to frame.

111. Define frame?

One of the shape photographs that a film or video is made of is known as frame.

112. What is key frame?

One of the shape photographs that a film or video is made of the shape of an object is known initially and for a small no of other frames called keyframe

113. What is pseudo animation? Pseudo animation is creating a sequence of stills, photographing or video graphing each still as one frame, and then later playing back the frames at a faster speed.

114. What is the normal speed of a visual animation?

Visual animation requires a playback of at least 25 frames per second.

115. What are the different tricks used in computer graphics animation?

a. Color look Up Table manipulation

b. Bit plane manipulation

c. Use of UDCS

d. Special drawing modes

e. Sprites

f. Bit blitting

116. What is color look up table?

In color display unit it is necessary to read 44-bit for each pixel from buffer. This very time consuming process. To avoid this video controller uses look up table to store many entries of pixel vales in RGB format. This look up table is commonly known as color look up table.

117. What is solid modeling?

The construction of 3 dimensional objects for graphics display is often referred to as solid modeling.

118. What is an intuitive interface?

The intuitive interface is one, which simulates the way a person would perform a corresponding operation on real object rather than have menu command.

119. What is Sprite?

A Sprite is graphics shape in animation and games programs. Each sprite provided in the system has its own memory area similar to but smaller than pixel RAM.

120. What is the UDC technique?

UDC stands for User Defined Character set. It is graphics animation trick, which is used in early microcomputer system.

121. What is the use of hidden line removing algorithm?

The hidden line removal algorithm determines the lines, edges, surfaces or volumes that are visible or invisible to an observer located at a specific point in space.

122. What is computer graphics realism?

The creation of realistic picture in computer graphics is known as realism. It is important in fields such as simulation, design, entertainments, advertising, research, education, command, and control.

123. How realistic pictures are created in computer graphics?

To create a realistic picture, it must be process the scene or picture through viewing-coordinate transformations and projection that transform three-dimensional viewing coordinates onto two-dimensional device coordinates.

124. What is Fractals?

A Fractal is an object whose shape is irregular at all scales.

125. What is a Fractal Dimension?

Fractal has infinite detail and fractal dimension. A fractal imbedded in ndimensional space could have any fractional dimension between 0 and n. The Fractal Dimension D= LogN / Log S Where N is the No of Pieces and S is the Scaling Factor.

126. What is random fractal?

The patterns in the random fractals are no longer perfect and the random defects at all scale.

127. What is geometric fractal?

A geometric fractal is a fractal that repeats self-similar patterns over all scales.

128. What is Koch curve?

The Koch curve can be drawn by dividing line into 4 equal segments with scaling factor 1/3. and middle 2 segments are so adjusted that they form adjustment sides of an equilateral triangle.

Computer Graphics Quiz

1. **Which of the following is NOT true about quaternions?**
   a) They are made up of 4 numbers
   b) They should always be normalized to length 1
   c) They can be used to represent all affine transforms
   d) They can be used to define the rotation of an object

2. **Which of the following does NOT figure into the Field of View of a pinhole camera?**
   a) The direction of projection
   b) The distance from the center of projection to the projection plane
   c) The size of the projection plane

3. **This projection technique has the direction of projection perpendicular to the viewing plane, but the viewing direction is NOT perpendicular to one of the principle faces.**
   a) Orthographic Parallel Projection b) Axonometric Parallel Projection
   c) Oblique Parallel Projection

4. **This projection technique does NOT have the direction of projection perpendicular to the viewing plane.**
   a) Orthographic Parallel Projection b) Axonometric Parallel Projection
   c) Oblique Parallel Projection

5. **This projection technique has the direction of projection perpendicular to the viewing plane, and the viewing direction is perpendicular to one of the principle faces.**
   a) Orthographic Parallel Projection b) Axonometric Parallel Projection
   c) Oblique Parallel Projection

6. **When transforming a random Axis-Aligned Bounding Box defined by the points ($near_x$, $near_y$, $near_z$) and (far_x, far_y, far_z) to the standard orthographic viewing box, which affine transforms are used?**
   a) shear and translation b) rotation and scale
   c) scale and shear d) translation and scale

7. **In class, we discussed the purpose of the front and back clipping planes in OpenGL. Which of the following was NOT a purpose for using clipping planes?**
   a) division by zero
   b) objects behind the center of projection mapping onto the projection plane
   c) avoiding the problems of infinite viewing volume size

8. In class, we discussed how the image of the Double Eagle Tanker was obtained for the large poster in the main hall of Sitterson. It required rendering several perspective images using OpenGL. Which of the following was NOT a step required in that process?

a) handling projection planes non-orthogonal to the viewing direction

b) cutting a single projection plane into many separate projection planes

c) rotating the viewing direction to be the same as the –z direction

d) handling several different centers of projection

9. In OpenGL, there are several different matrices. We have discussed two of them in class. Which one of the below would be used in conjunction with a glRotatef function call?

a) GL_MODELVIEW b) GL_PROJECTION

10. In OpenGL, there are several different matrices. We have discussed two of them in class. Which one of the below would be used in conjunction with glFrustum?

a) GL_MODELVIEW b) GL_PROJECTION

11. Which of the following is the order that geometry operations are performed in OpenGL (where we read the order from left to right)?

a) GL_PROJECTION ? GL_MODELVIEW ? Perspective division

b) GL_MODELVIEW ? GL_PROJECTION ? Perspective division

c) Perspective division ? GL_PROJECTION ? GL_MODELVIEW

d) GL_MODELVIEW ? Perspective division ? GL_PROJECTION

e) GL_PROJECTION ? Perspective division ? GL_MODELVIEW

12. For the next 4 questions, match the pictures on the right with the corresponding term on the left. The arrows in the picture denote light rays. The dashed lines represent the material type to be considered. The key is in the interaction of the light rays with the material.

a. Specular

(a)

b. Diffuse

(b)

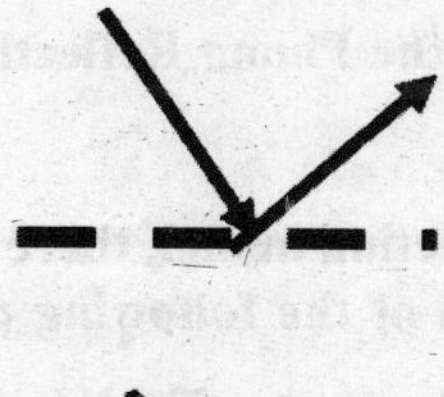

c. Transparent

(c)

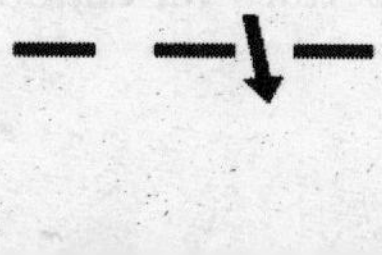

d. Translucent

(d)

answers: b,d,c,a

13. In "Utah" graphics, lights are simplified in order to approximate light/matter interaction with a minimum amount of work. Which of the following is NOT true about the simplifications made in "Utah" graphics lights?

a) Light intensity and color are folded into one value.

b) Lights are assumed to have zero size

c) Spotlights can not be handled

d) Soft shadows can not be handled

14. The Phong reflection model simplifies light-matter interactions into (essentially) 4 vectors and a number of constants. Each piece of the Phong model uses different vectors and constants. Which portion does NOT include taking a dot product?

a) Ambient b) Diffuse

c) Specular

15. The Phong reflection model simplifies light-matter interactions into (essentially) 4 vectors and a number of constants. Which piece of the Phong model is responsible for giving spheres their bright white spots?

a) Ambient b) Diffuse

c) Specular

16. The Phong reflection model simplifies light-matter interactions into (essentially) 4 vectors and a number of constants. Which of the following is NOT a vector needed for the Phong reflection model?

a) Surface Normal b) Direction to Viewer

c) Direction to Material Center d) Direction to Light

17. True or false: In the Phong Reflection model, ambient light is the same everywhere.

a) true b) false

18. In the Phong reflection model, there are 3 constants (a, b, c) which are used to describe the qualities of which of the following phenomena?

a) The material reaction to ambient, diffuse and specular light (respectively)

b) The amount to perturb reflection vectors as they are mirrored across the normal

c) The size (in each dimension) which the light is assumed to have

d) The attenuation of a point light source with distance

19. As discussed in class, when obtaining normals for a triangle, which of the following mathematical constructs is NOT used?

a) Point-Point subtraction
b) Vector dot products
c) Vector cross products
d) Vector normalization

UNSOLVED QUESTIONS

1. Which of the following tools allow the user to adjusts contrast of the edge detail and creates the illusion of a more focused image?

(a) Marquee tool
(b) Unsharp Mask Filter
(c) Custom Shape Tool
(d) None of the above

2. Which of the following is true?

(a) Digital sound is an example of data that does not degrade gracefully
(b) Digital image is an example of data that does not degrade gracefully
(c) Digital video is an example of data that does not degrade gracefully
(d) None of the above

3. Which of the following effects adds various combinations of highlights and shadows to a layer?

(a) Drop Shadow
(b) Bevel and Emboss
(c) Inner Shadow
(d) None of the above

4. Which of the following is known as text spacing?

(a) Kerning
(b) Leading
(c) Font
(d) None of the above

5. Which of the following is known as line spacing?

(a) Kerning
(b) Leading
(c) Font
(d) None of the above

6. In order to estimate the size of an image, you would need to know which of the following?

(a) The monitor resolution
(b) The image resolution
(c) The printing resolution
(d) All of the above

7. Which of the following is a characteristic of lossless compression?

(a) It has a high compression ratio
(b) It has a low compression ratio
(c) It is good for online delivery

(d) None of the above

8. In order to effectively print an image, you have to take into consideration which of the following?

(a) ppi (b) dpi

(c) lpi (d) kpi

9. If a 3-inch by 3-inch, 144-ppi image is displayed on a 72-dpi monitor, how big will the image appear to be?

(a) 3-inch by 3-inch (b) 6-inch by 3-inch

(c) 6-inch by 6-inch (d) None of the above

10. Which of the following is close to the maximum number of colours a regular human can see?

(a) 3 bits (b) 3 bytes

(c) 2 bytes (d) 2 bits

11. Which of the following file formats are not suitable for printing?

(a) TIFF (b) PICT

(c) PCX (d) EPS

12. Which of the following tools allow you to select a straight line around an area?

(a) Lasso tool (b) Magic Wand tool

(c) Marquee tool (d) Polygon lasso tool

13. Which of the following format is good for printing out an image?

(a) PICT (b) EPS

(c) PCX (d) JPG

14. Which of the following is true about bitmap images?

(a) They are better for illustrations and logos

(b) They can be resized easily without losing resolution

(c) They can represent subtle gradation of shade and colour

(d) None of the above

15. Which of the following is a common compression type?

(a) LZW (b) GIF

(c) CTV (d) None of the above

16. What is the maximum number of channels an image can have?

(a) 20 (b) 24

(c) 30 (d)

Appendices

Appendix A: Animation

CONVENTIONAL ANIMATION (KEY-FRAME ANIMATION)

The name "Key-Frame Animation" comes from combining the use of key frames and inbetweening. The name is also applied to computer-based systems that mimic this process.

- Storyboard (outline of the animation)
- Detailed layout (drawing for every scene in the animation)
- Soundtrack (instants at which significant occur are recorded in order)
- Key frames are drawn
- Inbetweening
- Pencil test
- Cels are painted, composition of foreground and background
- Assembled cels are ordered and filmed

INBETWEENING

*L*inear Int*ERP*olation (Lerping)

Given the values v_s and v_e of some attribute (position, color size) in the starting and ending frames, the value v_t varies smoothly from v_s to v_e.

vt = (1-t)vs + tve

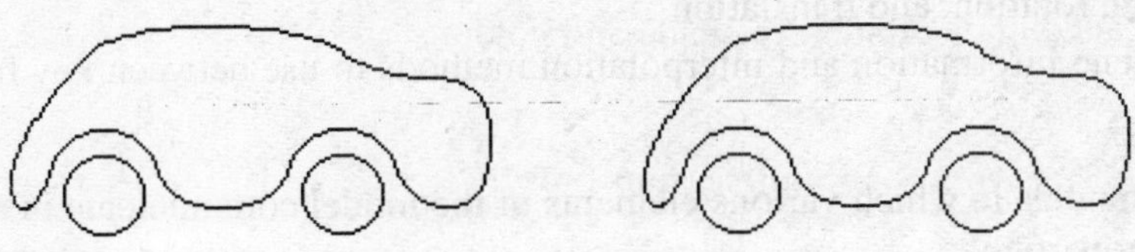

SPLINES

(Curves used to approximate a set of control points)

$$V_t = (1-f(t))V_s + f(t)V_e$$

- Smooth initiation and termination of changes (smooth-in and smooth-out)
- Relatively constant rate of change in between
- Example: f'(0) = f'(1) = 0, slope constant in middle of range

RIGID BODIES

Position

- Position of center of body is specified at certain key frames
- Intermediate positions are interpolated by some spline path
- Rate at which the path is traversed can be specified by:
  1. Marking equal time intervals on the key frames
  2. Rate is a function of time

QUATERNIONS

1. Have form [s,v] where v = (xv, yv, zv)
2. q1q2 = [s1,v1] [s2,v2]
   = [(s1*s2 - v1*v2, (s1v2 + s2v1 + v1 x v2)]
3. For a vector v, we rotate to position v' by
   $v' = q^{-1}\ v\ q$ v is treated as [0,v]
   $q^{-1} = (1/\|q\|^2)[s,-v]$, $\|q\|^2 = s^2 + v*v$

REALTIME ANIMATION TECHNIQUES

- Computation in realtime
- Zoom/Pan and double buffering
- Color map lookup table (LUT) animation

METHODS OF CONTROLLING ANIMATION

Full Explicit Control

Animator provides a description of everything that occurs in the animation

- Specifying scaling, rotation, and translation
- Providing key-frame information and interpolation methods to use between key frames

Procedural Control

- Uses procedural models in which various elements of the model communicate in order to determine their properties.
- Particle system of grass and wind

Appendix B: Illumination and Shading

BASIC ILLUMINATION

Light Source Independent Models

Depth Shading

- Color or intensity determined solely by "depth" of polygon.
- Darker colors or intensities at lower elevations.
- Effective in modeling terrain or surface data
- Avoids complex calculations of lighting dependent models
- Simulates realism

Depth Cueing

- Reduce intensity of pixel as the distance from the observer increases
- Simulates reduction in clarity as distances from the observer increases
- Image fades in the distance
- Often used in medical imaging

Light Source Dependent Models

What an object looks like depends on

- Properties of the light source such as color, distance from object, direction from object, intensity of source
- Surface characteristics of object such as color and reflectance properties
- Location of the observer

Light striking a surface of an object can be

- Reflected (Diffuse reflection & Specular reflection)
- Absorbed
- Transmitted (Translucent or transparent)
- Combination of all three

Diffuse Reflection Using Lambert's Law

Lambert's Law

The intensity of light reflected from a surface is proportional to the cosine of the angle between the vector L to the light source and the normal vector N perpendicular to the surface.

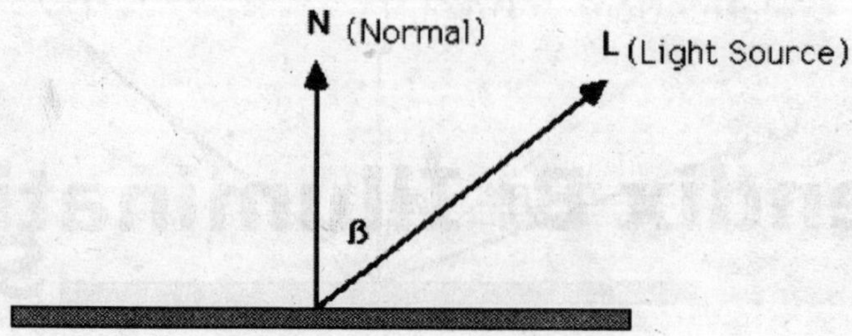

The amount of reflected light is dependent on the position of the light source and the object but independent of the observer's position.

Ambient Illumination

Ambient light is the illumination of an object caused by reflected light from other surfaces. To calculate this exactly would be *very* complicated. A *simple* model assumes ambient light is uniform in the environment.

Let

Ia = Ambient light intensity

ka = Ambient light reflected

Then we modify our previous illumination model to

I = Iaka + Ipkd (L*N)

Light-source Attenuation

Thus far we have ignored the inverse square law: energy decays with the inverse square of the distance dL to the light source. Including this term we get

I = Iaka + Ipkd (L*N)/dL2

However, due to our previous assumptions of a point light source and uniform ambient light, using the dL2 term gives too rapid of a decrease in illumination intensity to look realistic. The dL2 term is usually replaced by fatt where

fatt = MIN (1/(c1 + c2dL + c3dL2), 1)

I = Iaka + Ipkd (N*L)*fatt

Specular Reflection

- Light bounces off a glossy surface maintaining the color of the light source.
- Visible when the angle of incidence of the light from the point light source is equal to the angle of reflection toward the observer.
- For a nonperfect reflector, intensity of reflected light decreases rapidly as angle to observer

increases beyond the angle of incidence.

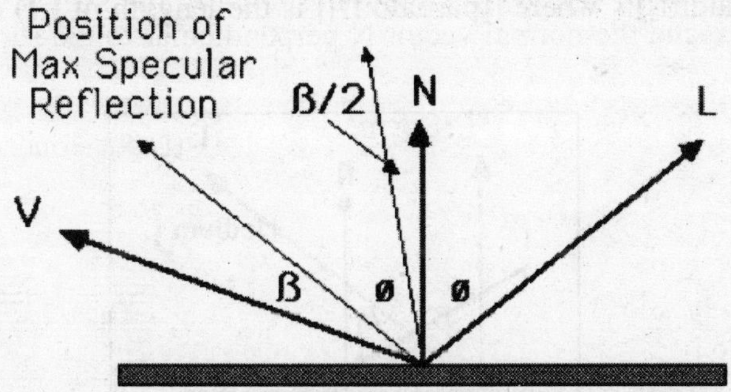

V = Observer Position , N = Normal Vector , L = Light Src Vector

Phong's Highlighting Term

Ipfatt W(ø) cosnß

Ip = Point light source intensity (white light)

fatt = Light-source Attenuation

W(ø) = Fraction of specullarly reflected light (usually a constant, ks)

n = Specular reflection exponent

cos ß = R * V

I = Iaka + Ipkd (N*L)*fatt

Specular Component = Ipfatt W(ø) cosnß

This term represents the amount of WHITE light that shouldbe added!

RAY TRACING

Reflection Vector

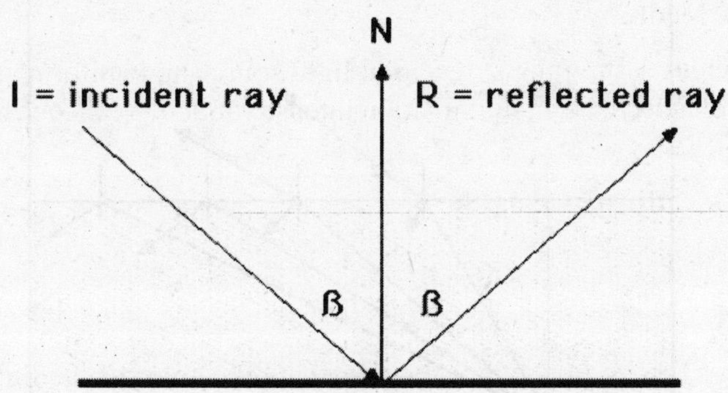

Assume that

||I|| = ||N|| = ||R|| = 1, I, R and N are coplanar.

We know: (-I)*N = R*N (unit vectors with same angle)

(-I) + R = [[partialdiff]]N where [[partialdiff]] is the lengyth of (-I) + R

Transmission

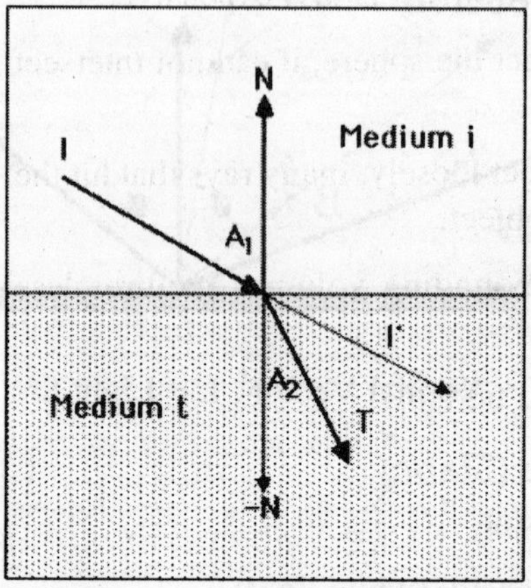

Let ui be the index of refraction of medium i with respect to a vacuum.

Let ut be the index of refraction of medium t with respect to a vacuum.

Snell's Law

sin(Ai) / sin(At) = ut /ui

We also know that

T = [[partialdiff]]I + ßN

Total Internal Reflection

TIR is a physical phenomonon when light tries to pass from a dense medium to a less-dense medium at too shallow an angle. The result is that the light glances off the interface between the media, and is specularly reflected instead of transmitted. At this point we just compute specular reflection.

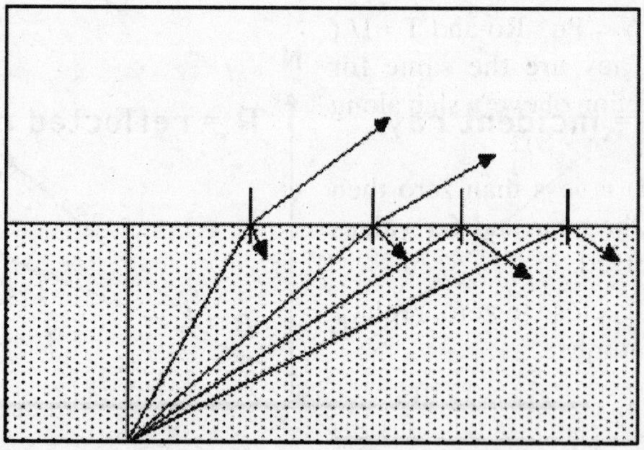

When the expression under the radical in the *T* calculation is negative then we have reached the critical angle.

Bounding Volumes

Bounding volumes are one way to decrease the amount of time spent on intersection calculations.

Enclose an object or objects that are expensive to intersect in a bounding volume whose intersection test is less expensive.

Example: If a ray doesn't intersect the sphere, it can not intersect the polygonal object inside.

If a bounding volume fits an object loosely, many rays that hit the bounding volume will miss the object.

Intersecting rays with simpler bounding volumes requires less calculations.

There is a tightness verses speed tradeoff!

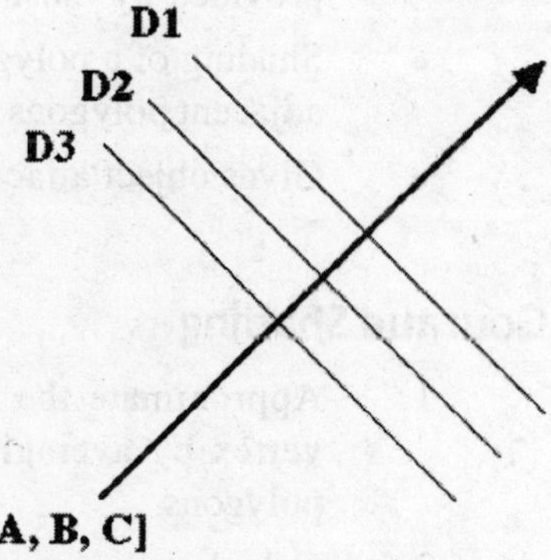

Bounding Volume Example (Slabs)

Ax + By + Cz + D = 0 A2+ B2+ C2 = 1 Normal, Pn = [A, B, C]

describes a plane in space lying D units from the origin.

If we leave Pn fixed and allow D to vary then we describe the set of all planes orthogonal to P_n.

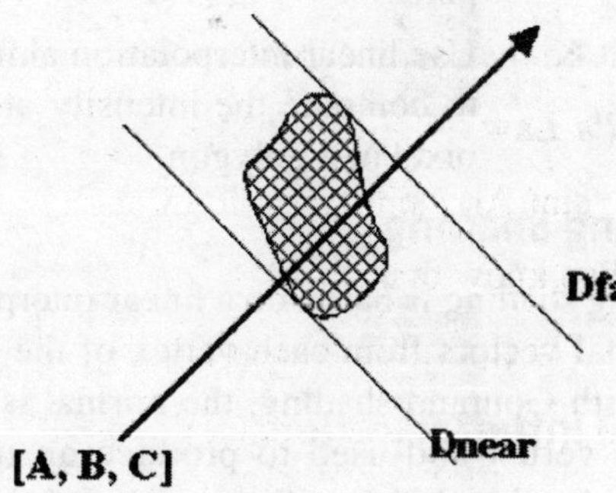

Ray-Slab Intersection

R(t) = Ro + Rd*t

t = (Dn - Pn* Ro) / (Pn * Rd)

so

t near = (Dnear - Pn* Ro) / (Pn * Rd)

t far = (Dfar - Pn* Ro) / (Pn * Rd)

- Precompute S = Pn* Ro and T =1/ (Pn * Rd). They are the same for every intersection of every slab along the ray! t = (Dn - S)T
- If (Pn * Rd) is less than zero then the roles of the near and far values must be reversed.
- If (Pn * Rd) is close to zero, replace it by a large number.

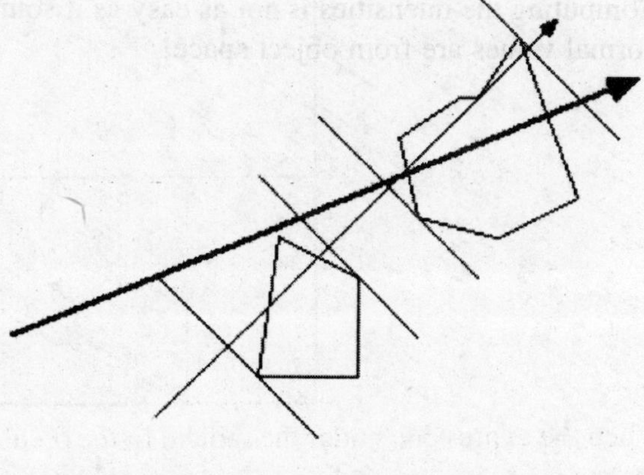

SHADING MODELS

Flat Shading

Every pixel interior to the polygon is assigned the same intensity. The normal at a point on the polygon is the normal of the plane determined by the polygon. (Use cross product of edge vectors to compute normal.)

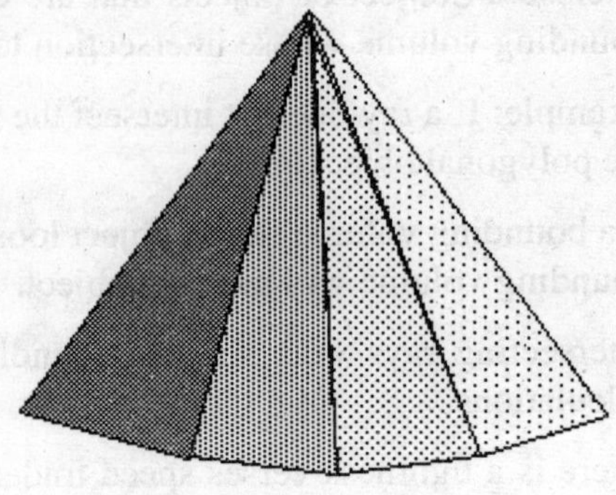

- Fast and simple, uses standard polygon fill provided by most frame buffers
- Shading of a polygon independent of shade of adjacent polygons
- Gives object a faceted appearance

Gouraud Shading

1. Approximate the normal to the surface at a vertex by averaging all normals of abutting polygons.
2. Calculate the intensity at each vertex using illumination equations.
3. Use linear interpolation along a polygon edge to compute the intensity at each edge pixel.
4. Use linear interpolation along a scan line to compute the intensity at each interior pixel of a polygon.

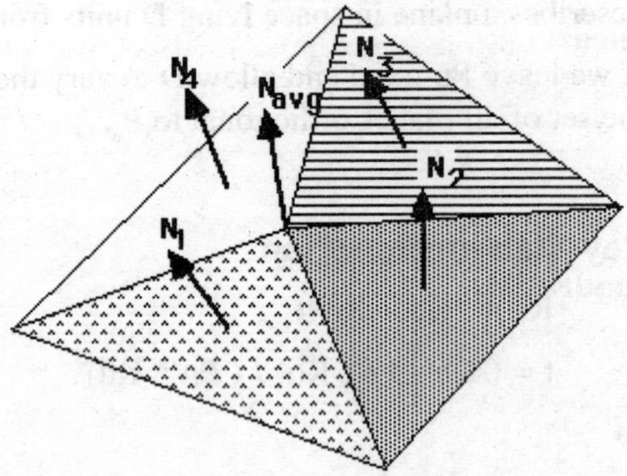

Phong Shading

Phong shading is based on a linear interpolation of the normal vectors from each vertex of the polygon. Just as with Gouraud shading, the normal is calculated at each vertex and used to produce an intensity. The intensity calculation will contain a term for a specular highlight. To fill the polygon, the normal vectors rather than intensities are interpolated from point to point. Using these interpolated normals, the intensities with a specular highlight are calculated at each pixel.

Computing the intensities is not as easy as it sounds since the pixel values are in image space and the normal values are from object space!

Appendix C: Representing Curves and Surfaces

MODELING CURVES

Parametric Curves

Linear:

x = axt + bx

y = ayt + by

z = azt + bz

Quadratic:

x = axt2 + bxt + cx

y = ayt2 + byt + cy

z = azt2 + bzt + cz

Cubic:

x = axt3 + bxt 2+ cxt + dx

y = ayt3 + byt 2+ cyt + dy

z = azt3 + bzt 2+ zczt + dz

Joining curve segments together

G_0 geometric continuity: Two curve segments join together

G_1 geometric continuity: The directions of the two segments' tangent vectors are equal at the join point

C_1 continuity: Tangent vectors of the two segments are equal in magnitude and direction

C_n continuity: Direction and magnitude through the nth derivative are equal at the join point

Hermite curves

Defined by two endpoints and tangents at the endpoints

Hermite Matrices

GH = (P1) MH = (2 -2 1 1)
(P4) (-3 3 -2 -1)
(R1) (0 0 1 0)
(R4) (1 0 0 0)

T = (t3 t2 t 1)

Q(t) = T MH GH

Hermite Blending Functions

Q(t) = T MH GH

Q(t) = (2 t3 - 3 t 2 + 1) P1 + (-2 t3 + 3 t2) P4 + (t3 - 2 t 2 +t)R1 + (t3 - t 2)R4

Bezier Matrices

GB = (P1) MB = (-1 3 -3 1)
(P2) (3 -6 3 0)
(P3) (-3 3 0 0)
(P4) (1 0 0 0)

T = (t3 t 2 t 1)

Q(t) = T MB GB

QUADRIC SURFACES

Quadric Surfaces

$$Ax^2 + By^2 + Cz^2 + 2Dxy + 2Eyz + 2Fxz + 2Gx + 2Hy + 2Jz + K = 0$$

or $P^T Q^P = 0$ where

$$P^T = (x, y, z, 1) \quad P = \begin{bmatrix} x \\ y \\ z \\ 1 \end{bmatrix} \qquad Q = \begin{bmatrix} A & D & F & G \\ D & B & E & H \\ F & E & C & J \\ G & H & J & K \end{bmatrix}$$

Example: Unit Sphere

$$x^2 + y^2 + z^2 - 1 = 0 \qquad P^TQP = 0$$

(x, y, z, 1) (1 0 0 0) (x)

(0 1 0 0) (y) = 0

(0 0 1 0) (z)

(0 0 0 -1) (1)

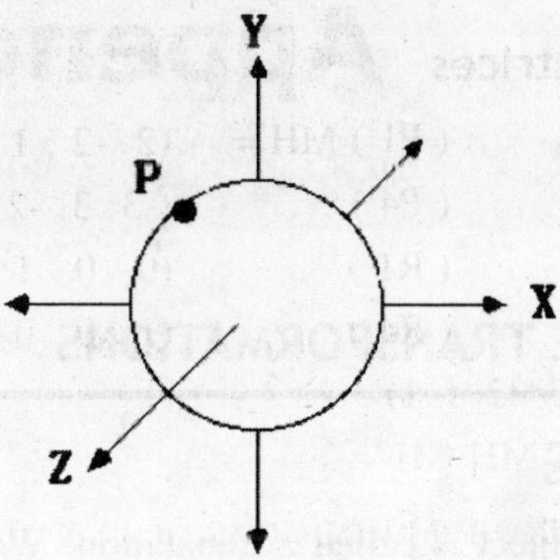

Ray/Quadric Intersection

Assume a ray with origin R0 = (x0,y0,z0)

and direction Rd = [xd,yd,zd], Rd a unit vector.

R(t) = R0 + tRd

Quadric Surface PT QP = 0

Substituting R(t) = R0 + tRd into PT QP = 0 and solving for t:

-Bq +/- [[radical]](Bq2 -4AqCq)

t = ———————————————

2Aq

Calculating the Normal Vector

F(x,y,z) = Ax2 + By2 + Cz2 + 2Dxy + 2Eyz + 2Fxz + 2Gx + 2Hy + 2Jz + K

To calculate the normal vector you take partial derivatives

of F with respect to x, y and z.

[[partialdiff]]F/[[partialdiff]]x = 2Ax + 2Dy +2Fz +2G

[[partialdiff]]F/[[partialdiff]]y = 2By + 2Dx +2Ez +2H

[[partialdiff]]F/[[partialdiff]]z = 2Cx + 2Ey +2Fx +2J

2 can be factored out so Rn = [xn, yn, zn] = [Ax+Dy+Fz+G, By+Dx+Ez+H, Cx+Ey+Fx+J]

We want the normal for the surface facing the ray so if Rn*Rd > 0 then Rn = -Rn

Appendix D: Geometrical Transformations

PRIMITIVE TRANSFORMATIONS

Translations

Moving an object is called a translation. We translate point by moving to the x and y coordinates, repectively, the amount the point should be shifted in the x and y directions. We translate an object by translating each vertex in the object.

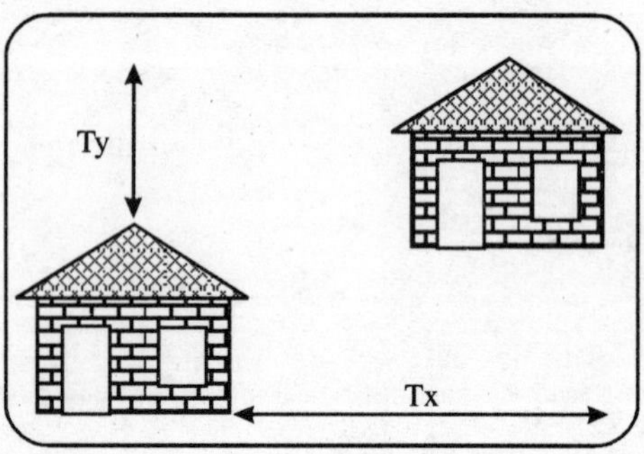

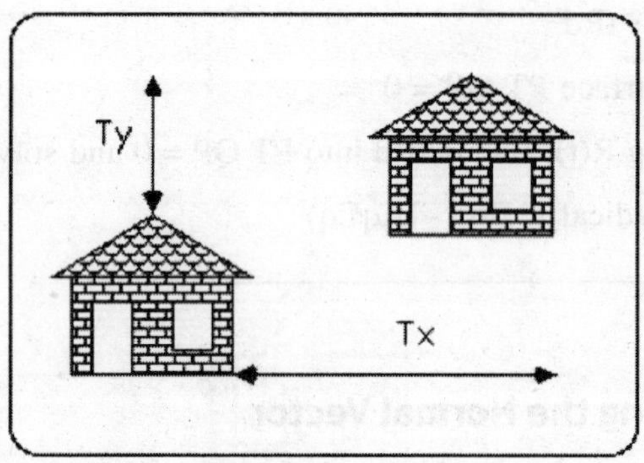

$$x2 = x1 + tx$$

$$y2 = y1 + ty$$

Rotation About the Origin

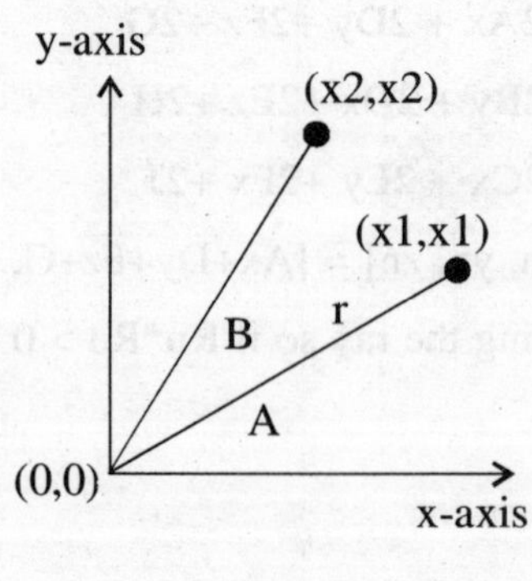

To rotate a line or polygon, we must rotate each of its vertices

To rotate point (x1,y1) to point (x2,y2) we observe:

From the illustration we know that

$$\sin(A+B) = y2/r$$

$$\cos(A+B) = x2/r$$

$$\sin(A) = y1/r$$

$$\cos(A) = x2/r$$

From the Double angle formulas

$$\sin(A+B) = \sin(A)*\cos(B) + \cos(A)*\sin(B)$$

Substituting

$$y2/r = (y1/r)*\cos(B) + (x1/r)*\sin(B)$$

Therefore: $y2 = y1*\cos(B) + x1*\sin(B)$

We have

$$x2 = x1*\cos(B) - y1*\sin(B)$$

$$y2 = x1*\sin(B) + y1*\cos(B)$$

Scaling

Changing the size of an object is called a scale. We scale an object by scaling the x and y coordinates of each vertex in the object.

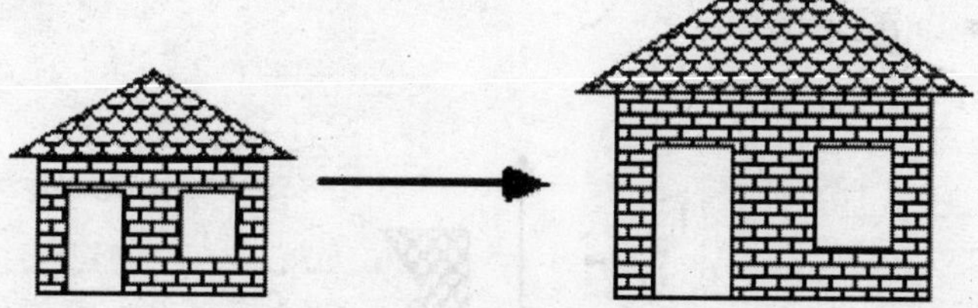

$$x2 = sx*x1$$

$$y2 = sy*y1$$

Shears

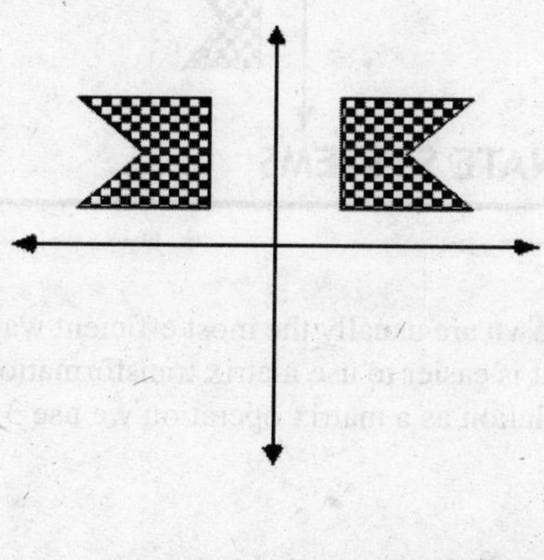

1 0 0	1 b 0
a 1 0	0 1 0
0 0 1	0 0 1

GRAPHICS —> x shear —> **GRAPHICS**

Reflections

Reflection about the y-axis

-1 0 0
0 1 0
0 0 1

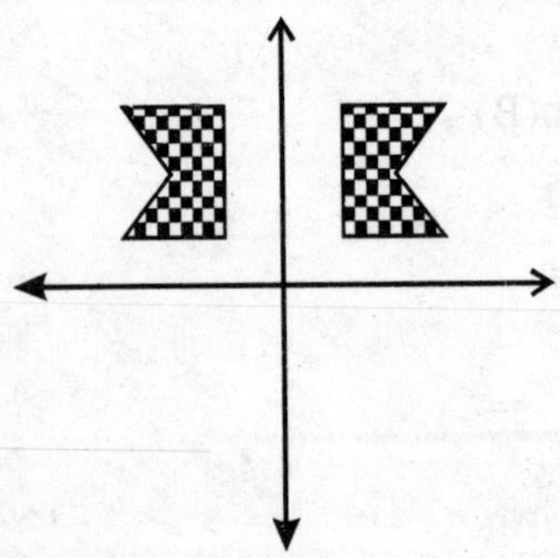

Reflection about the x-axis

1 0 0
0 -1 0
0 0 1

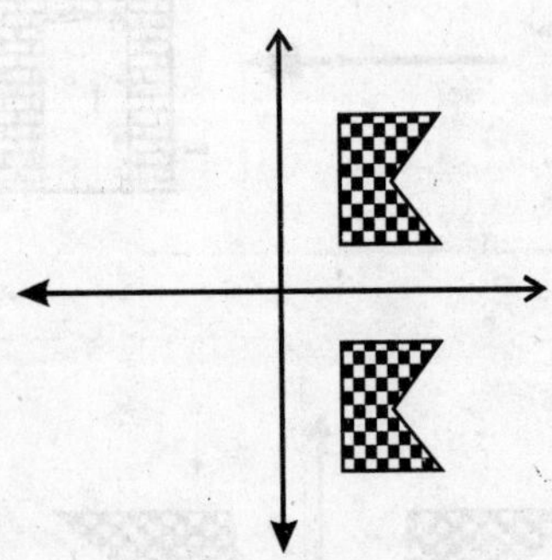

HOMOGENEOUS COORDINATE SYSTEMS

Homogeneous Coordinates

Although the formulas we have shown are usually the most efficient way to implement programs to do scales, rotations and translations, it is easier to use matrix transformations to represent and manipulate them. In order to represent a translation as a matrix operation we use 3x3 matrices and pad our points to bnecome 1x3 matrices.

Point P = (x,y,1)

Ro =

cos o -sin o 0

sin o cos o 0

0 0 1

S =

Sx 0 0

0 Sy 0

0 0 1

T =

1 0 Tx

0 1 Ty

0 0 1

WINDOWS AND VIEWPORTS

Windows, Viewports, and Clipping

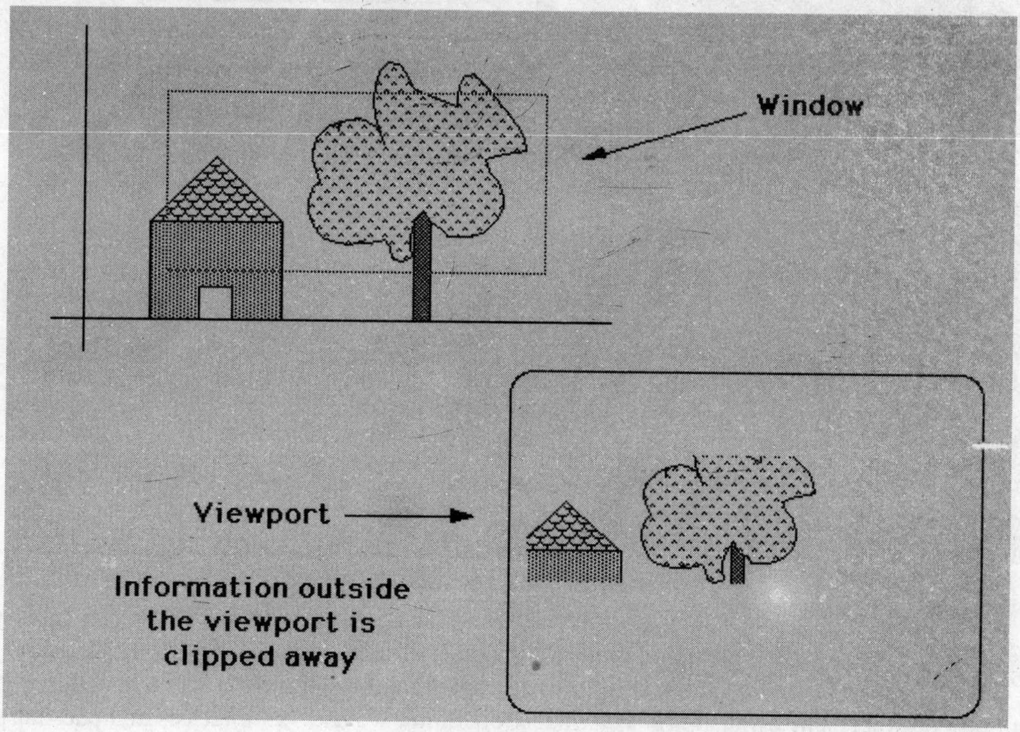

Viewing Transformation

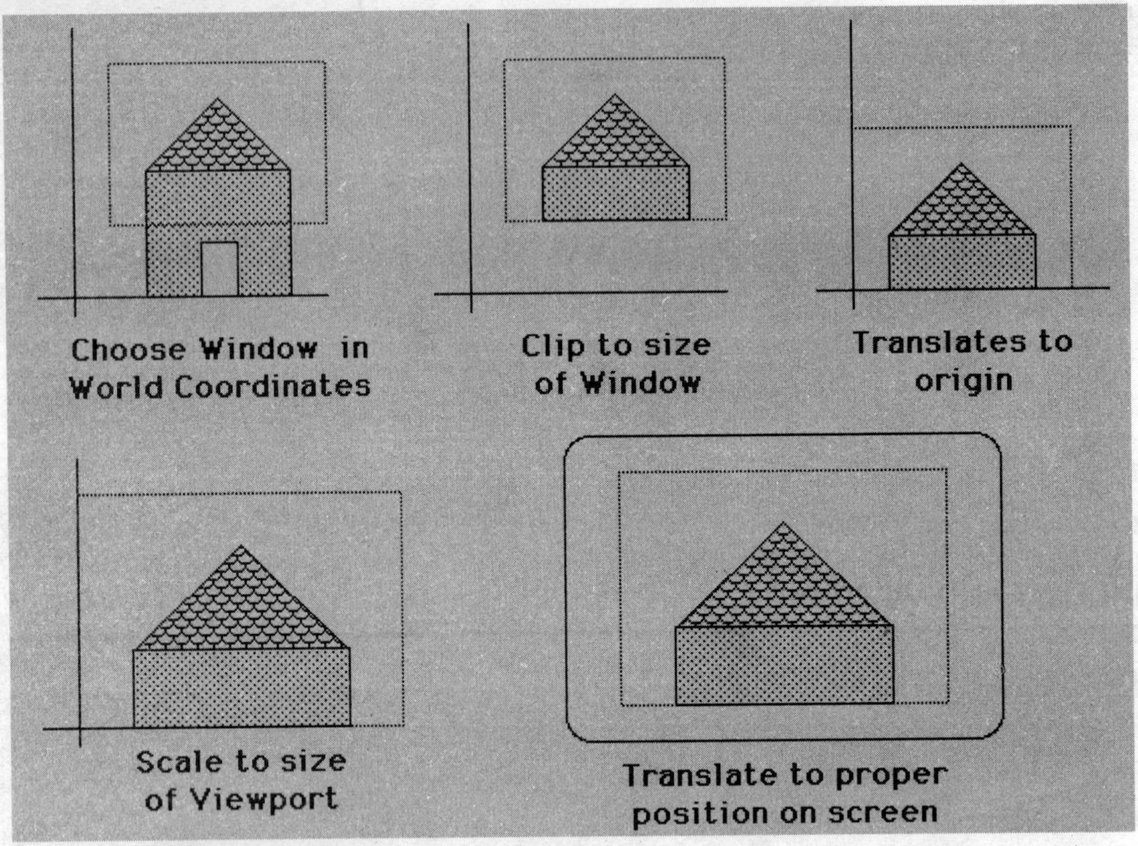

Glossary

1 A

1.1 aûne combination:

Let P_1 and P_2 be two points in an aûne space. The point Q = tP_1 + (1 “ t)P_2 with t real is an aûne combination of P1 and P2. In general, given n points {Pi } and n real values {ëi} such that “$_i$ë$_i$ = 1, then R = “$_i$ë$_i$P$_i$ is an aûne combination of the P_i.

1.2 aûne space:

A geometric space composed of points and vectors along with all transformations that preserve aûne combinations.

1.3 Aliasing:

If a signal is sampled at a rate less than twice its highest frequency (in the Fourier transform sense) then aliasing, the mapping of high frequencies to lower frequencies, can occur. This can cause objectionable visual artifacts to appear in the image.

1.4 Alpha Blending:

See compositing.

1.5 Ambient Reûection:

A constant term in the Phong lighting model to account for light which has been scattered so many times that its directionality can not be determined. This is a rather poor approximation to the complex issue of global lighting.

1.6 Antialiasing:

Aliasing artifacts can be alleviated if the signal is ûltered before sampling. Antialiasing involves evaluating possibly weighted integral of the (geometric) image over the area surrounding each pixel. This can be done either numerically (based on multiple point samples) or analytically.

2 B

2.1 B-spline:

A piecewise polynomial function whose shape is controlled by a discrete set of values and which automatically maintains continuity between segments. See also B´ezier splines.

2.2 Backfacing Polygons:

Polygons whose normal points away from the eye in screen space, after perspective, are considered backfacing. The enforcement of a polygon edge orientation is necessary to determine the polarity of the normal, usually via the right hand rule.

2.3 Barrel Distortion:

A distortion arising in lens and CRT technology.

2.4 Barycentric Coordinates:

The blending factors $ë_i$ in an aûne combination Q = “$ë_i P_i$ can be considered a coordinate system relative to the set of points {Pi}. For example, the 3 vertices of a triangle describe a barycentric coordinate system for the 2D aûne plane in which the triangle lies. Because the blending factors are constrained by “$ë_i$= 1, n + 1 coordinates are needed to parameterize an n-dimensional space.

2.5 B´ezier splines:

A representation of a polynomial controlled by a discrete set of values that have a geometric relationship to the curve. See also B-splines.

2.6 Bitblt:

Special purpose hardware for performing fast copying and logical operations on blocks of memory. Very useful in the support of windowing systems.

2.7 Bresenham's Algorithm:

Bresenham developed a fast algorithm which computes the raster representation of a line segment using only integer arithmetic. See also DDA.

2.8 Bump Mapping:

A form of texture mapping in which the normals of a surface are permuted. Can be used to simulate nonplanar surface texture.

2.9 Button:

A user interface widget composed of a portion of the screen which reacts to mouse clicks by issuing a callback or performing some other action, such as popping up a menu. Normally a button also changes its appearence when clicked, e.g. changes from a raised to a sunken relief mode.

3 C

3.1 Callback:

A UI library can be organized so that particular functions get called when certain events are detected. These functions are called callback routines and are registered with the UI library during initialization by passing a function pointer (in C).

3.2 Calligraphic Display:

A display device which draws line primitives directly, i.e. by sweeping an electron beam along the path of a line segment. As opposed to a raster display.

3.3 Cap Polygon:

When an object in a surface representation is clipped, it may be desirable to generate a cap polygon to hide the hole and maintain the illusion of a solid model.

3.4 Clipping:

Various operations in computer graphics require the removal of parts of objects or their primitives, typically through intersubsection with a convex polygon or halfspace.

3.5 Colour Map:

A colour map translates colour indexes stored in a frame buûer into display colour values, typically RGB values. This allows a degree of indirection which enables many tricks, as well as saving memory in the frame buûer while still providing a ûexible choice of colours. See also LUT.

3.6 Compensation Table:

When gamma correction is used to compensate for the nonlinearity of a display device, it is usually implemented with a look-up table.

3.7 Compositing:

To overlay pixels or images using an alpha channel to indicate relative opacity.

3.8 Concave object:

A concave object has the property that for some points within its support, a line can be formed that passes outside its support. See also convex objects.

3.9 Convex combination:

A convex combination is an aûne combination "ˌëiPi in which ëi e" 0 in addition to the aûne combination constraint of "ˌë = 1. The barycentric coordinates for the interior of a triangle form a convex combination.

3.10 Convex object:

A convex object has the property that any two points in its support can be joined by a line that consists of only points in its support. More generally, given any n points in a convex object, the set of all points formed by convex combinations of those points lie within the object. See also concave objects.

3.11 Cross product:

Valid only in three dimensions, the cross product of two vectors forms a new vector perpendicular to both whose magnitude is equal to the sine of the angle between the vector pair, measured in the right-hand sense, multiplied by the product of their magnitudes.

4 D

4.1 DAC:

A digital to analog convertor is typically used to convert digital colour speciûcations in a frame buûer into analog signals for analog display devices (such as CRTs).

4.2 DDA:

The digital diûerential analyzer is an algorithm which computes the raster representation of a line segment using a ûnite diûerence evaluation of the line equation. The Bresenham algorithm is typically more eûcient and accurate.

4.3 Diûuse Reûection:

A term in the Phong lighting model to account for light which is scattered equally in all directions.

4.4 Distributed Ray Tracing:

See stochastic ray tracing.

4.5 Dithering:

On a display device with a small number of quantization levels, spatial resolution can be traded for an apparent increase in the number of quantization levels by exploiting the spatial averaging property of the human visual system. Variations include ordered dithering and error-diûusion.

4.6 DMA:

Direct memory access is a form of peripheral interfacing in which the peripheral manages its own data transfer to and from the system's main memory, thus oûoading this work from the CPU.

4.7 Dot Product:

The dot product of two vectors is a scalar proportional to the cosine of the angle between them multiplied by the product of the magnitudes of the two vectors.

4.8 Dragging:

Pressing a physical button, moving a physical valuator, and releasing the button, when it constitutes a composite action accompanied with visual feedback, is called dragging. Normally dragging is accomplished with a physical device that has both buttons and xy valuators, such as a mouse, pen, or trackball.

5 E

5.1 ECL:

Emitter-coupled logic. A particularly power-hungry and hot bipolar technology whose main advantage is speed. Logic states are represented by constant current ûows down one of two alternate paths.

5.2 Error Diûusion:

A form of dithering in which quantization errors at one pixel are distributed to pixels that have not yet been quantized.

6 F

6.1 ûeld (even/odd):

In interlaced video systems, a frame of video is divided into two ûelds. The even ûeld contains all even scanlines, the odd ûeld all odd scanlines. These are presented in sequence.

6.2 ûicker:

If the refresh rate of a video or ûlm system drops too low, annoying ûicker will be apparent. The exact rate at which this occurs varies depending on the light level and the image; at low light levels a lower refresh rate can be used.

6.3 frame:

1. In n-dimensional aûne geometry, a point and n vectors deûning a coordinate system. In a barycentric coordinate system, n + 1 points can deûne a barycentric frame.
2. A UI widget meant to contain and organize other widgets.

6.4 Frame buûer:

6.5 Frustum:

See viewing frustum.

6.6 Fusion Point:

6.7 Function Box:

A hardware user interface device that has some collection of buttons and valuators (knobs, sliders).

7 G

7.1 Gamma Correction:

7.2 GKS:

7.3 Gouraud Shading:

Linear interpolation of colours deûned at the corners of a polygon. For each scanline, the colours are ûrst interpolated along the intersected edges and then along the scanline. For triangles, this interpolation technique corresponds to the use of barycentric coordinates and so is aûne invariant. For general convex polygons is it not.

See also Phong shading.

7.4 Fravity ûeld:

In physically-based animation, a constant downward acceleration applied to all objects. Note that a constant downward force is incorrect, although it is sometimes used.

8 H

8.1 hemi-cube:

8.2 Hertz:

A temporal frequency unit, equivalent to cycles per second.

8.3 HLS:

8.4 Homogeneous Coordinates:

8.5 Horizontal Retrace:

8.6 HSV:

The hue-saturation-value colour system is an alternative to the RGB colour system.

8.7 Hysteresis:

9 I

9.1 Image Space Algorithm:

9.2 Inking:

9.3 Ink jet:

9.4 In-line Gun:

9.5 Interlace:

9.6 Interpolating Spline:

A spline function which passes through its control points or values.

10 J

10.1 Jaggies:

10.2 Joystick:

10.3 Just Noticeable Diûerence:

11 K

11.1 Kerning:

11.2 Keypad:

12 L

12.1 Left-Handed Coordinate System:

12.2 Ligature:

12.3 Light Handle:

12.4 Light Valve:

12.5 Lightpen:

12.6 Linear Space:

12.7 Liquid Crystal Light Valve:

12.8 Local Control:

12.9 Locator:

12.10 Look-up Table (LUT):

13 M

13.1 Mach Bands:

An aliasing artifact that occurs with regular sampling of a pattern. The eûect is lines and possibly a false pattern appearing on top of the regular pattern.

13.2 Master Object Instancing:

A model may be placed more than one time in world space. In this case, an instance is a reference back to the master model. Changes to the master will be reûected in all instances.

13.3 Menu:

A panel of related buttons in a user interface.

13.4 Modelling Transformation:

13.5 Mouse:

14 N

14.1 Normalized Device Coordinates:

14.2 NTSC:

14.3 Nyquist:

14.4 Nyquist frequency:

15 O

15.1 Oû-axis correction:

15.2 On-axis correction:

15.3 Opponent colors:

15.4 Ordered dithering:

15.5 Orthographic projection:

15.6 Outcodes:

16 P

16.1 PAL:

16.2 Pan:

16.3 PDI protocol:

16.4 Persistence of Phosphor:

Once irradiated with an electron beam, a phosphor will glow for a short time, with an exponentially decaying intensity. Usually, in a CRT the decay is rapid, and persistence of vision is relied on to hide the scanning and interframe gaps.

16.5 Persistence of Vision:

The human visual system will retain for a short time an impression of an image, even if that image is only presented for a very short time. This simpliûes the creation of the illusion of motion by presenting a sequence of frames in rapid sucession. Most technologies cannot present images in sequence seamlessly, but must blank the screen. In video, persistence of vision is also used to hide the fact that the image is scanned temporally.

16.6 Perspective Space:

16.7 PHIGS:

16.8 Phong shading:

Normals deûned at the corners of a polygon are interpolated and applied to a lighting model (not necessarily the Phong lighting model) at each pixel. For each scanline, the normals are ûrst interpolated along the intersected edges and then along the scanline. For triangles, this interpolation technique corresponds to the use of barycentric coordinates and so is aûne invariant. For general (convex) polygons is it not. See also Gouraud shading.

16.9 Phosphor:

16.10 Phosphorescence:

16.11 Physical Input Device:

16.12 Physical Output Device:

16.13 Pick:

16.14 Pick id:

16.15 Pincushion Distortion:

16.16 Pixel:

16.17 Plasma Panel:

16.18 predictive Lightpen Tracking:

16.19 Pseudo-Color:

A method for shading an object where the colour represents some property of the surface.

17 Q

17.1 Quaternions:

A generalization of complex numbers, with three elements that sum to negative one. In computer graphics, unit quaternions are commonly used to represent rotations.

18 R

18.1 Rack:

18.2 Radiosity:

18.3 Random Dithering:

18.4 Raster Display:

18.5 RasterOP:

Short for Raster Operation. A copy or block logical operation for moving or combining blocks of pixels. May be implemented in hardware using a bitblt engine.

18.6 Ray Tracing:

A method for generating images by tracing the path of individual light rays through the scene.

18.7 Read/Modify/Write Cycle:

18.8 Retrace:

18.9 RGB:

A colour system that approximates the spectrum of light with three colours, Red, Green, and Blue.

18.10 Right-handed Coordinate System:

18.11 Rubber Banding:

18.12 Run Length Encoding:

19 S

19.1 Scanline Coherence:

19.2 Schlieren Optics:

19.3 Schmidt Optics:

19.4 Scroll:

Vertical translation of the camera. Synonomous to crane. Can also be used in a UI context for the vertical movement of text or images, often under the control of a scrollbar.

19.5 SECAM:

19.6 Segment:

19.7 Segmented Display List:

19.8 Seven Plus/Minus Two:

19.9 Shadow Mask:

19.10 Shadow Volume (or shadow polygon):

19.11 Sketchpad:

19.12 Solid Texture:

A method for adding texture to an object where a texture/material function is deûned over space. When shading a point on the object, the material for that point is determined by its location in 3-space.

19.13 Specular Reûection:

A term in the Phong lighting model to account for light which is scattered more strongly in the mirror direction (or close to the mirror direction) than it is in other directions.

19.14 SRL output:

19.15 Staircasing:

A form of aliasing which manifests itself as steps on line segments and polygon egdes, or along any sharp contrast edge. Also called jaggies in this context. Staircasing may occasionally refer to false edges induced by a low number of intensity levels during quantization.

19.16 Stochastic Ray Tracing:

A form of ray tracing where the ray directions are randomly perturbed as a means of anti-aliasing the image.

19.17 Storage tube:

19.18 Storage grid:

19.19 Stroke:

A single line segment primitive in a calligraphic display list.

19.20 Stroke Font:

A font composed of letters described by collections of strokes, i.e. line segments. This representation has the advantage of being independent of a raster, and so geometric transformations and device independence are possible.

19.21 Structured Display List:

A display list which may refer to other display lists in a hierarchical fashion, and usually allows database operations to read and modify its contents.

19.22 Subjective Spot Size:

19.23 Surface of Rotation:

A 3D surface created by sweeping a 2D curve about an axis of rotation.

20 T

20.1 Tablet:

20.2 Texture Mapping:

A method for adding detail to a surface by mapping an image onto the surface.

20.3 Tracker:

20.4 Trackball:

An input device where a rotational direction is speciûed by rolling a sphere in the desired direction.

20.5 Transformed Display List:

20.6 Turntable:

21 U

21.1 UIMS:

A User Interface Management System. Allows the creation and subsequent modiûcation of a user interface at a high level, visually or through a declarative special-purpose language.

22 V

22.1 Viewing Frustum:

A truncated pyramid that represents the volume which is visible to the eye under perspective, after near and far plane clipping. The canonical viewing frustum has sides which have slopes of plus or minus 1.

22.2 Viewing Transformation:

A transformation which converts from 3D World Coordinates to 3D View Coordinates.

22.3 Viewport:

A section of a screen to which the output of a rendering system is mapped. See also window and viewport transformation.

22.4 Viewport Transformation:

23 W

23.1 Wheel of Reincarnation:

What goes around, comes around. Also, in graphics, the tendency for "obsolete" issues and algorithms designed to address them to arise again and again in new contexts. In general, the balance between memory, CPU, and I/O is constantly shifting and this eûects the choice of algorithms as the pendulum swings back and forth.

For example, suppose an eûcient integer algorithm to perform some rendering task has been developed, deployed, but eventually dropped in general rendering systems in favour of a more general ûoating point algorithm as ûoating point performance increased. This integer algorithm may be reincarnated later as a special-purpose hardware algorithm, since integer arithmetic units take less space than ûoating-point units.

23.2 Window:

Two meanings, which are easily confused:

- Under a windowing system UI such as X Windows, a window is a portion of the screen whichacts as a virtual input and output device, and has its own device coordinate system.
- In 3D graphics, a window is a portion of the 2D projected view space which is mapped to a viewport on the output device.

The 3D terminology was developed before windowing systems were popular, hence the confusion. An X window should be thought of as a "display device" in the 3D context.

23.3 Window Edge Coordinates (WEC):

During clipping, it is useful to convert to a coordinate system relative to the clipping edge.

23.4 Window Coordinates:

Under X Windows, each window has its own virtual device pixel coordinates, relative to the window origin.

23.5 World Coordinates:

A space in which an entire scene is described independent of the position of the viewer.

23.6 Write Mask:

23.7 Write Through:

A cache system in which reads are cached but writes go directly to global memory.

24 X

24.1 X Windows:

A device independent 2D graphics and UI windowing system that functions across a network.

25 Y

25.1 yaw:

Rotation of the camera about the camera's vertical axis; this term is borrowed from aeronautics. Yaw is a synonym of pan.

26 Z

26.1 z-buûer:

A raster which stores, for every pixel in an image, the depth of the point on the object which is closest to the screen at that pixel. Used in hidden surface removal, and almost universal in hardware rendering.

26.2 z-depth:

In eye space, the distance from the camera to a point on an object.

26.3 zoom:

A change in perspective caused by decreasing the Field of View that causes the apparent size of objects to increase. A dolly should be used instead for most applications in animation. A zoom in a 2D context typically refers to the magniûcation of an image through interpolation.

Performance, Volume I, Sensory Processes and Perception, JohnWiley & Sons Inc (1986).

Boyer, C.B. (Revised by Merzbach U.C.), *A History of Mathematics* (2nd edn.), John Wiley & Sons Inc (1991).

17. Brown, S.F., 'Seeing Triple', *Scientific American*, pp. 88–89 (June 2007).

18. Bruce, V., Green P.R., and Georgeson M.A., *Visual Perception: Physiology, Psychology and Ecology* (4th edn.), Psychology Press (2003).

19. Burdea, G.C., *Force and Touch Feedback for Virtual Reality*, JohnWiley & Sons Inc (1996).

Burdea, G.C., and Coiffet, P., *Virtual Reality Technology* (2nd edn.), JohnWiley & Sons Inc (2003).

Campbell Swinton, A.A., 'Presidential Address', *The Journal of the Röntgen Society*, VIII (30), p. 1–13 (January 1912).

…s K., English, W.K., and Burr, B.J., 'Evaluation of Mouse, Rate-Controlled Isometric … Keys and Text Keys for Text Selection on a CRT,' *Ergonomics*, 21 (8), pp. 601–

…monstrate 3-D Volumetric Images', *Laser Focus World*, pp. 28–

References

1. Abramson, A., *The History of Television, 1880 to 1941*, McFarla

2. Agoston, M.K., *Computer Graphics and Geometric Modelli*
Springer-Verlag London (2005).

Performance, Volume I, Sensory Processes and Perception, JohnWiley & Sons Inc (1986).

16. Boyer, C.B. (Revised by Merzbach U.C.), *A History of Mathematics* (2nd edn.), John Wiley & Sons Inc (1991).
17. Brown, S.F., 'Seeing Triple', *Scientific American*, pp. 88–89 (June 2007).
18. Bruce, V., Green P.R., and Georgeson M.A., *Visual Perception: Physiology, Psychology and Ecology* (4th edn.), Psychology Press (2003).
19. Burdea, G.C., *Force and Touch Feedback for Virtual Reality*, JohnWiley & Sons Inc (1996).
20. Burdea, G.C., and Coiffet, P., *Virtual Reality Technology* (2nd edn.), JohnWiley & Sons Inc (2003).
21. Campbell Swinton, A.A., 'Presidential Address', *The Journal of the Röntgen Society*, VIII (30), pp. 1–13 (January 1912).
22. Card, S.K., English, W.K., and Burr, B.J., 'Evaluation of Mouse, Rate-Controlled Isometric Joystick, Step Keys and Text Keys for Text Selection on a CRT,' *Ergonomics*, 21 (8), pp. 601–613 (1978).
23. Chinnock, C., 'Researchers Demonstrate 3-D Volumetric Images', *Laser Focus World*, pp. 28–32 (November 1994).
24. Clements, A., *Principles of Computer Hardware* (4th edn.), Oxford University Press (2006).
25. Coleridge, S.T., *Biographia Literaria: Biographical Sketches of my Literary Life and Opinions*, Princeton University Press (1985).
26. Collender, R.B., 'The Stereoptiplexer: Competition for the Hologram', *Information Display* 4 (6), pp. 27–31 (1967).
27. Comninos, P., *Mathematical and Computer Programming Techniques for Computer Graphics*, Springer-Verlag London Ltd (2006).
28. Cook, R.L., Porter, T., and Carpenter, L., 'Distributed Ray Tracing', *Computer Graphics* 18(3), pp. 137–145 (1984).
29. Cooke, R., *The History of Mathematics: A Brief Course*, JohnWiley & Sons Inc (2005).
30. Cooley, P., *The Essence of Computer Graphics*, Pearson Education Limited (2001).
31. Coren, S., Ward, L.M., and Enns, J.T., *Sensation and Perception* (4th edn.), Harcourt Brace & Company (1994).
32. Cossairt, O.S., Napoli, J., Hill, S.L., Dorval, R.K., and Favalora, G.E., 'Occlusion-Capable Multiview Volumetric Three-Dimensional Display', *Applied Optics*, 46(8), pp. 1244–1250 (10 March 2007).
33. Cronly-Dillon, J.R., and Gregory, R.L. (eds.), 'Evolution of the Eye and Visual System', in *Vision and Visual Disfunction*, Vol. 2, The Macmillan Press Ltd (1991).
34. Cruz-Neira, C., Sandin, D.J., and DeFanti, T.J., 'Virtual Reality: The Design and Implementation of the CAVE', *Proceedings SIGGRAPH 93 Computer Graphics Conference*, ACM SIGGRAPH, pp. 135–142 (1993).
35. Cutler, L.D., Froehlich, B., and Hanrahan, P., 'Two-Handed DirectManipulation on the ResponsiveWorkbench', *1997 Symposium on Interactive 3D Graphics, Providence RI, USA*, ACM, pp. 107–114 (1997).

References

1. Abramson, A., *The History of Television, 1880 to 1941*, McFarland and Co. (1987).
2. Agoston, M.K., *Computer Graphics and Geometric Modelling: Implementation and Algorithms*, Springer-Verlag London (2005).

[illegible] Representation for Computer Vision', in *44th AFIPS National ComputerConference*, pp. 589–596 (1975).

4. Berkley, C., 'Three-Dimensional Representation on Cathode-Ray Tubes', *Proceedings of the IRE – Waves and Electrons Section*, pp. 1530–1535 (December 1948).
5. Bickley, W.G., and Thompson, R.S.H.G., *Matrices: Their Meaning and Manipulation*. The English Universities Press Ltd (1964).
6. Blake, D.T., Hsaio, S.S., and Johnson, K.O., 'Neural Coding Mechanisms in Tactile Pattern Recognition: The Relative Contributions of Slowly and Rapidly AdaptingMechanoreceptors to Perceived Roughness',
7. *Journal of Neuroscience*, 17 (19), pp. 7480–7489 (1997).
8. Blundell, B.G., '3-D Display Systems: Myth and Reality', *ITNow*, 48 (1), pp. 32–33 (2006a).
9. Blundell, B.G., 'Baird and the Volumetric Display', *IET Engineering and Technology*, pp. 36–40 (August 2006b).
10. Blundell, B.G., *Enhanced Visualization: Making Space for 3-D Images*, JohnWiley & Sons Inc (2007).
11. Blundell, B.G., and Schwarz, A.J., *Creative 3-D Display and Interaction Interfaces: A Trans-Disciplinary Approach*, JohnWiley & Sons Inc (2006).
12. Blundell, B.G., and Schwarz, A.J., *Volumetric Three-Dimensional Display Systems*, John Wiley & Sons Inc (2000).
13. Blundell, B.G., Daskalakis, C.N., Heyes, N.A.E., and Hopkins, T.P., *An Introductory Guide to Silvar Lisco and HILO Simulators*, Macmillan Education (1987).
14. Boden, M.A., *Mind as Machine: A History of Cognitive Science*, Vol. 1, Oxford University Press (2006).
15. Boff, K.R., Kaufman, L., and Thomas, J.P. (eds.), *Handbook of Perception and Human*

36. Cyrus, M. and Beck, J., 'Generalized Two- and Three-Dimensional Clipping', *Computers and Graphics*,**3**(1), pp. 23–28 (1978).

37. Davies, A.G.J., *Solid Geometry in 3-D*, Chatto andWindus (1967).

38. DeFanti, T., Cruz-Neira, C., Sandin, D., Kenyon, R., and Hart, J., 'The CAVE: Audio Visual Experience Automatic Virtual Environment', *Communications of the ACM* **35**(6), pp. 64–72 (June 1992).

39. Della Porta, G., *De Refractione Optices Parte* (1593).

40. Dodgson, N.A., Moore, J.R., and Lang, S.R., 'Multi-View Autostereoscopic 3D Display', *Proceedings International Broadcasting Convention* (September 10–14, Amsterdam), pp. 497–502 (1999).

41. Downing, E.,Hesselink, L.,Macfarlane, R.M., and Barty, C.P.J., 'Solid-State Three-Dimensional Computer Display', *CLEO '94* (1994).

42. Eberly, D.H., *Game Physics*, Elsevier Inc (2004).

43. Edgerton, S.Y., *TheHeritage Of Giotto's Geometry – Art And Science On The EveOf The Scientific Revolution*, Cornell University Press (1991).

44. Edgerton, S.Y., *The Renaissance Rediscovery Of Linear Perspective*, Harper and Row (1976).

45. Egerton, P.A., and Hall, W.S., *Computer Graphics: Mathematical First Steps*, Pearson Education Limited (1999).

46. Elkins, J., *How to Use Your Eyes*, Routledge (2000).

47. Encarnacao, J., and Schlechtendahl, E.G., *Computer Aided Design: Fundamentals and System Architectures*, Springer-Verlag (1983).

48. English, W.K., Engelbart, D.C., and Berman, M.L., 'Display-Selection Techniques for Text Manipulation', *IEEE Transactions on Human Factors in Electronics*, HFE-8 (1) (March 1967).

49. Fernandes, K.J., Raja, V., and Eyre, J., 'Cybersphere: The Fully Immersive Spherical Projection System', *Communications of the ACM*, 46 (9ve), pp. 141–146 (September 2003).

50. Foley, J.D., van Dam., A., Feiner, S.K., and Hughes, J.F., *Computer Graphics: Principles and Practice*, 2nd edn., Addison-Wesley Publishing Company (1990).

51. Gabor, D., 'A New Microscopic Principle', *Nature*, **161**, pp. 777–778 (May 1948).

52. Gabor, D., 'Holography, 1948–1971', Proc. IEEE, **60** (6) (1972).

53. Gauthier, J-M., *Building Interactive Worlds in 3D: Virtual Sets and Pre-Visualization for Games, Film & the Web*, Focal Press (2005).

54. Geddes, K., and Bussey, G., *The Setmakers: A History of the Radio and Television Industry*, The British Radio & Electronic Equipment Manufacturers' Association (1991).

55. Gibson, J.J., *The Perception of the Visual World*, Houghton Mifflin (1950).

56. Girling, A.N., *Stereoscopic Drawing: A Theory of 3-D Vision and its Application to Stereoscopic Drawing*,Arthur Girling (1990).

57. Glanz, J., 'Three-Dimensional Images are Conjured in a Crystal Cube', *Science* 273, p. 1172 (August 1996).

58. *GPIPG: Great Pictures in Private Galleries*, Cassell and Company Ltd (1905).

59. Halle, M., 'Autostereoscopic Displays and Computer Graphics', *Computer Graphics*

(ACMSIGGRAPH) 31(2) pp. 58–62 (1997).

60. Halle, M., 'Multiple Viewpoint Rendering', *Proceedings SIGGRAPH '96* (1996).
61. Harris, L.D., Camp, J.J., Ritman, E.L., and Robb, R.A., 'Three-Dimensional Display and Analysis of Tomographic Volume Images using a Varifocal Mirror', *IEEE Transactions on Medical Imaging*, MI-5 (2), pp. 67–72 (June 1986).
62. Hartwig, R., 'The Helix3D – A Three Dimensional Computer Display', invited presentation and demonstration, TELI – European Union of Science Journalists Association, German Study Tour, Heidelberg (November 5, 1982).
63. Hearn, D., and Baker, M.P., *Computer Graphics*, Prentice-Hall Inc (1986).
64. Hecht, S., andMintz, E.U., 'The Visibility of Single Lines at Various Illuminations and the Retinal Basis of Visual Resolution', *Journal of General Physiology*, pp. 593–612 (1939).
65. Hecht, S., Shlaer, S., and Pirenne, M.H., 'Energy Quanta and Vision', *Journal of General Physiology*, 25, pp. 819–840 (1942).
66. Helmholtz, H.H., *Popular Lectures on Scientific Subjects* (English Translation by Atkinson, E.), Longmans, Green, and Co. (1873).
67. Hill Jr., F.S., *Computer Graphics*, Macmillan Publishing Company (1990).
68. Hinckley, K., and Pausch, R., Two-Handed VirtualManipulation', *ACMTransactions on Computer-Human Interaction*, 5 (3), pp. 260–302 (September 1998).
69. Howard, I.P., and Rogers, B.J., *Seeing in Depth*, Vol. II Depth Perception, I. Porteous (2002).
70. Jiménez, P., Thomas, F., and Torras, C., '3D Collision Detection: A Survey', *Computers and Graphics*, 25, pp. 269–285 (2001).
71. Jones, A.,McDowall, I., Yamada, H., Bolas, M., Debevec, P., 'Rendering for an Interactive 360æ% Light Field Display'. *ACM Trans. Graph.* 26(3), Article 40 (July 2007).
72. Jones, G., Lee, D., Holliman, N., Ezra, D., 'Controlling Perceived Depth in Stereoscopic Images', *Proceedings SPIE (Stereoscopic Displays and Virtual Reality Systems VIII)*, 4297, pp. 42–53 (2001).
73. Jordan, D.W., and Smith, P., *Mathematical Techniques: An Introduction for the Engineering, Physical, and Mathematical Sciences* (3rd edn.), Oxford University Press (2002).
74. Kaczmarek, K.A., Webster, J.G., Bach-y-Rita, P., and Tompkins, W.J., 'Electrotactile and Vibrotactile Displays for Sensory Substitution Systems', *IEEE Transactions on Biomedical Engineering*, 38 (1), pp. 1–16 (1991).
75. Kamm, A., and Baird, M., *John Logie Baird: A Life*, National Museums of Scotland Publishing Ltd (2002).
76. Kandel, E.R., Schwartz, J.H., and Jessell, T.M., *Principles of Neural Science* (4th edn.),McGraw-Hill (2000).
77. Kemp, M., 'Science, Non-Science and Nonsense: the Interpretation of Brunelleschi's Perspective', *Art History*, 1 (2), pp. 134–161 (1978).
78. Kennedy, D.N., and Nelson, A.C., 'Three-Dimensional Display from Cross-Sectional Tomographic Images: An Application to Magnetic Resonance Imaging', *IEEE Transactions on Medical Imaging*, MI-6 (2), pp.134–140 (1993).

79. Kim, S., Berkley, J.J., and Sato, M., 'A Novel Seven Degree of Freedom Haptic Device for Engineering Design', *Virtual Reality*, 6 (4), pp. 217–228 (2003a).

80. Kim, Y.J., Otaday, M.A., Lin, M.C., and Manocha, D., 'Six-Degree-of-Freedom Haptic Rendering using Incremental and Localised Computations', *Presence*, 12 (3), pp. 277–295 (2003b).

81. Kubovy, M., *The Psychology of Linear Perspective and Renaissance Art*, Cambridge University Press (1986).

82. Land, M.F., and Nilsson, D.-E., *Animal Eyes*, Oxford University Press (2002).

83. Lang, S.R., Travis, A.R.L., Castle, O.M., andMoore, J.R., 'A 2nd Generation Autostereoscopic 3-D Display', *Proceedings* 7th *Eurographics Workshop on Graphics Hardware (Cambridge, UK, 5–6 September 1992)*, Lister, P.F. (ed.), pp. 53–63 (1992).

Index